CASTE AND EDUCATIONAL DEVELOPMENT

CASTE AND EDUCATIONAL DEVELOPMENT

(Before and After Independence)

M.L. MATHUR

KALPAZ

Published by

Kalpaz Publications
C-30, Satyawati Nagar,
Delhi – 110052
Ph.: 011-47034999, 9811692060
www.kalpazpublications.com
E-mail: kalpaz@hotmail.com

Distribution Network
gyanbooks.com
India, USA, Canada, UK, Australia, France

ISBN: 978-93-5722-906-7 (PB)

First Published, 2024

Printed at: Gyan Press, Delhi.

Caste and Educational Development: Before and after Independence
Author: M.L. Mathur

Contents

Preface

During British Raj in India, the modern education was spread in many parts of the country. In the early phase, the education was restricted to reserved sections of the society like children of employees of the company, Anglo Indian families and Indian Christians. This gave rise to birth of educational inequality. Missionaries also got encouragement to spread education for children of Christians. By the middle of 18th Century, a wave of education had swept across the province of Madras, which was forging ahead in the field and the educational pattern underwent total transformation. British policy of education was to lay emphasis on the English education. It was Lord Macaulay who was the Chairman of the Committee on General Instructions, though advocated for English education yet he felt need for vernacular education. He also advocated the theory of downward filteration with the purpose to consolidate the rule by educating the upper class and giving them upper high posts through the medium of instructions they understand. This was a step in the direction of education of Indian masses. To spread the education among the Indian masses, the British rulers recognized the role of private agencies in its first charter of 1854, i.e., Wood's Dispatch and in Indian Education Commission Report, 1882. It becomes historically significant to explore and study role of private agencies, e.g., castes, communities and missionary efforts to spread modern education in India. Princely rulers ruled many parts of India, even then they took keen interest to spread the modern education not only for boys but also for girls. The question also arises how did castes and communities manage and raise funds etc. for establishment of schools? Could they achieve their aim of educating their children? Sociological researches in the field of education began after the first study was conducted throughout the country under the title of Field Studies on Sociology of Education and Papers on the Sociology of Education (1967). This was the beginning of sociological research in various areas of education after twenty years of the Independence of the country. Some of the studies, were done by Madan and Haldar (1972) in three districts of Karnataka State viz. Belgaum, Dharwad and Mysore, Harold Gould (1972) in Faizabad District. The study of caste and education became a potent area of research.

When I was a post-graduate student, I first undertook an exploratory work on Caste Managed Secondary Schools in Jodhpur city in 1973-74 and submitted a dissertation. I persued this work further at the Doctorate level. The present book is based on revision of my work done earlier. This book is based on a study conducted in Jodhpur city of Rajasthan State which is one of the educationally backward State in India. Jodhpur city was earlier the capital of the erstwhile Marwar State. The State had always supported for the cause of expansion of education not only for boys but also for girls through private agencies like castes and communities. Both forward and backward castes and communities (Christian and Muslim) came forward and opened schools in Jodhpur city from 1887 to 1954. They were Brahman, Mahajan (Oswal, Agarwal, Maheshwari), Kayastha, Sanik Kshatriya (Mali), Rawna Rajput (Daroga), Kumhar, Suthar (Artisans), Muslim, Christian and Sindhi. This shows that forward castes, backward castes and minority communities got encouragement and support from the State to open schools for education of their children. This study also explored loyal relationship between castes and their rulers. This book is presented into the following chapters :

Chapter One : Introduction - Rise of Castes and Communities in the Field of Education

Chapter Two : Castes, Communities and Education in India

This chapter deals with caste as one variable of social status and social position in Indian society and in particular in Jodhpur city where nine castes opened schools. By using census reports of 1911, 1931, 1941 of Marwar State this chapter formed the basis for analysis of data on different variables such as literacy, rural-urban distribution, religion, occupation, population, etc. Castes above 1 per cent population at different level were chosen to find out their preponderance level.

Chapter Three : Educational Development : Historical Perspective

This chapter focuses on educational development before Independence. The schools were established during 1887 to 1954. As it was generally said that rulers were not keen to spread education among masses it becomes important to probe role played by State in educational development in the state and their policy towards private bodies to enter in the field of education. An attempt has also been made to analyse role played by castes in growth and development of their schools. This analysis was made in historical perspective based on all available historical records for all schools in the files of Rajasthan Historical Archives, Bikaner and other documents.

Chapter Four : Educational Policy and Its Implementation : An Analysis

The schools have completed more than fifty years to hundred years. This is a sufficient evidence to say that castes have been successfully managing schools in the society. During these period many recommendations were made by Educational Commissions, etc. Whether these schools have been implementing these recommendations to manage their schools well. Could they build prestige of the school in the society? An attempt has been made to estimate prestige score by computing on eight variables viz. caste, establishment, no. of students, no. of teachers, physical and library facilities, results of public examinations, average fee perstudent.

Chapter Five : School Management: An Analysis

The private aided schools are managed by a board of management or a managing committee as per rules of Registration of Societies Act, 1860 and Grant in Aid Rule, 1902 and 1963. This chapter analyses composition of the body, its functions etc. The main functions of the body are student' admission policy, recruitment of teachers, fund raising, courses and curriculum, examination etc. State government have got control and supervision over educational administration and educational management under rule by way of annual inspection, panel inspection in three-year period. Policy and decisions are two important dimensions of the management function, which have been analyzed in this chapter. This has been analyzed in management perspective.

Chapter Six : Selected Case Studies

This chapter discusses selected case studies of three schools. These schools were selected on the basis of combination of factors analyzed on historical, educational, and management perspectives.

Chapter Seven : Conclusion and Analysis

This chapter concludes that castes played contributory role in educational development in the city. We found that caste considerations continue to exist in educational institutions even after all legislative and executive measures are available. This does not mean that these educational institutions do not abide by the existing provisions of Rules and Regulations but they fit in all these to benefit their brethren.

Acknowledgements

The present research work could be completed with direct and indirect support received from many sources. First of all I would like to express my gratitude to Manager(s), Secretaries, Principals and selected teachers, school's office staffs for extending their kind cooperation in giving me all relevant information from time to time. I also express my sincere thanks to office staff of District educational office and office staff of Deputy Director, Directorate of Education, Jodhpur for giving me informations of educational institutions of Jodhpur city.

My research work required collections of data through primary and secondary sources. These sources of information are preserved in Sumer Public Library, Jodhpur, Rajasthan, Historical Archives, Bikaner and Jodhpur branch also. I collected historical data from unpublished official letters, reports and administrative reports of Jodhpur State, Census of Marwar State, etc. from these library. I also used extensively libraries of Indian Council of Social Sciences Research, New Delhi and National Historical Archives Library, New Delhi. There is a long list of persons who deserve to be acknowledged individually but due to limited space it could not be possible. I thank all of them who have helped me in making all materials available to me.

I got constant encouragement to bring out this work in a book form from Ehsahnul Haq, Professor J.S. Gandhi of School of Social Sciences, Jawaharlal Nehru University, New Delhi and Professor B. K. Nagla of M. D. University, Rohtak. I thank Shri Sanjay Mehrotra for typing the manuscript neatly and correctly.

I shall be failing in my duty if I do not record word of gratitude to my parents and thanks to my wife and children for bearing with me since I could not give sufficient time which they required. Their encouragement to me was a great boon.

1

Introduction

Rise of Castes and Communities in the Field of Education

Education is one of the areas of human activity and organization in any given society. It is through education that individual members of a social group or community acquire learning or socialize themselves as per norms and requirements of that society. It is through education that individual members of the society acquire not only information and knowledge but also pass them on to coming generation. Education thus helps to accumulate knowledge, to keep on improving and advancing it more and more to contribute vitally to the growth of society.

Education is also bound by a given society and its historical development. Historically speaking, in India, during ancient and medieval times, education was of traditional type and also restricted to a microscopic higher section of society. The access to education was not open and available to large sections of the population belonging to *Sudra* castes and also many *Vaishya* castes. Brahmans were occupying a special position in the context of education and learning. Even during Mughal period the situation did not change much except that Madarsas were opened to cater to the educational requirements of a section of Muslim and converted population. During the British period the situation did not continue like this and for various reasons (e.g. Rising employment opportunities in government jobs) education was becoming aspiration of certain castes, which had traditionally lagged behind other better off sections of society. Due to this education started becoming more open and widespread. (Saxena, R.N. 1967).[1]

During British period the first Indian charter of 1813 and 1854 (Wood's dispatch) and Indian Education Commission, 1882 recognized and recommended involvement of private bodies (e.g. Castes, religious organizations, etc) to spread modern education in India. However, there was no much progress in spread of modern education during this period (Madan and Halbar 1972).[2]

There was rise in number of privately managed and publicly managed educational institutions in India from the beginning of nineteenth century (Mishra 1962).[3] The laissez-faire policy enunciated in the Indian Education Commission (1882)[4] had led to rise of numerous privately managed schools and collages (Basu 1982).[5] Grant-in-Aid Rule, 1902 further attracted number of private bodies to open their schools, etc. The trend of increase in number of private educational institutions continued up to independence period due to flow of public donations and dedicated workers who sacrificed their careers for this cause but the trend declined after independence due to rise in prices and the effects of Second World War (Misra 1973).[6]

Growth of Educational Institutions

In 1881-82 there were 82,916 primary schools in India, which rose to 97,854 in 1901-02, i.e., an increase of 14,938 in two decades; in 1903-1910-11, the number rose to 1,18,262.

Aparna Basu tabulated data for different levels of educational institutions at different periods. The table explains the fact.

Table 1.1: Number of Educational Institutions from 1855-56 to 1946-47

S. No.	*Level of educational institutions*	*No. of educational institutions*			
		1855-56	*1901-02*	*1921-22*	*1946-47*
1.	Universities	-	5.005	14	17
2.	College of General Education	21	145	172	496
3.	Colleges of Professional and Other Education	13	46	74	130
4.	Secondary Schools (General)	281	1170	1248	5297
5.	Secondary Schools (Vocational and Technical)	-	94	292	665
6.	Special and Other Schools	7	990	3729	4746
7.	Middle Schools	-	4323	6739	11162
8.	Primary Schools	50676	97854	760070	172681
	Total	**50998**	**104627**	**173313**	**196891**

Source : Aparna Basu : *Essays in the History of Indian Education*, New Delhi: Concept Publishing Company: 1982, Table 1, p.14.

It is seen from the above table that there was an increase in number of educational institutions over the period of ninety years in the country from 50,998 to 1,96,891, i.e., an increase of 3.86 times ; primary schools

3.40 times; Middle schools 2.58 times in forty years; Secondary schools 18.81 times and so on. This shows an increasing trend in educational development.

As regards situation of educational institutions under private management in 1901-02 there were 82,372 educational institutions under private management including Christian Missionaries management which grew to 1, 25,563 in 1955-56. Comparing these figures with educational institutions under public management, it is seen that there were 22,250 institutions in 1901-02 which was about one-fourth of the private managed institutions. Surprisingly, the number of educational institutions under public management was 2, 41,078 in 1955-56 which was almost twice the number of educational institutions under private management. The table explains the growth of public and private management education, 1901-1955.

Table 1.2: Number of Privately Managed and Publicly Managed Educational Institutions and Pupils from 1901-02 to 1955-56

Year	*Under Private Management **		*Under Public Management*	
	No. of Institutions	*No. of Pupils*	*No. of Institutions*	*No. of Pupils*
1901-02	82372	2646852	22250	1239610
1921-22	117025	4398318	56274	3343907
1937-38	135758	7134523	83037	6299899
1946-47	94277	7608969	109596	10141294
1955-56	125563	11632140	241078	22291459

Source: A.N. Misra, *Education Finance in India.* Bombay : Asia Publishing House, 1962.

* Figure includes Christian Missionaries.

A Report on Growth of Schools1950-1992 (State-wise) (Government of India, Ministry of Human Resources Development, Department of Education, New Delhi, 1997) presents number of recognised schools in India since independence, i.e., from the year 1950-51 to 1992-93. At All India level, number of Primary/Junior Basic Schools has trebled from 2,09,671 in 1950-51 to 5,71,248 in 1992-93. In case of upper primary/ middle /Senior Basic schools these have increased from 13,596 in 1950-51 to 1,58,498 during 1992-93. The increase has been more than 11 times during this period. Further total number of High/Post basic/Higher Secondary/Sr. Secondary schools has increased by 9 times during the same period from 7,416 during 1950-51 to 84,608 during 1992-93. This astonishing increase is partly due to introduction of 10+2 system of education by the States in different years and partly due to the expansion of schooling facilities to make these facilities available nearby and also in order to cover uncovered areas/habitation.

The table shows number of schools of different types from the year 1950 to 1992.

Table 1.3: Number of Different Levels of Educational Institutions from 1950 to 1992

(in thousands)

Year	*Primary*	*Middle*	*HS/HSS*	*Total*
1950	209.67	13.60	7.29	230.56
1955	278.14	21.73	10.84	310.71
1960	330.40	49.66	20.43	400.49
1965	391.06	75.80	27.61	494.47
1970	408.38	90.62	37.05	536.05
1975	454.27	106.57	43.05	603.89
1980	494.50	118.56	51.57	664.63
1985	529.97	134.85	65.84	730.66
1990	560.94	151.46	79.80	792.20
1991	566.74	155.93	82.58	805.25
1992	571.25	158.50	84.61	814.36

Source: Growth of Schools 1950-1992 (State-wise) Govt. of India, Ministry of Human Resources Development, Department of Education (Planning, Monitoring and Statistics Division), New Delhi, 1997.

It is also seen from the report that there was an increase of 5,53,427 boy's school from 2,14,044 in 1950-51 to 7,67,471 in 1992-93 that is 3.6 times over the period of 40 years. In case of girl's schools, the increase was 30,294 from 16,639 in 1950-51 to 46,933 in 1992-93 that is 2.80 times over the period of 40 years. It would be an interesting analysis to go into detail State-wise and to arrive at the conclusion, which State was ahead on educational development than the other States *(Appendix I to VIII)*.

Education in India 1992-93 (Vol.I [S]) in its Statement I give growth of educational institutions in India during 1950–51 to 1992-93. These figures include all three levels of schooling, i.e., Primary, Middle, and High/Higher Secondary schools. There was a rise in number of schools from 2,30,560 in 1950-51 to 8,14,354 in 1992-93, i.e., about 3.53 times. This trend indicates a positive sign of development. Further it has been reported in the Table 1.02, p. 14 of the report that there were 1,31,915 (15.89%) out of 830393 selected educational institutions in India, which are being managed by private bodies (aided/unaided). Out of 131915 private aided/unaided schools 11698 (58.35%) and 35210 (55.49%) were Higher Secondary Schools (10+2 pattern) and High/Post Basic Schools respectively.

After Independence the education policy of British Raj continued for sometime. Education development was one of the topmost priorities before the Indian Government which they continued to encourage private bodies to run their schools as per State government education policy as per Grant-in-Aid Rule. This was also a positive step towards democratization of the education. As a result, different states were left to evolve their own policies.

Caste and Education: Policy and Development in Perspective before and after Independence in India

During British Raj in India some merchants obtained the permission from Queen Elizabeth I to enter into the trade with India and established the East India Company at Calcutta (now renamed Kolkata) in the year 1600.The Company obtained several rights through the letters of patent of 1698 and along with this it became easy for it to employ teachers and religious preachers in factories and workshops in India. After a few hundred years in India the merchants realized the need for education of children of sons of employees of the Company. The Company.opened schools at Madras in 1715 (now renamed Chennai), Bombay in 1718 (now renamed Mumbai) and Calcutta in 1731 (now renamed Kolkata). In these schools education was open to children of employees of the Company, Anglo-Indian families, and Indian Christians. However, other children also could get admission in these schools. These schools mainly depended on favours from the Company. These developments point out that the Company did not owe the responsibility for providing education to all till that time.

By the middle of eighteenth century a wave of education had swept across the province of Madras which was forging ahead in this field and the educational pattern underwent total transformation. German Missionary Schwartz deserved credit for this radical development. He impressed upon rulers of Tanjore and some other places need for education. Baptist Mission opened 115 schools nearby Calcutta-Serampore. Thus, it is evident that missionaries expanded education for children in their areas. These developments were indicators of reserving education for certain sections of the society. In other words education was not open for all sections of the society.

After battle of Plassey in 1757 the administration of Bengal had passed into the hands of the Company and the battle of Buxer in 1764 gave the final and finishing touches. In 1765, Shah Alam gave to the British, much against his wishes, the Dewani of Bengal, Bihar and Orissa. As a result of the treaty of 1765, the company acquired some important political rights and it was no more a trading concern but an actual ruler. The company had acquired all territories in India, ruled by Hindu and Muslim rulers. The Hindus and Muslims were lovers of higher education. The learned Pandits and Maulvis were honoured with titles and also with Jagirs (landed property) which provided them their livelihood. All these developments brought about great changes in educational development and consequently Sanskrit colleges were established at Calcutta, Madras and Banaras.

Besides the above-mentioned reasons there was a particular factor responsible for the expansion of education. According to the amended law of 1781, the judicial matters of the India were to be decided with due consideration of their customs, practices and ways of living etc. The English Judges were not acquainted with these, nor could they get to know about these without assistance of Indians. Hence it was deemed necessary to impart higher education to some Indians for gaining knowledge of these things. This gave birth to two important institutions in India, viz. Calcutta Madarsa in 1780 and Banaras Sanskrit College in 1791. These were open for children of all communities. They also received annual grant from the Company. By doing so the Company fulfilled its objective to appease two major religious communities - Hindu and Muslim. Persons of both high and low classes received higher education, got official jobs and became staunch supporters of the rulers. This was the hidden agenda of the Company to run its administration effectively.

British Policy of Education was to lay emphasis on the English Education. In 1788, a College was set up with the efforts of Brown and Mrs. Pitt. After twenty-two years another college, Fort William College, Calcutta was opened in 1800. During this period the Company thought of education of girls. This was the first time they showed concern for female education. There is no doubt higher education was important for acquiring jobs in government jobs. Some of reformists agitated in the British Parliament over the issue of providing education to children of poor. They moved the Bill in 1807 which they lost. Again they made an attempt and a committee was formed in 1815 to look into conditions of education of the poor. They again moved a bill in the Parliament but they lost. These reformists continued their agitation and did not get discouraged. Their main point of agitation was that the Company should take over the responsibility of providing education to children of the poor. One of the important causes for which the Company was not taking the responsibility of education was that the Company did not wish to educate the Indians because it was easier to rule over the illiterate and ignorant people. The company was also afraid that after being educated, the Indians would start criticizing it and try to set themselves free from its yoke. When the Company was being compelled to accept the responsibility of education, the British Parliament also expressed its sympathies for the Indian people with the aim of reforming social conditions. It was Charles Grant who advocated for use of both the native language and English as medium of instruction in his first Charter of 1813. Finally, the Company accepted the responsibility of providing education to Indians. A provision of Rs. 1 Lakh was also made to expend on education. Lord Minto and Lord Hastings continued the old system of education. In between the period of these developments oriental system of learning continued.

Lord Macaulay was the Chairman of the Committee on General Instructions. Though he advocated for English education yet he felt need to support for vernacular language. Lord William Bentinck agreed to the policy of Macaulay. He advocated the theory of downward filtration. The purpose of this theory was two fold: (i) to consolidate the rule by educating the upper classes and giving them upper high posts, (ii) to educate upper classes through the medium of instructions they understand so that education will automatically filter down to others. But Lord Macaulay was against the downward filtration theory. He was not in favour of educating masses but in favour of creating a group to disseminate education. In 1839, Bengal Committee on Public Instructions endorsed the views of Macaulay. But his policy failed on two fronts. First, number of English schools had multiplied. Second, Government could not provide jobs to so many people. It was the first time British Raj realized the need for adopting permanent education policy for Indians. In 1853, the Company received a new Charter of education. This Charter became known by Wood's dispatch on education, 1854. The foundation of modern education in India began after implementation of this dispatch. Some of the salient parts of the dispatch are mentioned briefly: (i) Unlike Macaulay the dispatch recognized the sentiments of Indian people; knowledge of Sanskrit, Arabic, and Persian useful, (ii) Organisation of education department at each province like Bombay, Madras, N.W. Province, (iii) Universities for higher education, (iv) Establishment of graded schools, (v) Grant-in-Aid to assist the smooth and continuous functioning of educational institutions, (vi) Schools to be looked after by influential persons of the area, (vii) Female education.

After twenty-eight years of Wood's dispatch (1854) the British Raj appointed Indian Education Commission (IEC) in 1882. The Commission had twenty members with William Hunter as Chairperson to find out state of primary education in India, position of religious missionaries, whether government schools are required or not, attitude of government towards indigenous schools, secondary education, adoption of grant-in-aid, education department, education of Muslims, backward classes, girls etc. It was first time that the IEC gave recommendations that included certain new measures to encourage education among Indians for neglected groups and private bodies by way of grant-in-aid. Princely states immediately implemented these recommendations.

Lord Curzon was the Viceroy for seven years from 1918 to 1925. This period is considered the best period of educational development in India. During those days nationalism was at its height. Curzon reviewed education situation at that time. In 1881-82 there were 82,916 primary schools in India, the number increased to 93,604 in 1901-02, i.e., an increase of 10,688 schools in two decades and these schools further rose to 1,18,262 in a decade, i.e., from 1903 to 1910-11. After review of the educational situation in India he suggested few measures for improvement of education in India. These measures were in direction of control over educational development in India and quality improvement in education; (i) Reform in curricula; (ii) Reform in Grant-in-Aid rules; (iii)Expansion of Secondary Education; (iv) Training of Teachers; (v) Recognition by the University, (vi)Restriction on the students of non recognized schools.

The national movement created an awakening among Indians. Gopal Krishan Gokhale moved a bill in 1911. In 1913 the Government adopted the education policy. Among other recommendations the most important was improvement of teachers' condition such as promotion policy, pension scheme, and provident fund. When the State did not find happy situation in the educational development the Hartog Committee gave its recommendations for improvement in education situation in 1929. During these periods of development education came into the hands of Indian Ministers in 1921. Education of harijans began to progress from that period only. This clearly indicates it was the first time government thought of education for downtrodden. There was no significant development in the field of education before Independence of the country though there were three schemes prepared in different periods Basic (Wardha) Scheme of Education, 1937 under the Chairman of Dr. Zakir Hussain, A. Abbott (1937) and Sargent (1944).

After Independence of the country the education policy continued with changes in the education structure on the basis of recommendations made by Radha Krishnan Commission (1948-49) on university education, Mudaliar Commission (1952-53) on secondary education, Kothari Commission (1964-66) and National Policy of Education (1968, 1986).

Report of the Secondary Education Commission (October, 1952–June 1953) contains recommendations, some of these are relevant and need to explore in context of the present study. These recommendations are:

Chapter IV – New Organizational Pattern of Secondary Education

(i) Multipurpose Schools should be established wherever possible to provide various courses of interest to students with diverse aims, aptitudes and abilities (Recommendations No. 8, p. 230).

Other Types of School

(ii) Public Schools should continue to exist for the present and the pattern of education given in them should be brought into reasonable conformity to the general pattern of national education. Such schools should gradually become self-supporting but during the transitional period of the next five years, State or Central assistance should be given to them on a gradually diminishing scale (Recommendation No.18, p. 231)

(iii) The States or the Centre should provide for certain free scholarships in them to be given on the basis of merit to selected students.

Chapter XII – Improvement of the Teaching Personnel

(iv) In all privately managed institutions and in schools maintained by local boards there should be a small selection committee entrusted with the responsibility of recruiting the staff, with the head master as an ex-officio member (Recommendation No. 2, p. 238).

(v) Teachers working in High Schools should be graduates with a degree in education; those who teach technical subjects should be graduate in the subject concerned with the necessary training for teaching it; teachers in Higher Secondary schools should posses higher qualifications somewhat similar to those prescribed in some Universities for teachers of the Intermediate colleges (Recommendation No. 4, p. 238).

(vi) The leave rules, should as far as possible be uniform for all educational institutions (Recommendation No. 14, p. 239).

Chapter XIII - Problems of Administration

Inspection of Schools

(vii) The true role of an Inspection should be to study the problem of each school and view them comprehensively in the context of educational objectives to formulate suggestions for improvement and to help the teachers to carry out his advice and recommendations (Recommendation No. 8, p. 241)

Management and Conditions of Recognition of Schools

(viii) Recognition of schools should be given on clear, defined conditions, which will ensure their proper running and the maintenance of proper standards (Recommendation No. 14, p. 241).

(ix) The Managing Board of all schools should be registered and should consist of a limited number of persons with the headmaster as an ex-officio member (Recommendation No. 15, p. 241).

(x) No member of the Managing Board should directly or indirectly interfere with the internal administration of the school (Recommendation No. 16, p. 241).

(xi) Every management should be required to draw definite rules of service wherein the condition pertaining to salary, leave,etc. should be definitely laid down (Recommendation No. 17, p. 241)

(xii) For proper running of a school every management should be required to provide an endowment and the income accruing from this should be shown in the receipts of the year (Recommendation No. 18, p. 241)

(xiii) The scales of fees fixed by the management of a school should be subject to approval by the Department of Education (Recommendation No. 19, p. 241)

(xiv) A committee should be appointed when necessary by the Department of Education to go into the question of levying uniform scale of tuition fees and other fees and all accounts of the school should be subject to audit by the Department (Recommendation No. 20, p. 242).

(xv) The management should satisfy the Department that qualified staff is available and will be appointed in accordance with the rules laid down by the Department for application (Recommendation No. 21, p. 242).

(xvi) The management should satisfy the Department that adequate accommodation and equipment, etc. have been provided for the efficient running of the school (Recommendation No. 22, p. 242).

(xvii) The number of sections in each class should be limited and before any increase in the number of sections is made, the prior approval of the department should be obtained (Recommendation No. 23, p. 242).

(xviii) The teaching staff should not be limited to any particular caste or community but should as far as possible be recruited on a wide basis (Recommendation No. 25, p. 242).

(xix) In view of the importance and urgency of providing diversified courses of instruction, financial aid and encouragement should be given to the existing schools as well as the new schools, providing diversified courses of study (Recommendation No. 26, p. 242).

School Building and Equipment

(xx) Normally, in designing buildings for schools, care should be taken to see that an area of not less than 10 sq. ft. is provided per student in the classroom (Recommendation No. 31, p. 242)

(xxi) The optimum number of boys to be admitted to any class should be 30 and the maximum should not in any case exceed 40; the optimum number in the whole school should be 500 while the maximum should not exceed 750 (Recommendation No. 32, pp. 242-43).

Hours of work and vacations

(xxii) As a rule the total number of working days in a school should not be less than two hundred, the working hours per week should be at least thirty five periods of about forty five minutes each, the school should work regularly for six days in a week one of days being a half day, when the teachers and students might meet informally and work together on various extra-curricular and social projects.

(xxiii) School holidays need not be identical with public holidays as declared by the Government and normally during the year there should be a summer vacation of two months and two breaks of ten to fifteen days at suitable periods during the year (Recommendation No. 40, p. 243).

Chapter XIV – Finance

(xxiv) The State Governments and the Centre should, wherever, possible assign lands to schools for playgrounds, buildings or agricultural farms and other necessary purposes without any change (Recommendation No. 9, p. 244)

(xxv) The educational institutions which have to obtain necessary scientific apparatus, workshop appliances and books for school library should be exempted from custom duty (Recommendation No.10, p. 241).

It is evident from the above historical account that castes and communities got encouragement from the British Raj before Independence and States after the Independence of the country to expand education in the society.

Caste and Education: Interplay

In the beginning of the twentieth century a significant tendency of caste organizations and caste associations emerged to enter into the field of education to spread education through establishment of institutions and also by building hostels for their own children. In a way this has been a notable contribution in India (Ruhela, 1981).[8] Kapadia (1959)[9] conducted his study in Navsari taluka of Gujarat. He found that Parsis came forward and opened schools for education of their own children. In Bihar state Bhumihar brahmans, Rajputs, and Kayasthas opened educational institutions as a result of separation of Bihar state from West Bengal and Orissa and political developments taking place there. They encouraged their members to take benefit of higher education for new opportunities in employment and declining profit in traditional occupations such as agriculture.[10] Madan and Halbar (1972)[11] studied educational institutions run by castes and communities in three districts of Karnataka state, viz. Belgaum, Dharwar, and Mysore. (Before formation of the Karnataka State, these three districts were under territorial control of erstwhile Mysore State). They found that some powerful communities did not trust government in providing higher educational facilities to their communities.

In Indian society caste associations opened schools in many parts of the country. The question is why did caste associations open educational institutions and build hostels in towns and cities? If lower castes had undertaken such activities it could be understood as an effort to seek their mobility from low social status to high status i.e. a process of sanskritisation. When upper and middle castes took responsibility of spreading education in the society can it be called a process of mobility of castes. In this regard Srinivas (1968)[12] states that caste associations came into existence for acceleration of mobility as well as for their social reform. Their initial aim was to reform their caste customs in the direction of sanskritisation to lay claims to high rank, to undertake such welfare activities for their caste fellows in building hostels, houses on cooperative basis and even colleges and hospitals in some areas, and to found journals and endowment scholarships. Similar was the findings of Baranbas and Mehta (1965)[13] ,

Khare (1970)[14], and Atal (1972)[15]. Baranbas and Mehta[16] had stated that it was the manifest aim of castes to undertake such activities. This can be true for some of castes like Sanik Kshatriyas (Mali), Rawna Rajput (Daroga), Kumhar and Suthar (Khati), of Jodhpur city. These castes have now been recognized among backward castes of Rajasthan in the State & Central list of Backward Classes (1994).

Mathur (1978)[17] found that nine castes and three communities opened schools and built hostels in different periods in Jodhpur city during erstwhile rule. Their primary aim was to provide education to their own children. There were factors which led few castes to open schools for education as well as for reform in their social customs through education, e.g., Mali (Sanik Kshatriyas), Rawana Rajput (Daroga), Suthar (Khati). All these castes are regarded as socially and educationally backward as such needed social reform in their customs. Rural castes preferred to build hostels to get benefit of education to their maximum number of children (e.g. Jat, Patel, Kumhar, Rajput, Rajpurohit, and Kayam khani Muslim). The development of such institutions in Jodhpur city is different from efforts made by religious bodies, and other bodies in other parts of the country.

In rural areas, for instance in 69 villages of Satara district, castes which were numerically dominant, held sizeable lands, took responsibility of spreading education (Gadgil and Dandekar, 1955).[18] In the same State, Kamat (1967, 1968)[19] studied Gulumb village and found that literate castes took initiatives and opened schools there. Joshi and Rao (1965)[20] found in villages of Punjab and U.P. that education development was associated with income and status of castes. Similar was the findings of Desai (1969)[21] and D.S. Survey (1974)[22]. They found that high caste people whose economic conditions were sound could get benefits of secondary and higher education. The middle castes also realized the importance of education and took interest in establishing institutions. Similar to the findings of these studies Mathur (1978)[23] found that in Jodhpur city literate castes first took opportunities and opened schools in the city. These castes were also occupying important positions in administration of the princely State. That is why they took advantage of their position and opened schools there.

Attributes like caste status, occupational status, literacy level, and numerical preponderance strengthen caste dominance in any society. These factors play very important role in Indian politics for politicians decide their vote bank strategy to win any election. Gould (!972)[24] observed that in Faizabad district of U.P. political parties and leaders have become educational zamindars. J.P. Naik (1972)[25] recorded views of local people of Faizabad that Congress has abolished zamindaris and given educational zamindaris. These same castes have built their political base in Indian society.

The question then arises do castes maintain their caste status. When caste associationa function as an educational enterprise, it loses its ritualistic and traditional function as a regulator of social behaviour for it becomes a service organization (Seminar, 1965).[27]

Whether it is a caste or class in any society, both try to build and improve its social status and social position in the society. Only a few castes or class succeed, while remaining does not. Are these elite castes located in any urban or rural society? Lall (1974)[28] listed eleven castes of Jodhpur city as urban elite based on their political, specialist, and economic status. Narain and others (1976)[29] have studied rural castes of Sriganganagar district (Rajasthan) and termed them rural elite. Chauhan (1967)[30] has stated that castes connected with administration took advantage of education. Thus the elite status in power structure and power relations gave them an advantageous position. Bottomore (1968)[31] termed such group as administrative elite. The present study supports the position that castes enjoy their social status by virtue of their numerical preponderance, etc. but exert influence in policy and decision making process. Three types of identifiable influences viz. local, cosmopolitan and neutral exert the influence of these castes in management process. Mathur (1980)[32] has found a close association between pattern of influence and caste status viz. high, medium and low through statistical analysis.

Caste members occupy different positions on the board of management; or management body. Secondary Education Commission (1952)[33] and Education Commission (1961-62)[34] suggested representation of the school head, parents' representative, teachers' and government's representative and non-managing caste members as representatives in the body to highlight its secular character, especially after independence. Before independence, Grant-in-Aid Rule, 1902 did not prescribe any such guidelines. Shukla (1967)[35] has analyzed composition and function of Board of trustees of educational institutions and termed these as decisive social groups. What decisions do these bodies take was raised by Gore (1982).[36] Rene Saran (1973)[37] discussed policy making issues in private secondary educational institutions in U.K. Chesler and Cane (1981)[38] found that management bodies were represented by parents which is a threat to teachers' position and civic elites who are nominated into it. Local political leaders (e.g., Municipal members, M.L.As etc.) are given in their berth to take benefit from them in respect of fund raising, recognition and grant release, etc. for their schools. One observation was that no Scheduled Caste members were given any nomination in the management body, which was similar to findings reported for some districts of U.P. by Chauhan and Narayana (1976).[39]

One of the functions of management body was to raise funds to meet school expenditure. This was one of the requirements under Grants-in-Aid Rule, 1902 and Grant-in-Aid Rule, 1963. Some of the studies (Sharp 1920, Richey 1923, UNESCO 1955, Naik 1963, Misra 1962, 1967 and 1973)[40] have discussed educational finances in the country from the beginning of modern education era. Misra (1973)[41] has reviewed Grant-in-Aid Rule of all States and found there were not many variations.

Management Body is also responsible for implementation of educational policies and educational management. The other policy issues are: student's admission policy and recruitment of teachers. Mathur (1980)[42] analyzed policy and decision making process in school management by using three dimensional action research model given by Pareek (1978)[43] and cybernetic by Rastogi (1979)[44]. Private bodies opened their educational institutes to expand education among their own group. This was not only the case in Indian Society but also in other countries too (Karbel, 1971,[45] Paulstiein, 1971,[46]). Does this factor lead to educational inequality? A few Scholars have studied this aspect (D'Souza 1969, 1975, Persell, 1977, Simkus et. al. 1982, Kerchoff, et. al. 1982, Jeonju 1984, Kundu and Rao, 1986, Valskar, 1990). These studies have found that educational inequalities exist even today. After Independence educational institutions have been showing off their outward secular mask. In reality, however, preferential treatment is always given to their caste brethren. Similar was also the case in the recruitment of teachers on caste considerations provided a teacher fulfilled minimum qualification, etc.

If caste based policy still exists in private aided schools, then it will be instructive to take a look at service conditions of teachers in these schools? J.C. Agarwal (1988)[47] has reviewed service conditions, benefits available to the teachers in these schools. He found that most of the schools have followed rules of age of superannuating, P.F scheme, medical benefits, and salary structure at par with the government teachers. But they are not equal in status which have led teachers to agitate for the principle of equal rights for equal work. These agitations have been converted into litigations and charged management body with anti-democratic and anti-secular policies in the society? Suresh Shukla (1985)[48] has raised this important issue in understanding the problem of education in society.

Literacy and Castes

Literacy is one parameter to measure the growth of any society. We found that it was also related to caste status. The 1891 census of

India, reported that approximately one-seventh of population was literate and belonged to higher castes and sub-castes of society. The literacy figures for different castes of different states are reported in Census of India 1911. This shows that only seven main castes, i.e., Agarwal, Arora, Baidya, Brahman, Kaysthas, Mahajan and Subarna Banik topped the list among literate Castes 49, 50.

The rise in literacy figures among castes in two decades period is one evidence to suggest that literate castes accepted modern education and sent their children to schools and colleges. In 1931, literacy among different castes was: Baidyas (782), Kaysthas (607), Nayar (603) males per 1,000 literate only, while 11 Bhils, 10 chamaras and 5729 Baidyas per 10,000 males were literate. In Bengal, Brahmans were surpassed by Baidyas, Subaran-Baniks and Agarwals in U.P. by Kayasthas and agarwals and Sayeed. Trading castes always had high male literacy (census of India 1931).[51]

In erstwhile Marwar State and Jodhpur city, a few persons of six castes knew English language and other languages in 1911. They were: Brahmans (797 and 2680), Kayasthas (159 and 668), Sheikh (24 and 247) Rawna Rajputs (21 and 263) Rajputs (27 and 213), and Saiyed (02 and 127) (Census of Marwar State, 1911)[52]. A comparative analysis of figure of 1911 of the country and Marwar State reveal that Brahmans, Kaysthas, Mahajans topped the list of literate castes. This was because the last two castes are "writers caste". As a rule the higher castes stood at the top and Scheduled Castes and Tribes at the bottom of the education ladder.

In 1941, there were 36 educated castes in Marwar State (Census of Marwar state, 1941)[53]. Out of 36 castes, only five castes having population above 10% were literate in other languages. These castes were: Mahajans (42,027), Brahmans (12,102), Rajputs (3,511), Sunars (2,019) and Kayasthas (1,390). These same castes were literate in English language but in different order: Brahmans (776), Mahajans (377), Kayasthas (305), Rajputs (113), and Sunars (08). Comparing figures of educated castes with other states, it is seen that Brahmans topped the list among literate castes.

The above review of literacy and castes in different states from 1911 to 1941 in the country and Marwar state reveals that education was though gradually becoming a necessity (Faure, et. al. 1973)[54] and some Indian communities were educated in their native languages as well as in English language also, but only a very few. This was because British opened public schools where English was taught and medium of instruction was English language, followed policy of downward filtration theory. This policy inevitably resulted in the emergence of a small group of educated elite from the upper wealthy castes. Certain religious group, and a small proportion of backward castes were also accorded special facilities by rulers (Desai, A.R. 1967).[55]

Joshi (1967)[56] found in two backward villages, one from the Chittor district of Andhra Pradesh and another from Bankura district of West Bengal that increase or decrease in literacy among different socio-economic groups was dependent on castes and economic social group over a period of time. In another study of growing industrial community of Dandeli, North Kanara district (Mysore state) it was found that caste and occupational backgrounds were determinate factors of literacy. Whether castes and communities were keen to spread education for their boys only or girls too?

Female Education

During the later phase of the British Raj education of girls also received some emphasis. When feelings of nationalism grew there was an awakening among Indians to provide education to girls also. After Independence of the country the situation started changing. Report of the National Committee on Women's education (May 1958 to January 1959)[57] reviewed educational situation of women's gave recommendations for improvement of their situations. This report mentions that the official survey of indigenous Education conducted in different parts of the country at the beginning of the nineteenth century threw some light on the conditions of women as it then existed. In Madras, Munro reported 5,480 girls attended the indigenous primary schools as against 1,78,630 boys (1822). In Bombay no girls were reported attending the public indigenous schools (1824-29) but there is enough evidence to show that the girls of the upper class families received some education at home. But in the beginning of education period (1813-54), several great Indians like Raja Ram Mohan Roy, Pandit Ishwar Chandra Vidyasagar contributed their services for the upliftment of women through various social reforms (e.g., abolition of sati, and education of girls). Thus, private efforts for education of girls got underway in this period.

Voluntary organisations play a very important role in collegiate, secondary, vocational and special education for women. In the field of secondary education, the usual activity of private effort is the establishment of High or Higher Secondary Schools for girls, some of which are partly or wholly residential institutions. In vocational and special education, however, private organizations are conducting a number of training institutions for primary teachers. In addition, they conduct a multitude of activities in the educational and allied fields. For example, number of such organizations have successfully organised training courses in crafts beneficial to middle class women who need to earn some supplementary income for the family, (e.g., tailoring, weaving, spinning, embroidery and dyeing). They are also conducting preparatory courses for women to enable them to go in for mid-wifery, nursing and craft teachers training. They have also been implementing after care rehabilitation and correctional programmes for rescued women. One of the most extensive programmes undertaken by them is for the training of Gram Sevikas for the Welfare Extension Projects of the Central Social Welfare Board and for the Coordinated Welfare Projects in Community Development Blocks.

One can easily understand that the State attitude towards Indian Private Effort was not very favourable under the British rule. Prior to 1854, such private efforts were so restricted that the question of formulating a general State policy towards it never really arose. But the Despatch of 1854 directed that full encouragement should be given to Indian private effort in education. In spite of this directive, the policies adopted by the Education Departments in dealing with private schools conducted by Indians were not very encouraging. The grant-in-aid rules were usually stiff, the quantum of grant was ordinarily low, and financial assistance to private schools was regarded almost as a patronage of the Department. These were not happy conditions and it is not a matter of surprise that private effort did not thrive. But the Hunter Commission of 1882 – its Report has been called the Magna Carta of private effort gave an entirely new lead on the subject. It categorically stated that private efforts could succeed only if certain fundamental principles are adopted as the basis of State policy viz., (i) abstinence from interference with internal management, (ii) provision of adequate grant-in-aid, (iii) elimination of any competition, direct or indirect, between private and government institutions, (iv) appointment of officers who can command the confidence of the private schools, and (v) acceptance of the 'equality' of private institutions with those conducted by the State. On this last issue, which is the crux of the problem, it said "But the way in which the Department should manifest its care for institutions, under private managers, may be briefly indicated. No desire for greater symmetry of system for any greater hold on the education of a locality should lead the Department to establish schools in places where aided effort can be made adequate. Again, if institutions under private managers are to be regarded as part of the educational apparatus of the country no less than those maintained directly by the Department, it follows that those who assist the State by managing them should have great influence in determining all questions of general educational policy. The Head of the Department must still be the controlling authority in the last resort; but if an aided institution is preferable to a departmental one when it is equally efficient, the opinion and advice of the managers of the former should be at least as carefully attended to and carry as great weight as the views of those who are intimately connected with the latter. In determining all such matters as the arrangement or conduct of public examinations, the rate of fees, the terms of admission, the course of study or the forms of periodical returns, in short, with regard to all that concerns the education of the community at large, the Director of Public Instructions should be guided as much by the laws of those interested in aided education as by those of departmental officers. He should employ the teachers and managers of aided schools as freely, if they so desire, as officials of the Department in carrying out what has been resolved on. We have decided, that the time has not come when a representative board should be set up to control or influence the educational executive but meanwhile a useful substitute for such a board may be provided by free and frequent consultation between the Director and those whom the State has invited to cooperate with itself. If aided institutions are thus to have the cordial sympathy of the Department, it follows that any success on their part must be as fully and warmly acknowledged as the similar success of a departmental institution. It follows, too, that when any changes are from time to time proposed, the bearing of such changes on the welfare and convenience of schools under private managers should be carefully weighed. It also follows that all scholarships and rewards that the State confers should be given without regard to the form of management of the institutions to which a candidate belongs".

This was too difficult a proposition for the foreign bureaucracy to follow and it is not surprising that these recommendations were not generally acted upon in the proper spirit, although the general conditions did improve to sum extent. With the beginning of the Curzonian era, the attitude towards Indian private efforts, which was often suspected to have a national leanings, became stiff and hostile. The position improved slightly with the transfer of education to Indian control; but on the whole, the old treatment of private efforts was generally kept up by all Education Departments till 1947 when the British power was withdrawn.

After the attainment of the Independence there has been a still further change and private effort now receives on the whole, much fairer treatment and a larger grant-in-aid than in the past. But even now, some vestiges of the old tradition are still left and they create difficulties. They are:- (i) Private institutions are still not accepted as equal partners with State institutions and several forms of partiality are still in evidence e.g., government stipends and scholarships are available in Government institutions only in some States, private institutions are still starved for funds in the first instance and then branded "inferior", the status accorded to them is generally lower etc.; (ii) the grant-in-aid is still not sufficiently liberal; (iii) there is too much of department control; and (iv) the procedures for release of grant are unduly complicated.

Steps will have to be taken to remove these difficulties if private efforts have to play the role which is really expected of it. The efforts made by government and private agencies have improved educational status of girls and women. Level of education of girls was estimated by their literacy percentage. National policy on Education (1986)[58] reported 24.82 per cent literacy among women in 1981, which has of course, increased from 7.93 in 1951, i.e., in three decades. This statistical fact still indicates that the much is required to be done for girls' education.

Table 1.4: Number of Girls per 100 Boys Enrolled in Schools

Year	*Primary (I-V)*	*Middle (VI-VIII)*	*Secondary (IX-X)*
1950-51	39	18	16
1955-56	44	25	21
1960-61	48	32	23
1965-66	57	37	30
1970-71	60	41	35
1975-76	62	46	39
1979-80	62	48	41
1980-81	63	49	44
1981-82	63	49	43
1982-83	64	51	41
1983-84	64	51	43
1984-85	65	52	44
1985-86	67	54	44
1986-87	69	54	46
1987-88	69	55	47
1988-89	70	55	50
1989-90	70	56	50
1990-91	71	58	50
1991-92	72	62	52
1992-93	72	61	51

Source: Education in India, 1992-93 Vol.1(S), Govt. of India, Ministry of Human Resource Development, (Deptt. of Education), Planning, Monitoring and Statistics Division, New Delhi, Statement 8, p.11.

The salient recommendations given in the Government of India Report of the National Committee on Women's education are reproduced here:

I. Special Recommendation

1. The education of women should be regarded as a measure and a special problem in education for a good many years to come and a bold and determine effort should be made to face its difficulties and magnitude and to close the existing gap between the education of men and women in as short a time as possible.
2. Necessary steps should be taken, without delay, to create a special machinery to deal with the problems of the education of girls and women and to assign adequate funds for the purpose.
3. The problem of the education of women is so vital and of such great national significance that it is absolutely necessary for the Centre to assume more responsibility for its rapid development. This responsibility will be three-fold:-
   (i) It should be a responsibility of the Centre to see that parity between the education of boys and girls is reached as early as possible, and also to see that the education of girls and women is developed evenly in all parts of the country.
   (ii) The Centre should prescribe targets to be attained and also guide the States in preparing comprehensive development plans for the education of girls and women in their areas.
   (iii) The Centre should assist the States financially in implementing the approved plans.
4. The magnitude of the problem of the education of girls and women is so great that it can be solved only if all the resources of Government and of non-official organizations are combined and fully geared to the task.
5. It is also necessary to enlist the cooperation of all semi-officials organizations, local bodies, voluntary organizations, teachers' organizations and members of the public to assist in the promotion of the education of girls and women.
6. To the extent that private effort is not forthcoming, direct action should be taken by the State to develop the education of girls and women and to establish special institutions for the purpose under immediate control.

II. Other Special Recommendations

Primary Education

7. The mere passing of compulsory legislation would be of no avail unless suitable conditions for encouraging parents to send

their daughters to schools are created. Greater emphasis, therefore, should be laid on the creation of such conditions rather than on giving the authority concerned more panel powers.

8. The Government should recognize the great importance of creating a strong public opinion in the country in favour of the education of girls and women and take all possible measures for the purpose.

III. Role of Voluntary Organizations

9. The services of the voluntary organizations should be extensively used in the field of middle, secondary, higher, social and vocational education of women. Their services should also be utilized in teacher-training and in providing special education facilities for adult women.
10. Some of the main difficulties experienced by voluntary organizations are as follows:
    (i) Private institutions are not treated on par with Government institutions, though their functions are identical.
    (ii) Grant-in-aid rules are not sufficiently liberal.
    (iii) There is irksome Departmental control.
    (iv) The procedure for the release of funds is unduly complicated.

Steps should, therefore, be taken to remove these difficulties and private effort enabled to play the part which is expected of it.

11. The existing grant-in-aid codes of the States need a thorough revision, on the following broad principles in so far as the institutions for the education of women are concerned:
    (i) There should be a substantial and significant difference in the rates of grants-in-aid as between girls' institutions and boys institutions at all level.
    (ii) The conditions of aid for girls' institutions should be made easier.
    (iii) The conditions generally imposed by Boards of Secondary Education and Universities in respect of buildings and reserve funds should be relaxed in the case of all educational institutions for girls.
    (iv) Institutions for the education of girls in rural areas should receive more liberal grants-in-aid, both recurring and non-recurring. The purpose of the non-recurring grants-in-aid should include building and equipment. In rural areas, hostels and staff quarters must be included where necessary.

(v) In the case of middle and secondary schools for girls, training institutions for teachers and institutions which provide special educational facilities for adult women, there should not be any condition requiring a matching contribution. In other cases, a matching contribution up to 25 per cent could be insisted upon.

(vi) The grant-in-aid given to voluntary organizations of established standing and repute for non-recurring purposes should be given on a hundred per cent basis (at least in so far primary, middle and the secondary schools and training institutions including the special institutions for adult women are concerned).

(vii) On the recurring side, the grant-in-aid should ordinarily cover the entire deficit, subject to the ceiling that the aid per capita will not be more than the cost per pupil in a State institution of a similar type.

(viii) In the case of other voluntary organizations matching contributions may be expected, but not more than half of what is expected in the case of boys' school.

12. (a) A scheme similar to the Central Government scheme to assist voluntary organizations doing some experimental or valuable work in education should be prepared for girls' institutions only and special funds allocated for it.

(b) A detailed scheme for giving loans for non-recurring purposes – particularly for hostels and staff quarters – should be drawn up for immediate implementation.

Education of Backward Castes

It is for nearly a hundred years that Provincial Government in India have been implementing special programmes for the welfare of depressed or deprived sections of society. The first such step was taken by Madras Government with the framing of Grant-in-Aid Code in 1885 to regulate financial aid to educational institutions, providing special facilities for students of depressed classes. Subsequently, in 1921, acting on a resolution passed by the State Legislative Council, Madras Government took steps for higher representation of non-Brahmins in Government services. The scheme was reviewed in 1927 and the scope of reservation was enlarged further, dividing all the communities in the State into five broad categories and earmarking separate quota for each category (Mandal, B.P. 1980).[59] In many States efforts were made to list out backward castes before Independence. After Independence, the First Backward Classes Commission was set up by a Presidential order under Article 340 of the

Constitution of India on January 29th, 1953 and it submitted its report on March 30th ,1955. The Commission is popularly known as Kaka Kalelkar Commission. It identified 2399 backward castes or communities for the entire country, and 837 of these were classified as the most backward. The report was not finally accepted and approved by the government [60]. After a lapse of twenty-four years, the Govterment of India appointed second Backward Classes Commission in 1979 under the chairmanship of Shri B.P.Mandal. The Commission submitted its report in 1980 and listed 3743 backward castes of India. From the reports of these two Commissions and earlier ones for different states it is clear that many backward castes were generally socially and educationally backward.

Education of Harijans

Among Hindu castes, the emergence of caste associations as educational entrepreneur was not in order of caste hierarchy. Middle castes were quick to respond to this opportunity. Why was this so? Why did not Brahmans respond first to modern education? Hutton (1951) and Ghurye (1957)[61] have discussed that caste hierarchy played major role in educational advancement because upper and middle castes were never deprived of educational benefits. But these varied from State to State. Castes connected with the administrative and record keeping functions were quick to respond to the incentives and took advantage of the rising opportunities (Chauhan, 1967)[62]. Since then, caste associations have opened schools for education of upper and middle castes. Who took the responsibility of education of scheduled castes?

Has any of upper castes opened any school for education of untouchables or scheduled castes. Attempts on the part of individual and government were unsuccessful. Chauhan (1967)[63] has discussed reasons for failure of separate schools for the scheduled castes in India. Caste differentiation was sharply in evidence in those days. An empirical study was conducted in five districts, viz. Agra, Bareilly, Mathura, Lucknow and Saharanpur of U.P. state. It was found that despite welfare measures taken for Scheduled Castes by the government the disparities in the educational levels and literacy rates between Scheduled Castes and general population continued to exist due to external factors (e.g., occupation, economic status, education level of family, etc.). The schools were established and managed by local influential drawn from upper castes and the teachers were recruited from upper castes (Chauhan and Narayana 1977)[64] . The literacy rate of Scheduled Castes population in general and female SC population for 1961 and 1991 is 10.27 and 37.41 and for female population is 3.29 and 23.76.

Marwar State : Erstwhile Princely State

The existing structure of the states of Indian union is partly the result of accident and the circumstances attending the growth of the British power in India and partly a by-product of the historic process of the integration of former Indian states. At the time of Independence of the country there were 566 princely states in the country. These princely states had been merged into different existing States.[65] These states had their own rulers during British Raj in India. The erstwhile rulers followed the policy of the British Raj which were in the interest of development of the State. Development in the State was also their topmost priority. These developments mainly included construction of roads, hospitals, educational institutions, etc. However, in the field of educational development it was reported that the Durbars (of Rajputana) took little or no interest in education.

Of the princely states in India the existing Rajasthan state is a product of integration of nineteen former princely states and British provinces. Among the princely States of the Rajasthan one of the largest princely state was Marwar (Maru Pradesh) which is located in western part of the State. Rajput ruler ruled the erstwhile State since its birth i.e., 1444 A.D. with Mandore as capital. Like other rulers the rulers of the Marwar State took interest in development of various fields such as health, education, etc.

According to Imperial Gazetteer of India – Provincial series Rajputana (1908)[66] the educational institutions at the end of March 1905, numbered altogether 647, of which 510 were maintained by several Durbars, 103 by private individuals, castes communities, etc., and 34 by missionary societies. These consist of 4 colleges, 86 secondary schools, 545 primary schools, including 53 for girls, and 12 special schools. The number on the rolls of these 647 institutions in 1905 was 37,670, and the daily average attendance during 1904-05 was 28,130.

The growth in number of educational institutions began from 1901 in the erstwhile Marwar state. There were 38 educational institutions in 1901-02 in erstwhile Marwar state, which increased to 64 in 1911, 80 in 1921, 158 in 1931 and 267 in 1941(Census of Marwar State,1941)[67]. This was a trend similar to country's development as reported by Misra (1962).

Table 1.5: Progress of Education in Marwar (1873-1923)

Year	Vernacular	State Schools			Aided Schools		
		Anglo Vernacular	High School and Colleges	Special Girls School	Boys	Girls	Total No. of Institutions
1873	12	2	-	-	-	-	14
1878	12	1	1	1	-	-	15
1883	13	2	1	2	-	-	18
1888	21	6	1	2	1	-	31
1893	25	6	2	3	1	-	37
1898	24	8	2	3	1	-	38
1903	28	9	2	3	1	-	43
1908	33	15	2	3	1	29	83
1913	47	18	3	3	1	23	95
1918	49	19	3	2	1	19	93
1923	54	20	3	2	1	17	96

Compiled from:

(i) Marwar Administration Report (1884-1923)

(ii) Reports on Administration of Rajputana States (1871-1904)

(iii) History of Durbar High School, Jodhpur

(iv) Rajputana Gazetteer, Vol. III A & B

Shah [1981] 68 compiled data for progress of educational institutions from 1878 to 1923 through secondary sources. The above table shows an increase in number of educational institutions from 14 in1873 to 98 in 1923, i.e., over the period of 50 years.

Selected Educational Statistics (As on 30th Sept. 1998) 1998-99 reports 55517 schools in the Rajasthan State. Of these there were 2219 schools in Jodhpur district. A close look on this table reveal that the city stands 5th at primary level, 6th at middle level and 3rd at high / higher secondary level of education among 32 districts of the state. (See Appendix Tables).

Jodhpur city was the capital of erstwhile Marwar State. The erstwhile Marwar State was founded in 1444 A.D. at Mandore as capital. Rao Jodha was the third ruler. In the nuclear stage (1459-1562), Rajputs ruled the State then in a transitory phase Mughals (1562-1678 and 1678-1803) came into power. British alliance started in 1803 to 1878. Developments in the State began from 1878 to 1918. During this phase Rathors ruled the State.

Modernization began from 1918-1947 and after (Kumbhat, 1969)[69]. It was during Maharaja Jaswant Singh Ji II (1873-1895) development in the erstwhile State was initiated. Sir Pratap Singh was the younger son of Maharaja Takhat Singh. He took all interest in the development of the State till he died in 1922 (Cox, A.P. 1968)[70]. Maharaja Sardar Singhji ruled the State from 1895-1911. Maharaja Kumar Sumer Singhji died at an early age of 21 years. Maharaja Umaid Singhji was vested with full powers to rule the State after 1922. After the death of Shri Umaid Singhji, Maharaja Hanuwant Singhji was made the ruler of the State (Reu. B.N. 1940)[71].

Marwar's history of the medieval periods abounds in the traditions of chivalry. With the downfall of the Moghul Empire and the establishment of the East India Company's rule Jodhpur State entered into an agreement with the Company's government in 1818. During the 1857 uprising the Britishers helped the erstwhile rulers and this brought induction of British civil servants in the State services. Apart from the impact on administration, the induction of British officers had its influence on the culture of the upper layer of the social hierarchy of Jodhpur, which started imitating certain modes of behaviour of the foreigners. It was largely due to the British influence that the State had an early start in medical and education fields. With educational field better than those in many other States in Jodhpur community consciousness about the country at large was far ahead of other States. (Lall, S.K., 1974: II)[71].

Jodhpur city is the second largest city in Rajasthan. According to 1991 Census population of Jodhpur city was 6,48,621 (Census of India, 1991, Rajasthan, Jaipur)[72]. There was an increase in population of Jodhpur city at every decade period from 1901 to 1991, except slight decline in 1921. Population of Jodhpur city in different decades were : 79,109 in 1901, 79,756 in 1911, 73,480 in 1921, 94,736 in 1931, 1,26,842 in 1941, 3,17,612 in 1971 and 5,06,345 in 1981. The rise in population in Jodhpur city has required educational expansion in Jodhpur city. (Census of India, 1981, Series-18, Rajasthan, District Census Hand Book, Jodhpur, Rajasthan, Jaipur)[73]. In Jodhpur city there were 3,65,967 persons literate (56.40%). This shows that percentage of literate persons is higher than that of state as a whole (38.81%) in 1991 and other cities of States.

In the city not only did the state play its major role of expansion of education but also they encouraged castes and communities to enter in the field of education. As a result number of forward castes, backward castes, and minority communities opened schools for education of both boys and girls. Even two Christian ladies with the support of two local jagirdars opened a school for education of girls in English medium. Another minority community Muslim also responded to this opportunity. This trend to avail of the incentives offered by the State is reflected in a tremendous rise in number of castes and communities in the city. It is interesting to note that Rajasthan state is an educationally backward state in the country and the Jodhpur city being second largest city in the state show large number of castes and community schools. These schools have been managed by castes for more than fifty years to hundred years.

History of Educational Development

It was observed that the erstwhile rulers were not keen on education expansion because they considered it below their dignity (Erskine, K.D.)[74]. Secondly, erstwhile rulers thought educated people would seldom bow down to aristocratic rule of one man and purposefully neglected education (Agarwal, B.D. 1979)[75]. This was not exactly true. Because there were few females who had received education at home in mid nineteenth century (Shah, P.R. 1981)[76]. Later on erstwhile rulers had thought of education in the field of education. Sir Pratap Singh, Regent and Shri Umed Singhji, His Highness and ruler of erstwhile princely State had always thought of education in the State (Vanwart, Robert, 1926, Cox, A.P. 1968 Lall, S.K. 1974, Singh,Vikram 1983)78. Development of modern education in Jodhpur city was initiated by Col. French in 1844. His efforts were unsuccessful to continue Vidya Shal School. Two educated persons Rao Raja Moti Singh, son of Maharaja Takhat Singh and Ratan Lal Manihar, a Marwari realized need of English education. They could impress upon Maharaja Takhat Singh, ex-ruler of the erstwhile State. In 1867, the erstwhile state opened a school which was earlier named as Durbar School, Jodhpur and now known as New Government Senior Higher Secondary School, Jodhpur. The erstwhile Marwar State opened two Rajput schools separately for education of Rajputs boys in 1875. Sir Pratap Singh Regent of the erstwhile State had always thought of education in particular of Rajput boys so that they could be placed in high offices in the princely State (Vanwart, Robert 1926)[78].

The year 1886 was important in the history of education in Jodhpur in following ways:

(i) It was in that year the first girls school named after Mr. Hewson (who was guardian to Maharaja Kumar Sumer Singh and he had died in August, 1886) was established (Agarwal, B.D. 1979)[79].

(ii) A department of public instruction was opened in that year.

(iii) Swami Dayanand Saraswati came to Jodhpur. His ideas had influenced Maharaja Takhat Singh, His Highness and Sir Pratap Singh, Regent of erstwhile Marwar State (Singh, Vikram 1983)[80].

(iv) Sir Pratap Singh, Regent of the State called a meeting of prominent persons of Jodhpur city. He asked them to open schools for education of their boys.

In response to a call given by the State, three middle castes viz. Kayasthas, Oswals and Sanik Kshatriyas (Mali) came forward and opened their schools for education of boy's only. Kayastha was the first middle caste that opened their Anglo vernacular primary boy's school in 1887. They named their school in honour of Sir Pratap Singh, Regent of erstwhile Marwar State. After nine years of first private aided school, the second middle caste Oswal came forward. They opened their Anglo vernacular primary school in 1896. This school was named after Shri Sardar Singh ji, the ruler of the erstwhile Marwar State. Like Kayasthas, Oswals also held key positions in various department of the Marwar State. A few educated persons of Oswal caste realized need of education because of modernization taking place in the country, erstwhile Marwar State and in Jodhpur city. Though traditional occupation of Oswal caste was business yet they took advantage of rising opportunities. In 1898, third middle caste Sanik Kshatriya (Mali) opened their Anglo-vernacular boy's school in Jodhpur city. They named their school after Maharaj Kumar Shri Sumer Singhji, who died at an early age of 21 years. He was son of Shri Jaswant Singh and brother of Shri Sardar Singh and Shri Umaid Singh, ex-ruler of the erstwhile princely State. Sanik Kshatriyas were influenced by Arya Samaj ideology and Swami Dayanand Saraswati.Their influence had motivated them to open first boy's school on outskirts of the city on Mandore road. By the end of 1900, there was rise in State-aided schools in this period. This was a period of educational necessity.

As per recommendations of Indian Education Commission (1882), British Government introduced a grant-in-aid rule, which is known as Grant-in-Aid Rule, 1902. In erstwhile Marwar State also, the Rulers in order to promote private effort in the field of education, introduced Grant-in-aid Rule, 1902 in 1904. In the erstwhile State, this rule was known as Grant-in-Aid Rule, 1902 (1904). There was a specific condition laid down in such rule that private-aided schools were required to maintain educational standards as per erstwhile State's education policy, and follow courses and curriculum accordingly to become eligible for State's aid. The conditions stipulated in the Grant-in-aid Rule (1902 (1904) attracted only two castes viz. Brahman and Rawna Rajput (Daroga) in 1912, i.e., eight years after introduction of the rule.

Pushkarna Brahman, a sect of Brahman caste opened their Anglo vernacular middle school in 1912. Like Sanik Kshatriya caste they also named their school in memory of ex-ruler Maharaj Kumar Shri Sumer

Singh who died at an early age. It was fourth State-aided private school in Jodhpur city. The question is: Why did upper caste Brahman respond in 1912 and not in 1886 and 1902 immediately? There were possible reasons of Pushkarana Brahmans responding to modern education in 1912.

(i) There was already one traditional school run by another sect Shrimali Brahmans of Brahman caste. Brahmans were keen in religious learning e.g., Sanskrit, Sandhya, etc. For this reason they did not respond to modern education immediately.

(ii) They realized need of modern education, because other castes have already opened their schools for education of their boys. (Kalla, Bansi Dhar Sharma, 1912). This was a case of ideological imitation because Brahmans were studying in State and three private-aided schools of Jodhpur city. Thus they were not educationally deprived.

(iii) One of their traditional occupations among others was cooking. On one social occasions, they felt insulted due to this occupation being the work of illiterate (Kalla, M.R.. 1947)[81]. This factor forced caste-elders to take immediate steps for education of their boys on modern lines of education so that they could also avail benefits of rising opportunities in Government jobs. (The question of other upper caste Rajput did not arise because State had already opened two schools for Rajput boys in 1875. State made all efforts to see that a school or two schools survived and finally a school took shape in 1912 as a first high school in Jodhpur city. After the end of feudal rule in 1949, Rajput school got status of private-aided school and renamed into Chopasani High School, Jodhpur in 1949).

In 1912, there was another caste Rawna Rajput (Daroga), which occupied low position in social-structure of Jodhpur city, opened their Anglo-vernacular boys lower primary school in that year. They named their school in honour of His Highness Shri Umaid Singh, ex-ruler of princely Marwar State, Why did they open their school when there were already one State run and three State-aided schools? The 1891 Census of Marwar State published some remarks about origin of this caste as illegitimate offspring of Rajputs in the State. This statement created a fire in mind of a few caste-conscious persons. They immediately realized need of social reforms through education (Chauhan, Panna Lal, 1927)[82]. Rawna Rajput (Daroga) caste has now been recognized socially and educationally backward caste in Rajasthan State and included in the State & Central list of Backward Classes. Thus Grant-in-aid Rule, 1902 (1904) could attract only two castes: Brahman and Rawna Rajput, which opened their boy's school in 1912. It was realized by ex-rulers that education was at slow progress. The erstwhile State took measures to accelerate educational expansions in the State by following actions:

(i) Reorganization of Education in Erstwhile Marwar State (1914)

A one-man committee of H.T. Knowlton, an educational advisor of Punjab was appointed to suggest measures of reorganization of education in erstwhile feudal State. This report suggested liberal-grant-in-aid policy to be followed to attract more number of private bodies. As a result of reorganization of education and liberal Education Policy, Maheswari caste opened their Anglo vernacular boy's primary school in 1918 and Anglo vernacular primary girl's school in 1920. It was a distinct phenomenon that Maheswaris named their school in 1902. It was a distinct phenomenon that Maheswaris named their schools after their caste only because State adopted open door policy to encourage private bodies. Another caste Pushkarna Brahman also opened first private-aided Anglo-vernacular girl's primary school in 1919 and named it after ex-chief Minister of Rajasthan State, Late Shri Jai Narayan Vyas later on. In this period private bodies also realized need of girl's education and they came forward.

(ii) Scheme of Expansion of Primary Education (1922)

On the recommendation of H.R. Knowlton's report (1914) on reorganization of education in Marwar State, the erstwhile State took further steps and Rao Sahib K.M. Bhattji prepared a scheme of expansion of primary education in 1922. This scheme encouraged all private bodies to open primary schools for boys and girls throughout the erstwhile Marwar State. This was a period of educational expansion. The scheme of reorganization of education in erstwhile Marwar State (1914) and scheme of expansion of primary education in Marwar State (1922) had attracted more number of private bodies in the field of education. In the erstwhile State there were 17 State aided schools in 1923, which had increased to 40 in 1944-45 (source: Annual Reports on Administration of Jodhpur State, 1923 to 1944-45)[83].

In Jodhpur city, Sanik Kshatriyas (Malis) caste (two different management bodies from boys' school) opened two girls school separately at different locations for education of their girls in 1925 and 1935. The first management body of Sanik Kshatriyas caste also preferred to name their schools after Shri Umed Singh, ex-ruler of the princely State like boys school which is located at Beriyon-Ka-Mohalla, Sojati Gate, Jodhpur. While the second girl's school was named after their religion Vedic Kanya Pathshala, which is located at Bagar Mohalla, Nagaori Gate, Jodhpur. As it was stated Sanik Kshatriyas were influenced by Arya Samaj ideology and Swami Dayanand Saraswati they thought of education of girls too, because this caste arranged marriages of their girls at an early age as per their traditional customs and social practices. They wanted to do social reforms. In 1931, Agarwal caste opened their boy's school and named it in honour of last ex-ruler Maharaja Shri Hanumant Singh. Their aim was to take advantage of erstwhile Marwar State's policy of educational expansion. Until now all castes aimed to educate their children in their schools, but a Pushkarna Brahman social worker of Jodhpur city took initiative and started a school named Sarvajanik School in 1943 i.e., school for children from all sections irrespective of caste, creed or sex and untouchables and Harijans. His attempt to provide education to untouchables and Harijans failed, similar to efforts made by erstwhile State also. It was the period after Second World War and people were involved in national struggle and Quit India Movement.

Like castes, minority communities also took advantage of rising opportunities in the field of education. These communities were local and immigrated. The first minority community was Christian. Local Christian ladies who resided in Jodhpur city mobilized support of local rural persons. These ladies had connections with British officials in the State. They approached the princely ruler through the English lady and obtained permission to start a girls' school on the English education pattern. Such types of schools were not opened either by State or by any caste in Jodhpur city. One uniqueness and distinct feature of this development was that it was not missionary movement to spread education like in other parts of country. Though this school later on received funds from mission sisters of Ajmer.

Another immigrant community was Sindhi, which immigrated to India from Pakistan (Sindh area). As a result of partition of India after Independence Government of those days took measures to resettle them in refugee camps in Jodhpur city. A separate Department of Resettlement and Rehabilitation was opened. The erstwhile government also realized language problem of Sindhis for they could communicate in Sindhi language only. There was no school in Jodhpur city, districts and the erstwhile Marwar State, which were providing instructions in Sindhi language. A few educated Sindhis approached erstwhile government and opened two schools for education of Sindhi boys and girls separately. They were allowed to recruit teachers from Sindhis so that they could teach them properly. It was a case of rehabilitation of migrant community through education, which began in 1947.

In Jodhpur city, the Muslims had strong beliefs in Madarsa education. They opened many madarsas in Jodhpur city and in the erstwhile State. Muslims were famous and good workers for construction work.

They constructed a modern well designed home for ex-ruler Maharaja Umaid Singh, which is known as Umaid Bhawan. The ex-ruler was very much impressed by their work. He asked a few prominent and educated persons of Muslim community to open a school for education of Muslim boys on line of modern education like other State and State-aided schools. They took benefit of advice of the ex-ruler. In 1937, Marwar Muslim education society opened a school named Muslim school. They managed their school well. Like other state-aided schools, they were also required to raise funds for upgradation of their school. By the time they could raise funds in 1949, the erstwhile feudal state was merged into present Rajasthan State. Popular government came into power. Popular government of those days took over control of their school only in the State and renamed it into Mahatama Gandhi School, Jodhpur. This was the first case Government of Rajasthan took such steps in the city. Due to their decisions, Muslims of Jodhpur city felt very bad and considered government's approach apathetic.

A few prominent persons of Muslim community and Marwar Muslim education society approached to Government of Rajasthan. They were given permission to start a primary school with madarsa also in1954. (They continued their fight with government to compensate them for earlier school. Recently Government of Rajasthan has granted them land and permission to start a senior higher secondary school which has been named after national leader Maulana Abdul Kalam Azad. The school is known as Maulana Abdul Kalam Azad Senior Higher Secondary School, Jodhpur that is located at Kamla Nehru Nagar). The present study covered Isaquia Secondary School, which was named after the founder person Mohd. Isaq Sahib.

After 1954, there was no rise of secondary and higher secondary schools in Jodhpur city. Government of Rajasthan reframed grant-in-aid rule, which is known as Grant-in-Aid Rule, 1963. Grant-in-aid Rule, 1963 attracted a few individuals and religious organizations. Four secondary schools were opened by the time. These were not included in the study since these schools did not fall into our criteria of selection of school as discussed in detail in methodology section.

Educational Profile of Jodhpur City

In Jodhpur city there is one university, now known as Jai Narayan Vyas University, Jodhpur (formerly known as Jodhpur University) and six colleges and schools at different levels. Table 1.6 shows educational profile of Jodhpur city.

Table 1.6 : Educational Profile of Jodhpur City

S.No.	Type of Institution	No. of Institutions				Total
		Govt.	Private		Autonomous	
			Aided	Unaided		
1.	University	-	-	-	1	1
2.	Colleges					
	A. General Courses					
	(i) Science college	-	1	-	-	1
	(ii) Commerce college	-	4	-	-	4
	(iii) Girls college*	-	-	-	-	1+1
	(iv) National Law College	1				
	B. Technical Courses					
	(i) Engineering	-	-	3	-	3
	(ii) Medical college	1	-	-	-	1
	(iii) Polytechnic	1	-	-	-	1
	C. Professional					
	(i) B. Ed.	-	1	-	-	1
3.	(ii) Sanskrit college	1	-	-	-	1
4.	Training centre for teachers (STC)	1	-	-	-	1
	Schools	169	106	94	-	369
	Total	**174**	**112**	**97**	**1**	**384**

Source: 1. Directory of Year Book on Education (Jodhpur), Jaipur: Govt. of Rajasthan
2. Office of District Education Officer, Rajasthan, Jodhpur, 2004.

* *Note: Engineering and Girls College are part of the University*

It was found that there were 384 educational institutions in Jodhpur city. University is a State University, which is financed from State and UGC budget. It has got four engineering colleges and one girl's college besides all other faculties of Science, Arts, Commerce, Social Sciences, etc. There are three state controlled govt. colleges: Medical, Polytechnic and Sanskrit. There is one govt. run teachers' training centre (School Teachers Certificate Course for primary school teachers). This city has six private aided colleges, which are run by individuals and castes (Brahmans, Maheswaris and Oswals). Recently, a National Law College has been opened recently in the city, i.e. in 2001.

At school level, there were 369 schools in Jodhpur city. Out of 369 schools, 169 (45.80 Per cent) schools were govt. run schools, 200 (54.20 Per cent) were private schools. Again out of 200 private schools, there were 106 private aided schools and 94 private unaided schools but recognised, which was fairly high as compared to the State and Country Statistics.

Table 1.7 : Educational Institutions (only schools) by Type of Management and Different Stages of Schools in Jodhpur City in 2004-05

S. No.	*Type of School*	*Number of Schools by type of Management*											
		Government			*Private aided*			*Private unaided*			*Total*		
		Boys	*Girls*	*Total*	*Boys*	*Girls*	*Total*	*Boys*	*Girls*	*Total*	*Boys*	*Girls*	*Total*
1.	Pre-Primary	-	1	1	-	4	4	-	-	-	-	5	5
2.	Primary	74	26	10	32	23	55	41	18	59	147	67	214
3.	Upper Primary	33	12	45	15	12	27	31	4	35	79	28	107
4.	High School	8	5	13	5	3	8	-	-	-	13	8	21
5.	Higher Sec.	5	5	10	10	2	12	-	-	-	15	7	22
	Total	**120**	**49**	**169**	**62**	**44**	**106**	**72**	**22**	**94**	**254**	**115**	**369**

Source: Office of District Education Officer (Boys), Jodhpur District and Office of Dy. Director (Woman) Jodhpur District, Jodhpur, Rajasthan, 2001.

It was found the only two types of agencies viz. govt. and private agencies are managing schools in Jodhpur city from pre-primary stage to senior higher secondary stage. Table 1.2 shows that there were only 5 pre-primary govt. run and private aided schools, which were very small. This shows that private agencies did not prefer to prepare children for education from pre-primary age i.e., 3-5 years. However, individuals have opened pre-primary schools, which are unrecognised. It is also very difficult to give their statistics. At primary stage there were 214 (58%) schools, which was less than country's figures. Out of 214 primary schools, there were 100 (46.70%) govt. run primary schools, 55 (25.70%) private aided schools and 59 (27.60%) private primary schools. Overall, private agencies managed 53.30% of primary schools in Jodhpur city, which was slightly more than govt. schools.

At middle stage of education there were 107 (29.00%) upper primary schools. Govt. and private bodies also managed these schools. Out of 107 upper primary schools, govt. managed only 45 schools

(45.05%), private bodies managed 62 schools (57.95%). There was a decrease in number of private-unaided schools from 59 primary schools to 35 upper primary schools and not single unaided secondary and senior higher secondary schools. This trend indicates that private agencies (it includes individuals) could manage schools without aid at primary and upper primary stage, but not at later stage since it involves considerable expenditure.

Out of 369 schools, there are 43 secondary and senior higher secondary schools in Jodhpur city during 2000-01. There were 23 (53.50%) govt. run schools and 20 (46.50%) private aided schools. Out of 20 private aided schools, there were 12 senior higher secondary schools and 8 secondary schools. Only 16 private aided schools were chosen for the study because other four schools (1 senior higher secondary school and 3 secondary schools) were established after Independence. Three schools are managed by individual bodies and one by Rashtriya Swayam Sevak Sangh (RSS). The schools which are not included are namely: (i) Lal Bahadur Shastri Senior Higher Secondary School, Jodhpur (established in 1968), (ii) Adarsh Vidya Mandir, Jodhpur (managed by RSS), (iii) Brig. Jaber Singh Secondary School (1976), (iv) Central Academy, Jodhpur (1978).

Data analysis revealed that there were 254 boys schools (68.85%) and 115 girls schools (31.15%). Ratio of girls and boys schools was 1:2.20, i.e., girls schools were comparatively less. There was variation in boys and girls schools by type of management and stage of education. Out of 169 govt. schools, there were 120 boys schools (71.00%) and 49 (29.00%) girls schools. Private agencies managed 134 boys schools (67.00%) and 66 girls schools (33.00%). Also there was variation in boys and girls schools at each stage of education.

There were four girls' schools only at pre-primary stage. At primary stage, there were 147 (68.70%) boys schools and 67 (31.30%) girls schools; govt. run boys and girls schools were 74 (74%) and 26 (26%) privately managed boys schools 73 (64.00%) and girls schools 41 (36.00%). There were 107 upper primary schools; 79 (73.85%) boy's schools and 28 (26.15%) girls' schools. Again govt. run 33 (73.35%) boys schools and 12 (26.65%) girls schools, while private bodies managed 46 (74.20%) boys schools and 16 (26.80%) girls schools. At secondary stage, there were 21 schools. There were 13 (61.90%) govt. run schools and 8 (30.10%) private bodies run schools. Among govt. run schools there were 8 (61.55%) boy's school and 5 (39.45%) girls' schools. In the category of private managed schools there were 5 (62.50%) boys' schools and 3 (37.50%) girls schools. Last stage of education further showed decline in girl's schools managed by both govt. and private bodies. Govt. managed equal number of 5 boys and 5 girls' schools, while private bodies managed 10 (83.35%) boys' schools and 2 (16.65%) girls' schools. It was observed that there was sharp decline in number of girls schools from primary stage to senior higher secondary stage; number decreased from 67 to 7, about 90% decline. Sociological fact is most of girls are sent for education up to upper primary stage only and then they are normally married off at an early age as a custom prevalent in Rajasthan State and particularly among low caste and rural caste.

Sixteen private aided schools were selected on the criteria of those schools which were established during Princely State, and are providing education up to X or XIIth standard.

Out of 20 private aided secondary and senior higher secondary schools, 4 schools did not fall into the above criteria, which were excluded.

Table 1.8: Year-wise and Managing Castes of Private Aided Secondary and Higher Secondary Schools in Jodhpur city

S.No.	*Year of Establishment*	*Managing Caste*	*Name of the School*
1.	1887	Kayastha	Sir Pratap Senior Hr. Secondary
2.	1896	Oswal	Sardar Senior Hr. Secondary
3.	1898	Sanik Ksyastha (Mali)	Sumer Senior Hr. Secondary
4.	1912	Pushkarna Brahman	Sumer Pushtikar Sr. Hr. Sec.
5.	1912	Rawna Rajput	Umed M.P. Sr. Hr. Sec
6.	1918	Maheswari	Mahesh M.P. Sr. Hr. Sec.
7.	1919	Pushkarna Brahman	Jai Narayan Vyas Kanya Sec.
8.	1920	Maheshwari	Mahalaxmi Kanya Sr. Hr. Sec.
9.	1925	Sanik Kshatriya (Mali)	Umed Kanya Sec.
10.	1931	Agarwal	Hanuwant Sr. Hr. Sec.
11.	1938	Sanik Kshatriya (Mali)	Vedic Kanya Sec.
12.	1937	Christian	St. Patrics Vidya Bhavan Sr.Hr. Sec.
13.	1943	Pushkarna Brahman	Sarvajaneek Sec.
14.	1947	Sindhi	Modern Sr. Hr. Sec.
15.	1875*	Rajput	Chopasani Sr. Hr. Sec.
16.	1954	Muslim	Isaquia Sec.

** Chopasani Sr. Hr. Sec. School, Jodhpur became private aided since 1949. That is when Marwar State was merged into present Rajasthan State.*

This book deals with sixteen caste-managed secondary schools established in Jodhpur city from 1887 to 1954 during erstwhile rule of Marwar State. They opened both for boys and girls schools for education of their children. The details are given in Table 1.9.

Table 1.9: Number and Types of Schools by Managing Castes

Managing Caste/ Community	*Number of Schools*						
	10+2			*10th*			
	Boys	*Girls*	*Total*	*Boys*	*Girls*	*Total*	*Grand Total*
I. Forward Castes							
1. Brahman	1			1	1	2	3
2. Rajput	1	-	1	-	-	-	1
3. Oswal	1	-	1	-	-	-	1
4. Maheswari	1			-	-	-	2
5. Agarwal	1	-	1	-	-	-	1
6. Kayastha	1	1	2	-	-	-	1
		-	1				
		-	1				
II. Backward Castes							
7. Mali (Sanik	1			-	2	2	3
Kshatriya)		-	1		-	-	
8. Rawana Rajput	1			-			1
(Daroga)		-	1		-	-	
III. Minority							
9. Muslim	-			1		1	1
10. Christian	-	1	1	-	-	-	1
		-	-		-	-	
IV. Migrant							
11. Sindhi	1		1	-			1
		-	-		-	-	
Total	**9**	**2**	**11**	**2**	**3**	**5**	**16**

The focus of the book is to study role played by castes and communities in educational development in Jodhpur city of Rajasthan State. At present the city is second largest city in the state. Before Independence the city was the capital of one of the biggest princely states, Marwar. It has been reported that erstwhile rulers seldom took interest in education development for masses. In the city large number of castes and communities came forward and opened schools, built hostels, etc. from the beginning of modern education era. Therefore it draws attention of researcher to probe the factors that led many castes and communities to open schools in different period of time before independence of the country.

Some of the important questions which immediately strike to one's mind to probe are:

- Which are those castes and communities? What were their aims to open schools?
- Did they open schools for education of girls as well.
- Did any backward caste, minority community open schools in the city.
- Did any caste think of education of untouchables.
- Why did only literate castes open schools?
- Were these castes connected with the administration of the princely State.
- How did they raise funds at the time of opening schools, their upgradation, recognition, acquiring land, etc.
- Whether there was any case of inter-caste solidarity in terms of giving donations, etc.
- Could they withstand the financial crisis if they faced or die of their slow death.
- What was the method of collection of fund?
- What was the student admission policy and recruitment policy of teachers followed by castes and community schools in Jodhpur city?
- What kind of role did the erstwhile rulers play in giving support to castes and communities?

To achieve the objectives as outlined above, the methodology followed for collection of data and presentation of the work into different chapters are discussed:

Methodology : Method andTechniques of Data Collection, Analysis and Interpretation of Data

The present research work was aimed to study in three perspectives: historical, educational and management. Data were collected through primary (unpublished and published) and secondary sources. Information schedules were used separately for heads of schools e.g., Principals and key functionaries, e.g., Manager or Secretary of the management body. A questionnaire was used to collect data from selected sample teachers.

Data were analysed through statistical techniques by using rank score analysis and F-test. Action research model given by Pareek and Khanna (1978) and cybernetic model given by Rastogi (1979) were used to analyse and interpret policy and decision issues in management process. Methodological approaches are discussed here:

Use of Census Reports

The present research work selected castes as one system variable to status and social position in Indian society and in particular in Jodhpur city where nine castes opened educational institutions in Jodhpur city. Census reports for 1891, 1911, 1931 and 1941 of Marwar State and India were examined to collect data on population of castes, literacy of castes, rural-urban distribution at city, district and erstwhile Marwar State level, religion, occupation, etc. Castes above1 per cent population at these three political boundaries was chosen to find out preponderant castes. Their occupational position in princely State and traditional occupation revealed social status of castes in Jodhpur. Education of a few castes members knowing English language and native language in 1911 and 1941 combined with occupational position gave them an advantageous position in erstwhile Marwar State. Numerically preponderance also determined caste preponderance.

Use of Historical Records

What was the contribution of castes and communities in growth and development of their schools? Data on this aspect were collected from unpublished and published primary and secondary sources of document, which are preserved at Rajasthan Historical Archives, Bikaner. Files of individual schools, which contained unpublished official letters, reports of schools, etc. were examined to collect historical facts. Administrative Reports of Jodhpur State (from 1873 to 1949) were examined to collect information on education policy, grant-in-aid policy, amount of grants given to state-aided schools, curriculum and examination policies, etc. The historical development of all sixteen schools has been described (in Chapter 3) based on data analysed through these sources.

Use of Structured Schedules: Information Schedule

What is the present status of these schools? Are these schools implementing state educational policy and guidelines? For instance Secondary Education Commission (1952) has recommended normal capacity of students in a class. Private-aided schools are generally charged with over-crowding of students because these are known as profit-making institutions like publicly managed educational institutions. Data from all schools were collected on establishment, upgradation, subjects taught (Arts, Science and Commerce), number of students class-wise in schools, number of teachers according to teachers hierarchy, their list and year of joining the school, Physical and library facilities, fees charged per class in each schools. Was there any difference in average period of upgradation of schools from lower primary or primary school to secondary or higher secondary schools? Is there any difference among schools charging fees at different rates? Do these schools provide educational facilitates as per educational norms and educational standards? Have these schools been able to create impact in the society and build their educational prestige? Rank score analysis was used to determine educational prestige of schools which they have build in the society and F-test was used to measure variance between and within schools on all individuals variables and total variables (Chapter 4).

Private-aided schools are being managed by a management body. These schools are registered under Societies Act. After Independence, a separate body from parent body was formed to run schools for all students of country irrespective of caste, creed or sex. Management body plays very vital role in school management. Data were collected on structure of management body, composition of social background of members etc. The purpose of collection of such information was to find out any social group, e.g., politicians, educationists, lawyers, industrialists, etc. Do these members play any manifest or latent role? Do these members exert any influence in policy and decision making process? These are some of important issues in context of research in educational management.

Use of Structured Schedule for Respondents

The dynamics of educational administration and educational management was analysed through responses collected from 16 principals and 15 key-functionaries of management body (one management body Pushkarna Brahman are running one boys and one girls schools in Jodhpur, hence number of respondents were 15).

Use of questionnaire for Sample Teachers

Out of 369 teachers, 42 teachers were selected on the criteria of one teacher from each category of teacher's hierarchy and second by those who have completed median years of service in the school. They were administered a questionnaire to collect responses on school administration and school management. The purpose of collection of data from these categories of respondent was to understand and analyse organizational environment in private-aided schools. Management body of a school perform following functions: (i) Overall school management, (ii) Fund raising, (iii) Student admission policy, recruitment of teacher, service benefits of teachers, etc. What was the form of fund raising? Caste's individual contribution, endowment fund, contribution in cash and kind, (e.g., construction of class rooms in memory of their kin and on occasion of birth, marriage, etc.) Was there any inter caste contribution? Was inter-caste contribution a unilateral or bilateral one? Have any schools been downgraded or closed due to poor financial status of schools or due to improper functioning of financial misappropriation?

Teachers in any school occupies important place in school organization. What was or is mode of recruitment of teachers followed in these schools? Have non-caste teachers been appointed on the post of principal/head master/head mistress of the school? What were factors responsible for recruitment of non-managing caste teachers?

An attempt has been made to analyse data related to policy and decision aspects and management issues on three dimensional action research model given by Pareek and Khanna (1978) and cybernetic analysis given by Rastogi (1979).

Private-aided schools are not given full autonomy at the level of management body to manage schools independently. Who supervise and control these private-aided schools? Is the State government effective in their supervision and control of private-aided educational institutions? What is the role of the management body in supervision and control of these schools? Data were collected from key functionaries of management body and analysed. The Chapter 6 presents analysis and interpretation of data on school management.

Use of Case Study Technique

Three approaches of data analysis and interpretation of data in historical, educational and management perspectives were used. Out of five schools, three schools were selected for case studies by using rank score analysis on eight variables individually and on all variables. These three schools were: (i) Sir Pratap Senior Higher Secondary School, Jodhpur. This is managed by Kayastha caste, which opened their school in 1887, a first private-aided school. (ii) Sardar Senior Higher Secondary School, Jodhpur – This is managed by Oswal caste which opened their school in 1896, a second private-aided school in Jodhpur city. (iii) Sumer Senior Higher Secondary School, Jodhpur. This is managed by Sanik Kshatriya (Mali) caste, which opened their school in 1898. All these three schools were opened before the end of the nineteenth century.

The schools namely: (i) Chopsani Senior Higher Secondary School, Jodhpur, and (ii) Mahesh Senior Higher Secondary School, Jodhpur also scored above mean score on educational prestige obtained by rank analysis but these two schools were not included in case studies for (i) Chopsani school got its status of private aided school in1949 when erstwhile Marwar State was merged into Rajasthan State. Erstwhile rulers financed this school cent-per-cent hence there was no caste contribution for this school. The other school was opened in 1918 by Maheswari caste. This caste took advantage of erstwhile State's liberal policy of educational expansion.

Hence there was no sociological and historical fact, which decides about selection of school for case study. Hence this school was also dropped in case-study analysis.

Case-study technique was used to understand growth and development of schools in historical, educational and management perspectives. What was caste's contribution in development of their schools? The Chapter 6 describes and presents analysis of case studies of three selected schools.

The last chapter (Chapter 7) presents conclusion of study aimed at. Could caste castes and communities achieve their aims founded at the time of establishment of schools?

References

1. R.N. Saxena, Traditional systems of education in India (Chapter) in papers in the Sociology of Education in India (ed.) by M.S. Gore, et .al. New Delhi: National Council of Educational Research and Training, 1967.
2. T.N. Madan and B.G.Halbar, Caste and community in the private and public education of Mysore State (Chapter) in *Education and Politics in India: Studies in Organisation, Society and Polity (ed.)* by Susana Hoebar Rudolph and Loyld. I Rudolph, Delhi: Oxford University Press, 1972.
3. A.N. Misra, *Education Finances in India.* Bombay: Asia Publishing House, 1962
4. See for details Indian Education Commission (1882) report.
5. Aparana Basu, *Essays on the History of Indian Education,* New Delhi: Concept Publishing Company, 1982.
6. A.N.Misra, *Grant-in-Aid of Education in India Delhi,* The Macmillan Company of India, 1973, p.177.
7. Suresh Chandra Ghosh, *Education Policy in India since Waren Hastings.* Calcutta, Naya Prokash, 1989.
8. S.P. Ruhela, Education and Social Transformation: Religion, Caste and Tribe (Chapter) in the *Teacher and Education in Emerging Indian Society* (ed) by C.L. Anand, et.al. New Delhi: National Council of Educational Research and Training, 1981.
9. K.M. Kapadia, "Progress of Education in Navsari Taluka" in *Sociological Bulletin.* 1959, Vol. VII, No. 1.
10. R.C. Prasad, "Educational Development in Bihar in Seminar (107). 1968.
11. T.N.Madan and B.G.Halbar, 1972, *Ibid.*

12. M.N. Srinivas Mobility in the caste system (Chapter-8) in *Structure and Change in Indian society* (ed.) by Milton Singer and B.S. Cohen. Chicago: Aldiem Publishing Co., 1968.
13. A.P. Baranbas and Subhas. P.C. Mehta, "Caste in Changing India" (Mimeograph). New Delhi, IIPA, 1965.
14. R.S. Khare, *The Changing Brahmans: Associations and elites among Kanyakubj of North India.* Chicago: The University of Chicago, 1970.
15. Yogesh Atal, "Changing Patterns of Caste". A working paper presented in Indian Sociological Society XIth All India Sociological Conference, Panel III, April 28-30, 1972.
16. A.P. Baranbas and Subhas, C.Mehta, Ibid.
17. M.L. Mathur, " Caste and educational institutions in Jodhpur City: A Sociological Study". *The Journal of Social Sciences.* Samaj Vigyan Jagat, Vol. I. No. 1 & 2, June/December, 1978.
18. D.R. Gadgil and V.M Dandekar, Report of two investigations: Primary Education in Satara district. Poona: Gokhale Institute of Politics and Economic Change, 1955.
19. A.R. Kamat, "Education in Gulmb". Indian Educational Review, 1967, Vol. 2. and "Some features of the growth of education in Rural Maharashtra". *Indian Education Review,* 1968, Vol. 3 (2).
20. P.C. Joshi and M.S.A. Rao, "Changes in literacy and education study of villages in U.P. and Punjab". *Economic Weekly,* 1965, July.
21. A.R. Desai, *Rural Sociology in India* (ed). Bombay Popular Prakashan, 1969.
22. D.S. Survey, "Social and Political Influence on Indian Education during the later half of the nineteenth century". *Indian Dissertation Abstracts,* 1974. Oct.-Dec.
23. M.L. Mathur, Ibid. 1978.
24. Harold Gould, Educational Structures and Political Processes in Faizabad district, U.P. (Chapter 7) in *Education and Politics in India: Studies in Organization, Society and Policy* (ed) by S.H. Rudolph and L.I.Rudolph. Delhi: Oxford University Press, 1972.
25. J.P. Naik, The role and problem of private enterprises in education in I.S.S Feres Consultation of Principles of Christian Colleges, Tambram. The Christian College and National Development, 1967 (Comment recorded in Gould's work, 1972, *op. cit*).
26. M.N. Srinivas, "The Dominant Caste in Rampura" in *American Anthropologists,* 1959, Vol. 61. No. Feb.
27. Seminar 1965. Special Issue on Caste "The Problem".
28. S.K. Lall, 1974, Urban Elite. New Delhi : Thompson Press.
29. Iqbal Narain, K.C. Pande, and M.L. Sharma. The Rural Elite in

Indian State: A Case Study of Rajasthan. New Delhi: Manohar Book House, 1976.

30. B.R. Chauhan, 1967, Ibid.
31. T.B.Bottomore, The Administrative Elite. (Chapter) in *New Sociology: Essays in Social Science and Social Theory* (In honour of C.Wright Mills) (ed.) by I.L. Horowitz. New York: A Galaxy book, Oxford University Press, 1968.
32. M.L. Mathurm, "Caste, Elite and Education: A Sociological analysis of School's Board of Management" in *The Journal of Social Sciences: Samaj Vigyan Jagat,* 1980, Vol. 3, No. 1&2, June/ December, pp. 36-46.
33. A.L. Mudaliar, Report of the Secondary Education Commission (October 1952 to June, 1953). New Delhi; Govt. of India, Ministry of Education, 1954.
34. D.S. Kothari, 1966, Ibid.
35. Suresh Shukla, Controls and Decision-making in the education system (chapter) ed. in *The Papers in the Sociology of Education in India* (ed) by M.S Gore, et.al, *Ibid.* 1967.
36. M.S.Gore, *Education and Modernization in India.* Jaipur: Rawat Publications, 1982.
37. Rene Saran. *Policy making in Secondary Education: A Case Study.* London: Oxford & Claredon Press, 1973.
38. Mark Chesler and William M. Cane. Community Groups and Community Schools (Chapter 4) in *Sociology of Education. New York:* McMillan Publishing Co. Inc. 1981.
39. B.R.Chauhan, and G.Narayana, "Problems of education among Scheduled Caste Students in Uttar Pradesh" *Social Change,* 1976, (6) Vol. 1 & 2.
40. I.H.Sharp, Selections from Educational records (Pt. I). 1920. J.A.Richey, 1922, Selections from Educational records. UNESCO Report on Financing of education. Geneva: UNESCO, 1955. J.P.Naik Selections from Educational Records Vol. II, 1860-67. New Delhi; National Archives of India, 1963. A.N. Misra, 1962, 1967 and 1973 *op.cit.*
41. A.N. Misra, 1973, *op.cit.*
42. M.L. Mathur, 1980, *op.cit.*
43. Udai Pareek. "The Role of Action Research in building Self-sustaining system". *Indian Journal of Social Work,* 1978, Vol. XXX VIII, No. 4. Jan.
44. P.N.Rastogi, Cybernatic Studieo. 1979.
45. Jerome Karabel, Community Colleges and Social Stratification: Submerged class conflict in American Higher Education (Chapter

11) in *Power and Ideology* (ed.) by Jerome Karabel and A.H. Hasley. New York: Oxford University Press, 1971.

46. Rolland, G. Paulston, Educational Stratification and Cultural hegemony in Peru (Chapter 24) in *Power and Ideology* (ed.) by J.Karabel & A.H. Halsey, *Ibid.* 1971.
47. J.C.Agarwal, *Teacher's Role, Status, Service conditions education in India. A Reference to committees and Commissions.* Delhi; Doaba House, 1988.
48. Suresh Shukla, 1985, *Ibid.*
49. *Census of India, 1891.* Calcutta: Superintendent, Government Printing Press, India 1892.
50. *Census of Marwar State,* 1911. Jodhpur: Govt. of Marwar Press, 1912.
51. *Census of India,* 1931. Calcutta: Govt. of India Press, 1932.
52. *Census of Marwar State,* 1911, *Ibid.*
53. *Census of Marwar State, 1941.* Jodhpur: Govt. of Marwar, Press 1942.
54. Edgar Faure, Felipe Herrera, Abdul Razzak Kaddoura, Henri Lopes, Arthur.V.Prtorovsky, Majid Raheama, Fredireck Champion Ward. *Learning to be: The World of education today and tomorrow.* Delhi: Sterling, 1972.
55. A.R. Desai, 1967, *Ibid.*
56. P.C. Joshi, *Literacy and Education in backward regions* (Mimeographed 1967).
57. *Government of India Report on National Committee on Women's eduction* (May 1958 to January 1959).
58. *National Policy of Education: Programme of action.* New Delhi: Govt. of India Deptt. of Education, 1986.
59. B.P. Mandal, *Govt. of India Report of the Backward Classes Commission.* First Part, Vol. I & II. 1980.
60. Kaka Kalelkar, *Government of India Report of the Backward Classes Commission Part I&II,* 1955.
61. J.H.Hutton. *Caste in India: Its Nature, Function and Origins.* London: Oxford University Press, 1951. G.S.Ghurye. *Caste and Class in India. Bombay* : Popular Book Depot.
62. B.R.Chauhan, 1967, *Ibid.*
63. *Ibid.*
64. B.R. Chauhan & G.Narayana, 1977, *Ibid.*
65. Govt. of India Report of the States Reorganisation Commission, New Delhi: Govt. of India Press, 1955.
66. *Imperial Gazetter of India – Provisional Series Rajputana,* New Delhi. Usha (1908) 1989 (Reprinted)

67. *Census of Marwar State, 1941, Ibid.*
68. P.R. Shah, *Raj Marwar during British Paramountancy (A Study in Problems and Policies up to 1923), Jodhpur :* Sharda Publishing House, 1981, p.170.
69. P.C. Kumbhat, Urban Geography of Jodhpur city. Ph.D. Dissertation submitted to University of Jodhpur, Jodpur, 1969 (Unpublished).
70. A.P. Cox, Forty years of reminscence. 1968 and 1960 Reu, B.N., *Ibid.*
71. Lall, S.K., 1974, *Ibid.*
72. *Census of India – Rajasthan – 1991.*
73. *Census of India – Series 18, Rajasthan, District Census Handbook,* Jodhpur,Rajasthan, Jaipur
74. Erskine, Administrative Report of Jodhpur. Govt. of Jodhpur Press, Jodhpur, 1911, Vol IIIA, Chapter XIX, p.116.
75. B.D. Agarwal, Education and culture (Chapter XV) in *Rajasthan District Gazetteers :* Jodhpur. Jaipur Directorate Gazetteers, Govt. of Rajasthan, 1979, p. 400.
76. P.R.Shah, *Raj Marwar during British Paramountancy (A Study in Problems and Policies up to 1923).* Jodhpur: Sharda Publishing House, 1981, p. 170.
77. See for detail information on education policy followed in Marwar State-Robert. B. Vanwart: *The life of Lt. General His Highness Sir Pratap Singh.* London Oxford University Press, 1926, P. 73. A P. Cox, *Forty years of reminiscences.* New eland; Christ Church, 1968, p. 166. S.K.Lall. *Urban Elite.* New Delhi: Thompson Press, 1974, P. 1. Vikram Singh. *Sir Pratap and His contributions.* Jodhpur: Rajasthan Shodh Sansthan Chopasani 1983, p. 65.
78. Robert Vanwart, *Ibid.*
79. B.D. Agarwal, 1979.
80. Vikram Singh, 1983.
81. M.R. Kalla, 1947.
82. Pannalal Chauhan, 1927; Sudha Saroj.
83. Annual Reports on Administration of Jodhpur State 1923 to 1944-45.

2

Castes and Educational Institutions in Jodhpur City

Education in India has mostly been the concern of the private sector. In the ancient and medieval times it was the private teacher who held sway. The Britishers too recognized this fact as well as their limitations to organize the education of a big sub-continent and depended mostly on private enterprise (Misra 1973)[1] .This was the reason the British had thought of encouraging private enterprise through grant-in-aid system. By this time modern education era had begun. There was a shift in policy from traditional system of education to modern education system, since western impact has created new opportunities in employment, which required educated persons.

Role of private agencies in the field of education was recognized in the first dispatch of 1854. The Missionaries and Indian agencies took up the responsibilities and helped the government in expansion of education. Misra (1973)[2] has identified four factors were responsible for growth of private enterprises. These four factors were:-

(i) Keen desire of the people to get education in order to drive away ignorance and poverty by improving their status and earning capacity. Gopal Krishna Gokhale often expressed it in the legislatures and on the public platform.

(ii) Rise of militant nationalism in the last quarter of the last century and swept the whole sub-continent in the first half of the twentieth century. It was very critical of hurdles placed in the expansion of education.

(iii) Public munificence, which flowed freely for the spread of education. Inspired and goaded by the feelings of piety and patriotism which overtook the people as a result of several religious, social and political movements in Indian life in the last and first quarter of two centuries.

(iv) Dedication of a large number of selfless talented workers who sacrificed their careers for education for removal of ignorance, illiteracy and in absence of lucrative government jobs.

These factors have led caste associations, caste organizations to establish educational institutions and built hostels for welfare of their own castes. Private educational institutions form a very heterogeneous group. It is categorized into : (i) recognized and aided, (ii) recognized and unaided, or independent institutions, and (iii) unrecognized institutions (Kothari, 1966)[3] . The first category of institutions forms large percentage among private enterprise. For instance, caste associations and caste organizations, religious organizations have entered in the education field as educational entrepreneurs.

V.M.Sirsikar (1965)[4] has reported that castes have built their inroads into the education field. That is, caste organizations are running schools and colleges. He further mentions that it is not an accident that some of our Universities have been 'Unofficially' called 'Brahmin', 'Chettinad', Lingayat' and 'Kayastha' Universities. At school level also, innumerable caste associations have come forward and established their schools and colleges and awarded scholarships for the benefit of their student members (Rao, 1967)[5]. Kapadia (1959)[6] studied progress of education in Navasari taluka of Gujarat State. He found that Parsis were the first to realize the importance of English education for the progress of their religious group. They established a school for Parsis boys, which later admitted students belonging to other castes and religious groups. There were similar efforts to establish educational institutions in villages in Maharashtra by Anvil Brahmins, Patidars and Kolis, they also built caste hostel. It was not only Hindu castes that realized need of English education but also the Muslims grew conscious of the advantages of English education and established their educational societies. Muslims established Universities like Aligarh Muslim University and Dar-ul-Islam at Deoband. In east U.P., Azamgarh district Muslims has established Shibili Institutions (Azmi, 1967)[7]. Certain religious organizations like Arya Samaj, Sanathan Dharm Society, etc. have established educational institutions. Jains and Sikhs have also come into field in later years.

T.N. Madan and B.G. Halbar (1972)[8] have studied castes and communities in the Private and Public Education of erstwhile Mysore State, covered three districts viz. Belgaum, Dharwar and Mysore of Karnataka State. This study found that only few castes viz. Brahman, Christian, Lingayat and Muslim have come forward and established their schools. In erstwhile Marwar state, Department of Public Instructions was established in 1886.The erstwhile rulers gave a call to private bodies in the same year. This call was responded by only three middle castes of Jodhpur city before the end of 19th century. These three middle castes were: Kayastha (1887), Oswal (1896) and Sanik Kshatriya (1898). Then other castes have also come forward after introduction of Grant-in-Aid Rule, 1902 (1904) and upto 1937, i.e., a period of beginning of nationalist movement. After national movement gained momentum, there was shift in policy of upper castes from education of upper caste children to untouchables. That was in the year 1943, when Brahmans came forward and took responsibility to spread education among Harijans and untouchables on the principle of basic education given by Gandhiji. Another interesting development after 1920 was spread of female education by private enterprises (e.g., caste bodies). The late initiative by caste bodies for spread of female education in Jodhpur city has sociological relevance in historical reality. This historical reality was early marriage of girls at the age of adolescence and particularly in Rajasthan. Though State opened first girl's school named after Hewson in late 19th century, before private bodies came forward to spread education in Jodhpur city.

Based on ethnographical material available in the People of India (1998) – All India Series and Rajasthan State and other sources, the castes and communities, which entered in the field of education, are discussed in detail in the following paragraphs [9] :

FORWARD CASTES

1. Brahman

Hutton (1951)[10] writes about brahmans "religious works of the post-Vedic period consisting in theological treatises explaining the Vedas. They expound the sacrificial ceremonial in minute detail with speculation as to origin, etc. the brahmans probably belong to about the seventh century B.C."

Brahman is a *Varna* category traced to the Vedic period and also a *jati.* Population of the Brahman, as reported in the 1931 Census was 15,207,277, concentrated in the United Provisions, Bihar, Orissa, Bengal and Madras. The majority of the Brahman communities live in the plains, followed by the coastal areas, in hilly terrain and in the valleys. They consider themselves as occupying the top position in the Hindu society or Varna order; others also concede this position. Majority of the Brahman communities (97.4 per cent) are engaged in Government service as against the national average of 66 per cent followed by other pursuits such as private service, self-employment, business, trade, industrial work, settle cultivation. The Brahmans are a major land owning community. Due to reservation in Southern States, the Brahmans switched to self-employment sector as professional engineers, administrators, leaders, artists and scholars.

In Madhya Pradesh, most of the Brahmans own agricultural land but barring a few, they do not plough it themselves. Being a priestly community, most of them are educated and exercise dominance in political spheres and are prominent in modern occupations, such as Government service and professions. In Rajasthan, though traditionally the Brahmans are priests, their primary occupation is agriculture; others in government service, private service, business or trade (POI, National Series and Rajasthan)[11] .

There are many castes, among Brahman communities in Rajasthan. Of them, Pushkarna Brahmans and Srimali Brahmans occupy higher position in the social order. According to Sherring (1881)[12] and Ibbetson (1916)[13] , the Pushkarna Brahman were originally Ods and a section of them were engaged in digging Pushkar lake (Ajmer) and hence began sacred and religious works. In Rajasthan they are found in Jaisalmer, Bikaner, Jodhpur and some parts of Western Rajasthan. While the Srimali Brahman are believed to have originated from Srimal in Jalore district. Sherring describes the Srimali Brahman as a sub-group of Brahmans of Marwar. But according to Major Walter, there is no such group of Brahmans in Marwar. In 1891 Census, the Srimali Brahmans have been referred to as a caste of Marwar.

Census of Marwar State (1941)[14] reported 28 castes/sub-castes of brahmans. There were 1,13,172 persons in the State and 17,089 in Jodhpur. Brahmans were residing all over the erstwhile Marwar State. Among brahmans, Pushkarna brahmans and Srimali brahmans opened their schools in Jodhpur city. Total population of Pushkarna Brahmans was 20,015 in Marwar state and 9,921 in Jodhpur city and Srimali Brahmans 11,963 in Marwar state and 2,530 in Jodhpur city. Pushkarna brahmans are said to have come to the erstwhile Marwar State from Sindh (Pakistan) to which place language has a close affinity. However, Kalla (1916)[15] has reported origin of Pushkarna, a religious place in Ajmer district. While Srimali brahmans are said to have originated from Srimal village in Marwar state, near Jalore district. However, Pushkarna are largely clustered in Pokarna district. They had little concern with any trade and chiefly followed agriculture, but a large proportion of urban population was employed in Rajasthan service "the members of this caste, says Col. Walter, rose to eminence during the reign of Maharaja Takhat Singh and held the office of Diwani and Bukshish (Marwar Marudamsumari 1911)[16] . Their loyalty to the Raj is exemplified here:

"When the Jodhpur fort was built by Rao Jodha, a purohit, as is generally believed, cut his finger and sprinkled the blood in the foundation, uttering a blessing for the stability of Rathor, power as long as Pushkarnas would exist (Singh).

Brahmans topped in literacy rate among all castes in 1911 (797) and second (12,102) among all 36 castes in 1911 (Census of Marwar state, 1911.[17] While in southern and western states, literacy per 1000 for brahmans males in Madras was 719, Mysore 707, Cochin 621, Travancore 571 and Bombay 591 (Census of India 1911).[18] Comparing figures at state and country level, brahmans were ahead in literacy rate in erstwhile Marwar state. They responded to modern education in 1912 after 26 years of State call and eight years of Grant-in-aid Rule, 1902 (1904) was implemented. One of the reasons was Srimali Brahmans had opened one school for education of their children on traditional system of learning, which was later on merged with the school managed by Pushkarna Brahmans, i.e., the present school. Social factors led Pushkarna Brahmans to open their school, however, late it was. (A detail discussion will be made in the next chapter). They were first to open a girl's, school in Jodhpur city.

Brahmans enjoyed social positions in the society. They entered in the field of politics, too. Late Shri Jai Narayan Vyas was the first Chief Minister of Rajasthan Brahmans has elected their representative at Municipal election level and State assembly. Nine candidates have been sent at this level, but not to Lok Sabha. This observation holds the belief that brahmans have strong hold now in urban areas after reorganization of election constituency in the present Rajasthan state. In Jodhpur city, brahmans opened two boys' schools and one - girls schools in different periods.

2. Rajput

The name Rajput is derived from the Sanskrit word *Rajputra,* meaning son of a ruler. In the Vedas, the term occurs as a synonym of *rajanya* in the sense of Kshatriya, meaning one who is the scion of one endowed with a kingdom. The word has been used with different connotations by different authors. The Rajputra constitutes a class of nobility, whereas the Kshatriya was a social group, a *varna* category or a cluster of communities associated with political power. The Rajput class emerged further as a dominant community in the north and western India in the colonial period.

The Rajput was a heterogeneous community of traditional warriors, rulers, landholders, peasants and workers. Their total population in India in 1931 was 10,743,091.The Rajputs are at present spread in Bihar, Orissa, West Bengal, Assam and to some extent in Karnataka and in the Andaman & Nicobar Islands. However, Rajputana, the homeland of the Rajput to which they lend their name or a few of their lineages, continues to serve as a model of Rajputization.

The Rajputs are mainly a rural (64.5%) community. Some of them are also distributed in rural/urban (30.6%) and urban (6.5%) settlements.

The Rajputs are land-owning community. Traditional occupation of 67.7 per cent of them is in settle cultivation; this percentage is much higher when compared with the 35.1 per cent of all communities. It was so because the Rajputs were a ruling class who owned vast tracts of land. They still continue to pursue settle cultivation (66.1%) but at present this percentage is not so high when compared with that of the total number of communities (54%).The Rajputs are shifting to other occupations such as government service (82.3% against 65.85), business (58.1% against 44.3%), private service (56.5% against 47.9%), self employment (46.8% against 52.0%), animal husbandry (33.9% against 21.6%), trade (22.6% against 18.9%), in industry (16.1% against 8.92%) etc.They are also the categories of the landless (14.5%), skilled labourers (6.5%) and unskilled labourers (2.1%). The Rajput communities have traditional caste councils to settle the matters arising out of social dispute.

The Rajputs of Rajasthan are divided into four categories: (i) the Rajputs who were the former rulers like Sisodia, Rathor, Chauhan, Bhati (ii) the Natrayat Rajput who practice widow remarriage; (iii) the Rawna Rajput who are the progeny of the concubines of the Rajput rulers but do not enjoy the same status and are represented by the Daroga, Hajuri, Wazir, Gola, etc. and (iv) the Muslim Rajput, Kaimkhani and Sipahi. Literacy among the Rajput is widespread. Both boys and girls study upto postgraduate level.

Rajputs are generally known as aristocratic caste, widely spread in western, northern and central India. Its traditional functions were fighting and ruling. They represent the ancient Kshatriya *varna,* and rank next to the brahmans socially. Tod (1919)[19] has described Rajputs in its classical work Annals and Antiques of Rajasthan. The Rathors settled in Jodhpur in the thirteenth century. However, Rao Jodha established his throne in 14th century and Marwar State was born. In erstwhile Marwar state there were ten castes of Rajput clan, viz. Rathor, Bhati, Chohan, Kuchhawaya, Sisodiyas, Tunwar, Jhala, Panwar, Solunki and Parihar (Marwar Marudumsumari 1891)[20] .

Rajputs, being the ruler of the State and noble caste were sending their children to Mayo College, Ajmer when they enlightened about educational needs of other Rajput boys. State opened two schools; one for education of Noble's children (i.e., Sons of jagirdars, thikanas, etc. and second one for poor Rajput boys in 1875). State financed these schools, which finally came into one school in 1912.

Rajputs were residing all over the Marwar State. Their main occupation was chief military class.

According to 1941[21] census population of Rajputs were 2,18,583 in erstwhile Marwar state. This forms 8.55% of total population of the erstwhile state.

A few Rajputs were educated in English language (113) and other language (3511). They sent their children to Mayo College, Ajmer for education. They enjoyed position by virtue of ritual status, economic and ruling caste of erstwhile Marwar state. They were known by three characteristics, viz. (i) the possession of land, (ii) the parda system of female, and (iii) Ruler of the state (Marwar Marudumsumari, 1891)[22]. In Jodhpur city, the princely State initially opened schools for education of children of Nobles and poor separately which finally merged into one school after undergoing different stages of metamorphosis and finally got the status of State-aided school in 1949.

3. Mahajan

Literally the term *mahajan* means great folk. The terms mentioned in ancient literature also, though with different shades of meaning implying a great or respectable persons, which has nothing to do with caste. This name had been bestowed on the Bania or trading class. As such it is synonymous with Shah (King), the popular term for money orders in the hills (Rose, 1919).[23] Ibbetson (1916)[24] states that they appear to be a mixed caste sprung from the intermarriage of migrants from the plain belonging to the Bania or Kayastha castes. Traditionally they were engaged in money lending and associated economic pursuits.

There are many castes of Mahajan community. Here we discuss about Oswal, Maheswari and Agarwal castes.

Oswal

Hutton (1951) described Oswals "a trading caste from Mewar Rajputana. This caste is very largely Jain by religion, but Hindus and Jain Oswals recognize each other as caste brethren".

The members of Oswal community are largely engaged in trade.

They are spread over many States. A great majority of them are followers of Jainism. Crooke (1896)[25] has a story regarding their conversion to Jainism. According to Gandhi (1984)[26] there are four groups of Jain based on the language they speak. They are Oswal (Marwari and Mewari speakers),Gujarati Oswal (Gujarati Speakers) and Multani Oswal (Multani Speakers). The Oswal from these groups have migrated to various places in India in due course of time.

In Rajasthan, the Oswal mainly inhabit the districts of Jodhpur, Bikaner, Pali, Nagaur, Churu and Ajmer. The name Oswal owes its origin to an ancient town of Upkesh. Others believe that it has come from Osia, a town near the desert city of Jodhpur. In both the cases they claim that their community got its name from the place of their original settlement. From there they have migrated to different parts of the country. Traditionally, the Oswal are in business and do farming. They are landowning farming farmers. During the princely regime, they were also engaged as kamdars of Managers of the jagirs and held important positions in the government particularly of Mewar and Marwar State. They have their own community Panch who solve their social disputes and is responsible for the maintenance of their religious establishment. They have made significant progress in the field of education and support female education.

In Marwar the Oswal formed large proportion of the writer group. They belong to one of the castes of Mahajan community. In comparison with other Mahajan castes, a great number of them were employed as mustadis or writers in the State. Other members of this caste became traders and generally well off in the Marwar as well as in other parts of the country (Marwar Marudumsumari, 1891)[27] . Population of Oswal caste was 1,03,052 in Marwar state, and 7552 in Jodhpur city in 1941.

Oswals were residing in rural and urban areas of Marwar State. They established schools and colleges for education of children of Jodhpur city and erstwhile Marwar State. This was second caste in Jodhpur city, which opened their schools in 1896 for education of their boys and girls later on. Oswals being a business caste, also hold political status in Jodhpur city and the State. They have elected representatives at Municipal level, State assembly and Lok - Sabha (see Table 2.6). Following Oswals were elected to Lok Sabha S/Shri Jaswant Raj Mehta, Laxmi Mal Singhvi, Late N.K. Sanghi and Ranchor Das Gattani, Guman Mal Lodha and Birad Mal Singhvi were elected to State Assembly. This caste has opened schools for education of boys and girls and also colleges. They were very ahead in vertical and horizontal educational expansion.

Maheswari

The Maheswari are also called Mahajan, a broad generic term for the mercantile communities. In existing ethnographic account they are described as descendants of Sujan, the son of Khargasen, the Chanchem raja of Ninth Century who ruled in Khandela. They were so named because of their faith in Lord Shiva (Mahesh). Maheswari interpret the word Mahajan as an educated person (maha or great, i.e., educated jan or person). It is said that in the erstwhile princely States they were employed as advisors and accountants the job which requires education. Later, they shifted to trading. Trading is their economic pursuit. Some possess cultivable lands, which they give on sharecropping. Nowadays some are joining service and professional jobs. They have doctors, engineers among them.

The community is distributed in the districts of Bikaner, Jodhpur, Ajmer and Udaipur. They also participate in politics of the regional level (Chakraborty, Karkali, 1998, POI)[28]

This caste is known to be descent of Rajput Class. They are as Revd. M.A. Sherring says, "Opium traders, bankers and the like and their business is generally far from house." In Marwar they are for the most follower of Hinduism. They believed in "Mahesh" or Mahadeo God (Marwar Marudumsumari; 1891, quotes Revd. Sherring).[29]

Hutton (1951) has used term "Marwari" for business Class. It is an inhabitant of Marwar in Rajputana, "loosely used for Baniya from the region". He described baniya for those who were involved in trade, moneylenders, and shopkeepers, and often used for various trading castes, particularly those of Rajputana and western India. Maheswari caste is one of the Mahajan community (others are Agarwal, and Oswal). There are 25,453 in Marwar State and 2490 in Jodhpur city (Census of Marwar State, 1941).[30] This shows that 9.78% population resided only in Jodhpur city. This caste is rural based also. It has sent its representatives to Municipal Council. This caste has opened schools for education of boys and girls, also colleges and built hostels. They were very ahead in vertical and horizontal educational expansion.

Agarwal

Agarwals are generally known as "mercantile caste of upper India with traditions of descent from a Naga (snake) ancestress. Many of them are Jains by religion (Crooke, 1896)[31] . This caste is one of the major groups of Mahajan community, vaishya group. They are originally said to be Rajputs and descendents of Agrasen and hence called Agarwals.

Mr. Ibbetson remarks "the great saint from the neighbourhood of Agroha bears testimony to the truth of the tradition". A community distributed over many States, the Agarwal is largely engaged in trade and allied economic pursuits. Crooke (1896) has given different etymologies of the name of the community in the northwest and has mentioned a legend, which traces, their origin, to the Kshatriya ruler Agrasen, who established his capital at Agra and Agora.

The Agarwals are is a most enterprising community in terms of business, trade and industry, including small-scale industries and general merchandise, which are their traditional occupations. They have now diversified into government and private service and have also taken up agriculture. In most of the States the Agarwal have reported the emergence of scholars; administrators' teachers and white-collar workers and leaders at the regional and national levels. Education is encouraged for both boys and girls almost in all the States.

In Rajasthan the Agarwals are concentrated in the urban areas. They have a community organization for the welfare of the community members. Political leadership has encouraged at the local as well as regional levels. They have made significant progress in the field of literacy.

"Agarwals in Jodhpur city were known as thakurs"(Marwar Marudumsumari, 1891: 133 Quotes Ibbetson)[32] . According to Census of Marwar state, 1941, population of Agarwals in Jodhpur city was 1706 and in Marwar state as a whole 10,854. (see Table 2.3). This caste was included among Mahajans. This caste was rural and urban predominated. Agarwals opened a school for education of their children in 1931, when there were number of state and state aided schools in Jodhpur city. They took benefit of State's liberal education policy of expansion of primary education in the State. Out of 36 educated castes, Mahajans topped the list among educated castes. The Mahajans.and "Baniyas topped the list in literacy in Rajputana (450), Central India (456), C.P. and Berar (456). Agarwals occupied the second position in U.P. and Punjab with literacy rate at 412 and 381 respectively. (Census of India, 1891).

The other two castes of Mahajan community viz. Oswals and Maheswaris had already opened their schools in 1896 and 1918 respectively. This might be one of the reasons Agarwals did not respond to open one more school of their own because their children were receiving education in Maheswaris and other schools in Jodhpur city. Agarwals could elect their members at municipal council. Agarwals opened a school for education of boys in Jodhpur city.

The Writer caste: Kayastha

Kayastha is known as the "writer caste". According to Hutton (1951)[33] , this caste was found in "upper and eastern India". They formed the second most in occupational group of professional class B, the priests only exceeding them in number, while its population was 6.16% of total population in the Marwar State in 1891.

Kayasthas, "who stood next to brahmans in general estimation in Bengal seem to have been regarded in the eighteenth century simply as a clean sudra caste, but it is probable that nowadays they are more generally regarded as a twice-born caste whose claims to Kshatriyas status need not be caviled at" (Hutton 1951). While the observation given by Verma (1904) and Rowe (1968) stands same. He quotes Verma, that the Kayasthas of Bombay, Bengal and the United Provisions claimed the rank of Kshatriyas (warriors) in a forceful and persistent manner over many decades. While these people were steadily improving their secular status during the last nineteenth century. British court ruled that they were shudras. However, the ruling of Calcutta High Court in early seventy's was on British courts' thought, but was rejected by Allahabad High Court on the pretext that this caste enjoyed high literacy status and social position in society. In view of this position, this caste was not declared shudras as reported earlier.

Kayasthas claimed their origin from Chitragupta, the son of Brahma as mentioned in the Padma Puranand, the Kayastha Ethnology. Sir John Malcom says that "their origin is coeval with the invention of letter" that they were created to be an intellectual not a labouring class and they in consequence deem themselves to learning. Sir H.M. Elliot derives the word Kayastha from Sanskrit *Kaya*-body and *stha* – the remaining. When Parsu Ram, says he, destroyed the Kshatriyas, the pregnant woman of that caste fed the children to whom they subsequently gave birth, having been conceived during the massacre in the wombs of the mothers, were called 'Kayastha (Marwar Marudumsumari, 1891 : 109, Quotes Sir John Malcom and Sir H.M. Elliot)[34] .

A well known and widely distributed community, they are addressed by various synonyms like Lala, Kaith, Kait or Kayasth. The recorded evidence of the Kayastha as a caste appeared for the first time during the ninth century A.D. (B. Roychoudhary, 1968)[35]. They are distributed in 40 districts of the country in the State of Uttar Pradesh, Madhya Pradesh, Himachal Pradesh, Bihar, West Bengal, Tripura, Assam, Delhi and Chandigarh besides their sporadic presence in all other States.

Most Kayastha communities are engaged in Government service, private service, self-employment business, trade, industry and industrial work.

There are twelve castes under Kayastha community such as Asthana, Bhatnagar, Mathur, Saxena, Srivastava, Nigam, Surajdhaj, Amisht, Gour, Karan, Balmik, Kalsarisht (Singh,1894)[36].

In Rajasthan, Mathurs are largely distributed in Jodhpur, Nagaur, Ajmer, Jaipur, Bhilwara, Udaipur, Kota etc. The Mathurs are mainly in service. Their preference lies in administrative jobs. They are also found in substantial number in professional service of medicine and engineering. They are essentially an urban people.

According to Census of Marwar State, 1941[37] , population of Kayasthas was 3811 in Jodhpur city and 6780 in Marwar State as a whole. A few persons of this caste were literate in English language (1390). Literacy percentage of this caste was 25% of Kayastha population in the Marwar State. At all India level, Kayasthas topped among all castes in literary rate. In 1911, Kayasthas had literacy figure per 1000 for males as 603 for Bihar and Orissa, 544 for U.P. and 569 for Bengal. In Marwar State, it stood second to Brahmans. Kayasthas elected their representatives at Municipal level only. However, Late Shri Harish Chandra Mathur was a Member of Parliament in Rajya Sabha and Shri Mathura Das Mathur, ex-Minister in Rajasthan State Assembly. Shri Mathura Das Mathur had been elected from Didwana constituency from Nagaur District.

This was the first caste, which opened a school for education of boys in Jodhpur city in response to the State's call in 1886.

Kayastha was a urban caste and enjoyed its social and occupational position in the erstwhile state. This was the first caste to respond to State's call and opened their private aided school in 1887. Late Shri Mathura Das Mathur, ex-Minister of Rajasthan State opened a science college in memory of his brother and named it Lachoo Memorial College of Science, Jodhpur in 1967.

BACKWARD CASTES

Backward Classes include Scheduled Castes, Scheduled Tribes and other Backward Classes (OBCS). For sociological reasoning the term 'backward caste has been performed over OBCS. Here we discuss about two backward castes.

The concept of backward castes emerged after a historic Mandal judgment in 1992[38]. Sanik Kshatriyas and Rawna Rajputs castes have been included in the State and Central List of Backward Classes of Rajasthan and some other state's being socially and educationally backward castes. Here we discuss about these two castes, which opened schools in Jodhpur city.

Sanik Kshatriya (Mali)

According to People of India (All Communities: H-M, 1998)[39] the word Mali is derived from the Sanskrit word *mala*, meaning garland. The Malis are widely distributed in West Bengal, Bihar, Orissa, Andhra Pradesh, Uttar Pradesh, Maharashtra and Gujarat.

The Malis are also distributed in all the districts of Rajasthan. Presently, the Malis are engaged in business, service, daily wage labour and agriculture. They have their caste council *(panch)* to settle their problems. This caste has been included in the Central and State List of Backward Classes in Rajasthan and other States too as socially and educationally backward caste.

Hutton (1951)[40] writes about this caste, which is involved in "domestic and market gardeners in all India except south".

Population of this caste in Marwar State was 68,756 and in Jodhpur city 7,934 persons in 1941 (Census of Marwar State, 1941).[41] There were only 26 men who were literate in English language and 221 in another language, which forms 0.35% of total population of Marwar State. They were influenced by Arya Samaj ideology and Swami Dayanand Saraswati's ideas on education. However, this caste could not expand education among boys and girls as is evident from literacy percentage.

Numerical preponderance has certainly helped this caste to build its political influence in outside area of Jodhpur and the district. This caste has elected representatives at Municipality, State Assembly and Lok Sabha seats. S/Shri Anand Singh Kachawaha, Dr. Om Dutt Bhati, Amrit Lal Gehlot, Madho Singh Kachwaha, and Man Singh Deora were elected for Vidhan Sabha Assembly. Shri Ashok Gehlot was elected for Lok Sabha seat and Assembly seat. In Jodhpur city, Sanik Kshatriyas (Mali) opened a boy's school in 1898 and two girls' schools in 1925 and 1935 for education of their children.

Rawna Rajput (Daroga)

The emergence of the Daroga traced to the Rajput rule in the medieval period. *Gahlot* (1981)[40] writes that the Daroga include Chakar, Chela, Hazuri and Pas Bania. They were connected with the ruling families and are called 'daories' in Marwar, 'badran' in Jaipur and 'bai' in Bundi.

This caste also claims their origin from Kshatriya *varna* and considers them Rajput. But Census of Marwar State (1891)[41] termed this caste as 'Gola' means slave. This report further remarks about this caste as "illegitimate offspring of Rajputs upon whom they attended as hereditary servants". This caused embarrassment to members of this caste who decided to take measures of social reforms. For this reason Rawna Rajputs opened their school in 1912, first for boys and then for girls education.

This caste was found in almost all the paragans of erstwhile Marwar and includes as many class as those of their fathers. Those connected with ruling family occupied a superior position and were not associated in any way with those attached to the lower grade mustadis. They mostly follow the customs of Rajputs and Nata (Relations) is permitted among them.

In Jodhpur, the 'golas' or Rawna Rajput were called 'Sheri-Sirdar' probably for their mostly residing in the city. They were commonly known as 'Chakaras' and are also styled 'Daroga', Khawas *(nai or Barber)* Pasban or chela. In the western part of erstwhile Marwar they were generally known as wazirs and in Marwar they were known as 'dars' servant. This caste was known to have been giving their daughters as 'dowry' in the marriage of Rajput girls.

Population of this caste was 57,693 in the erstwhile Marwar State and 3,352 in Jodhpur city in 1941 (Census of Marwar State, 1941).[42] There were only 24 persons literate in English language and 562 persons in language other than English. Literacy percentage was 1.01%. This caste does not enjoy political influence in the city and State. In Jodhpur city, Rawna Rajputs opened a boys school, which was upgraded upto 10+2 stage, and then a school for girl's education, which remained upto middle level of education.

MINORITIES COMMUNITIES

Minorities constitute Muslims, Christians, Sikhs, Buddhists Parsis and Zorastrians. Their problems are by no means common; these differ in many respect and community to community. Here we discuss about two religious minority communities viz. Christians and Muslims from another Sindhi community, which entered in the field of education in India and in Jodhpur city in particular.

Muslim

Muslims are spread all over the country from the highest concentration in Jammu & Kashmir to the lowest density in Orissa. Muslims had strong belief in traditional education through Madarsas. They also responded to modern education.

Not only did Hindu castes but also Muslims responded to modern education. Muslims were generally educationally backward (Jayaram, N.1990)[43] and politically alienated after the end of Mughal period. Due to Muslim alienation from the society, the impart of western education on

Muslims was noticed very late (Hashmi, 1989)[44] . They grew conscious of the advantages of English education and established their educational societies. Muslims established Universities like Aligarh Muslim University, Aligarh, Dar-Ul-Islam at Deoband. In East U.P., Azamgarh district, they established Shibli Institutions (Azmi, 1967)[45] In U.P. urban Muslims of three districts of Allahabad, Gorakhpur and Jaunpur were ahead of Hindus in English education. While they were equal in Benaras. It was because these three districts were Muslim dominated.

In Jodhpur city, the Muslims had strong beliefs in Madarsa education. They opened many madarsas in Jodhpur city and in the erstwhile State. Muslims were famous and good workers for construction work. They constructed a modern well designed home for ex-ruler Maharaj Umaid Singhji, which is known as Umaid Bhavan. The ex-ruler was very much impressed by their work. He asked a few prominent and educated persons of Muslim community to open a school for education of Muslim boys on line of modern education like other State and State-aided schools. They took benefit of advice of the ex-ruler. In 1937, Marwar Muslim education society opened a school named Muslim school. They managed their school well. Like other State-aided schools, they were also required to raise funds for upgradation of their school. By the time they could raise funds, in 1949, the erstwhile feudal State was merged into present Rajasthan State. Popular government came into power. Popular government of those days took over control of their school only in the State and renamed it into Mahatma Gandhi school, Jodhpur. This was the first case Government of Rajasthan took such steps in the city. Due to their such decision, Muslims of Jodhpur city felt very bad and considered government's approach apathetic.

A few prominent persons of Muslim community and Marwar Muslim Education Society approached to Government of Rajasthan. They were given permission to start a primary school with Madarsa also in 1954. (They continued their fight with government to compensate them for earlier school. Recently, Government of Rajasthan has granted them land and permission to start a senior higher secondary school which has been named after national leader Maulana Abdul Kalam Azad.The school is known as Maulana Abdul Kalam Azad Senior Higher Secondary School, Jodhpur which is located at Kamla Nehru Nagar).The present study covered Isaquia Secondary School which was named after the founder person Mohd. Isaq. Sahib.

Christian

Christians are next to Muslims in terms of population among

minority communities. According to the 1981 census [46], the Christian population is 16,165,447. They constitute 2.43 per cent of the total population of India. Their sex ratio is 992 females per 1000 males. Though they are mostly rural population (70.84 per cent), a substantial number of them (29.16 per cent) also are urban dwellers. The highest concentration of the Christian is in Kerala (32.38 per cent), followed by Tamil Nadu (17.31 per cent), Andhra Pradesh (8.87 per cent) and Karnataka (4.73 per cent). Thus, the majority of their population (63.29 per cent) is concentrated in the southern States. The area of their next highest concentration is the north-eastern region of the country. They are a majority when compared with the total population of some States, like Nagaland (80.21 per cent), Mizoram (83.81 per cent) and Meghalaya (52.62 per cent).They also have a considerable population in Manipur (29.68 per cent).The other areas of their concentration are Goa, Daman & Diu (29.28% per cent) and the Andaman and Nicobar Islands (25.58 per cent).

The Christians are distributed all over the country, particularly in the Southern States, West Bengal, Himachal Pradesh, Orissa, Chandigarh, Daman and Diu and Maharashtra. (POI, 1998)[47]

According to the Report on Minorities (Vol. I, 1983)[48] – High Power Panel on Minorities, Scheduled Castes, Scheduled Tribes and Other Weaker Sections, Ministry of Home Affairs, Government of India, New Delhi, dated 14th June, 1983 Christians has shown progress vertically and horizontally in all sphere of life. The Christian missionaries were able to spread literacy and offer healthcare services not only to the Christians but also to the other communities. The Christian community, therefore, ranks above the general population in several major indices of social and economic development, particularly in literacy and education. The first Christian institution to develop the general community welfare was founded by St. Francis Xavier as early as 1540. From the beginning of 18th century onward, the European missionaries began setting up schools and the number of Christian missionaries in the country has increased considerably after Independence. The Roman Catholics, being the largest among Christians in India conduct 7072 primary schools, 1198 secondary schools, 114 colleges, 183 technical schools and 74 teachers' training colleges by 1969. Apart from the Roman Catholic institutions, other Christian denominations have also set up a number of social service institutions for the spread of literacy and health care but accurate statistics are not available.

By the middle of eighteenth century a wave of education had swept the province of Madras, which was forging ahead in this field, and the educational pattern underwent total transformation. German Missionary Schwartz deserved credit for this radical development. He impressed upon rulers of Tanjore and some other places need for education. Baptist Mission opened 115 schools nearby Calcutta-Serampore. Thus it is evident that missionaries expanded education for children in their areas. These developments are indicators of reserving education for certain sections of the society. In other words, education was not open for all sections of the society.

In Rajasthan, the Roman Catholic Christians are distributed in Ajmer, Jodhpur, Jaipur, Kota, etc. There are two dioceses, one at Udaipur and the other at Ajmer. They speak Hindi and use the Devanagari script. They run schools, hospitals and hostels and are consequently able to forge wider linkages. In Jodhpur city, two Christian ladies took initiative with the help of local business men and jagirdars and opened a girl's school for education of girls of Jodhpur city on the line of English education.

Sindhi

According to a Sindhi Scholar, Hiranandani, the Sindhi community before partition was unique in many ways. They were prosperous and well employed in administrative jobs and trade. There were no Brahmans and no Sudras including sweepers, washermen, ploughmen and masons among them. The Arabs had destroyed Brahmans. However, a few brahmans who were later invited became a part of the Sindhi society. The Sindhi Hindus were preponderant, Vaisyas, traders and businessmen. The divisions within their ranks were based primarily on sub-occupation of territory. Those who were in administration (Amils) also came to own land in lieu of their services, in the pre-partition period and became Zamindar or jagirdar. The Bhaibands who belonged to Hyderabad, Shikarpur, etc. were mainly engaged in trade and banking, inside and outside the country. After partition, the Sindhi were uprooted from their ancestral home, they lost their predominant position and migrated to urban centres in India where they became entirely an urban community (POI, 1998).[49]

The Sindhis form a large part of Musalman Rajputs in Marwar. They are mostly found in Shed, Mallani and Sanchor where they are chiefly cultivators and herdsmen. They originally belong to the Yadu family of Chanderbans; Rajputs but now consist of various tribes such as Bhati, Sodhi, Tanwar and Rathore. Their conversion dates to a period 1200 years back, when Mohammad Kasam commenced his invasions of Sindh from Arabia (Singh, 1894)[50] . In Jodhpur city, Sindhis migrated from Pakistan after partition of the country in 1947. They opened two schools in Jodhpur city in 1947 for education of their children and built *dharmsalas* later on.

Jodhpur City: The Study in Context

Like in other parts of the country Hindu castes and Muslim community have established their schools, colleges and built their hostels in Jodhpur city. Christians opened a school for girls' education on the pattern of the English education. Sindhi, a immigrated community opened their two schools to rehabilitate them in all spheres. Table 2.1 shows 13 castes and community opened 30 educational institutions in Jodhpur city upto 1954. After independence, individual bodies have opened their schools at primary and upper primary levels, which are continuing even now.

It was found that ten Hindu castes, three communities opened educational institutions in Jodhpur city. Except Christians twelve castes opened boys school (It is mentioned here that two schools, one school run by Suthar (Artisan) and another school run by Sindhis have been closed). Brahmans, Sanik Kshatriyas, Maheswaris and Rawna Rajputs opened girl's schools, Christians opened only girl's school in 1937. Only three castes could rise upto college level.

Table 2.1 Castes and Educational Institutions in Jodhpur City

S.No	*Castes/communities*	*No. of Educational Institutions*			
		Schools+		*Colleges*	*Total*
		Boys	*Girls*		
	A. Forward Castes				
1.	Brahman	2	1	1	4
2.	Rajput	1	-	-	1
3.	Oswal	1	2	1	4
4.	Maheswari	2	1	2	5
5.	Agarwal	2	-	-	2
6.	Kayastha				
7.	Charan				
	B. Backward Caste				
8.	Sanik Kshatriya	1	2	-	3
9.	Rawna Rajput	2	1	1	4
10.	Kumhar	1	-	-	1
	C. Minorities				
11.	Muslims	2	-	-	2
12.	Christian	-	1	-	1
13.	Sindhi	1	-	-	1
	Total	**17**	**8**	**5**	**30**

Source : Based in Data collected from Directorate of Education, Rajasthan, Jaipur (Jodhpur office).

It is mentioned here that first private-aided science college was opened in memory of Late Shri Man Mohan Mathur (popularly known as Lachoo) by political mentor of Rajasthan State, Shri Mathura Das Mathur, Ex. Minister of the State. He realized that there was growing demand in science subjects as one University in Jodhpur could not cope up increasing demand of student rush towards science subjects in Jodhpur city. Similarly demand for commerce subject also grew. Brahmans, Oswals and Maheswaris opened their colleges in different years. Of all these castes, Maheswari caste realized that number of high schools has increased considerably and there was no professional college in Jodhpur city. They opened a B.Ed. College in 1958. It was also found that Charans, Kumhars and Rawna Rajputs (girl's school) could not raise their schools upto secondary level whereas other traditional castes have run race at a faster speed. However, rural castes have preferred to first build hostels in towns and cities than educational institutions. These rural castes were Charans, Rajpurohits, Jats and Patels. If two rural castes viz. Charans and Kumhars are minus, then it is seen only eight castes are in the field of education. The question is: why only eight castes have continued to manage educational institutions for more than four decades to a century? Secondly, were these castes literate castes? Thirdly, were these castes connected with social and occupational positions in administrative hierarchy of princely state?

Literacy and Caste

The 1881 Census of India[51] reported that approximately one-seventh of the population were literate and belonged to higher castes and sub-castes of society (Petrov 1978).The literacy figure for different castes of different States are reported in Census of India, 1911. The Kayasthas had literacy figure per 1000 for males as 603 for Bihar and Orissa, 544 for U.P. and 569 for Bengal. The Mahajans and Baniyas topped the list of Rajputana (450), Central India (146), C.P. and Berar of Bengal Second in the State returned the highest figures at 683. The Baidyas in the State returned the highest figure at 720. Agarwals occupied the second position in U.P. and Punjab with literacy rate at 412 and 381, respectively whereas the Khatris returned the figures as 405 and Arora 361.

In southern and western States also literacy per 1000 for Brahmans males in Madras was 719, Mysore 707, Cochin 621,Travancore 571 and Bombay 591 (Census of India, 1911)[52] .This shows that seven main castes were literate castes. These castes were Brahman, Subarna Banik, Mahajan, Agarwal, Arora, Baniya and Kayastha.

In erstwhile Marwar State and Jodhpur city there were few educated persons from only six castes. They learnt English language and other languages: Brahmans (797 and 680), Kayasthas (159 and 668), Sheikhs (24 and 247), Rawna Rajputs (21 and 236), Rajputs (27 and 213) and Saiyed (2 and 127)/(Census of Marwar State, 1911).[53] A comparative analysis of figures of 1911 of country and Marwar State reveal that Brahmans, Kayasthas and Mahajans topped in the list of literacy rate. This was because they were among "Writer-Castes".

But in two decades progress, there were extreme variations in literacy among different castes. According to Census of India, 1931[54], literacy figures of different castes were: Baidyas (782), Kayasthas (607), Nayars (603) males per 1000 literates only. 11 Bhils and 10 Chamars were also literate. While 5729 Baidyas males per 10,000 were literate in English and 2418 Kayasthas. Castes such as Chamars had 3 and Bhils 1 male literate in English per 10,000. In Bengal Brahmans were surpassed by Baidyas, Subarna Baniks and Agarwals in U.P. by Kayasthas, Agarwals and Saiyeeds. Trading castes had high male literacy (Census of India 1931).

Literate castes continued to take advantage of literacy facilities. In Marwar State, there were 36 main castes, which were educated in English language and other language in 1941. Out of 36 educated castes, there were only five castes who are 10 per cent or more population was literate. These five castes whose 10 per cent or more population was literate. These five castes were: Mahajans (42,027), Brahmans (12,102), Rajputs (3,511), Sunar (2,019) and Kayasthas (1,390).

These same castes were literate in English language but in different order: Brahmans (776), Mahajans (377), Kayasthas (305), Rajputs (113) and Sunars (8) (Census of Marwar State, 1941: 162). From these figures of Jodhpur city and country as whole it is observed that Brahmans topped in the list among literate castes as in case of Bengal and than other castes literate in English language. Again figures from 1911 to 1941 of literacy among castes in the country as a whole and in Marwar state give a clear picture about a few upper castes that were literate and responded first to the education.

Religion and Caste

According to Census of Marwar State, 1941[55], there were 122 castes in Jodhpur city. Population percentage of different religious groups were: Hindus (68.25%), Muslims (25.25%), Christians (0.55%), Jains (5.45%),

Sikhs (0.15%) and Parsis (0.25%). Table 2.2 shows distribution of no. of castes into various religious groups. It is seen from the table that 66.15% were Hindu castes and 28.65% were Muslim castes. It was observed that Hindu and Muslim castes were religiously and numerically preponderant. However, literacy percentage of religious groups were in different order. Christians, Sikhs and Jains surpassed Hindus and Muslims of Jodhpur city. Thus emergence of traditional castes as private enterprise was based on numerical preponderance and social position in caste hierarchy.

Table 2.2. Caste Religion, Literacy of Population of Jodhpur City in 1941

S.No.	*Type of Religion*	*No. of Castes*	*%age*	*Population*	*%age*	*Literate*	*%age*
1.	Hindu	90	66.15	86,594	68.25	21743	25.10
2.	Muslim	39	28.65	32,040	25.25	4286	13.35
3.	Christian	2	1.50	892	0.70	378	42.40
4.	Sikh	1	0.75	179	0.15	75	41.90
5.	Jain	3	2.20	6921	5.50	2880	41.60
6.	Others	-	-	77	0.05	-	-
7.	Parsi	1	0.70	139	0.10	1	0.70
	Total	**136**	**100.00**	**126842**	**100.00**	**29363**	**23.14**

Source : Census of Marwar State, 1941. Jodhpur: Govt. of Jodhpur Press, 1942: p 325 (Table V).

Note : 1 Actual number of castes were 122, while total number shown in the table was 136 for population of 14 castes belonged to either Hindu or Muslim religions.

Caste and Population

An attempt was made to analyse preponderant castes according to its population. Population of Jodhpur city was 1,26,842, Jodhpur district 1,71,996, Paraganas 24,29,062 and erstwhile Marwar State 25,55,904. There were 122 castes, 82 castes,129 castes at different political boundaries. For convenience and estimation of preponderance, population above 1per cent in 1941 was taken as a base. Table 2.3 shows that there were 22 castes above 1per cent population at Jodhpur city level, 15 castes at Jodhpur district, 23 castes at paraganas and 22 castes at Marwar state level. A close observation of this table reveals that there was large variation of castes in terms of its population size at different political boundaries. Further, the percentage of population has varied indifferent order at these levels.

Table 2.3. Population of Castes Distributed at Jodhpur City, Jodhpur District, Parganas and Marwar State Level Based on 1per cent above to Total Population in 1941

S. No.	Castes (N=122)	Population (N=1,26,842)	%age	S. No.	Castes (N=82)	Population (N=1,71,996)	%age	S. No.	Castes (N=129)	Population (N=24,29,062)	%age	S. No.	Castes (N=129)	Population (N=25,55,904)	%age
1.	Brahman	17089	13.45	1.	Jat	47872	27.85	1.	Jat	352213	14.5	1.	Jat	354342	13.85
2.	Mahajan	11820	9.3	2.	Rajput	18073	10.5	2.	Rajput	212923	8.75	2.	Rajput	218583	8.56
3.	Sanik Kshatriya	7934	6.25	3.	Bhambis	16454	9.6	3.	Bhambis	187290	7.7	3	Bhambis	189879	7.4
4.	Rajputs	5660	4.45	4.	Bishnol	10581	6.15	4.	Mahajan	147395	6.05	4.	Mahajan	159215	6.2
5.	Kayastha	3811	3	5.	Sanik	9197	5.35	5.	Rebari	113068	4.65	5.	Brahman	113172	4.4
6.	Rawna Rajput (Daroga)	3352	2.65	6.	Rebari	6474	3.75	6.	Kumhar	98224	4.05	6.	Kumhar	101517	3.95
7.	Kumhar	3293	2.6	7.	Mahajan	5769	3.35	7.	Brahman	96083	3.95	7.	Sanik Kshatriya	68756	2.7
8.	Ghanchis	2298	1.8	8.	Brahamn	5001	2.9	8.	Sanik Kshatriya	60822	2.5	8.	Bishnoi	59342	2.3
9.	Sunars	2192	1.7	9.	Purohit	4759	2.75	9.	Bishnoi	59185	2.45	9.	Rawna	57693	2.25
10.	Jat	2129	1.65	10.	Kumhar	3975	2.3	10.	Sirwis	54862	2.25	10.	Sirwi	54879	2.15
11.	Mirasi	1971	1.55	11.	Patel	3856	2.25	11.	Rawna Rajput (Daroga)	54341	2.23	11.	Khati	49845	1.95
12.	Nai	1766	1.4	12.	Balai	3590	2.1	12.	Bhil	49420	2.03	12.	Balai	49637	1.94
13.	Jogi	1690	1.35	13.	Rawna Rajput (Daroga)	3571	2.05	13.	Balia	48978	2.01	13.	Bhil	49500	1.93
14.	Dholi	1653	1.3	14.	Khati	3374	1.95	14.	Khati	48714	2	14.	Purohit	46341	1.8
15.	Mochi	1364	1.07		**Minority**			15.	Purohit	46044	0.1	15.	Sindhi	44901	1.75
16.	Khati	1355	1.06		Bhil	3463		16.	Sindhi (m)	43890	1.8	16.	Sheikh (m)	44531	1.74
17.	Darzi	1305	1.02					17.	Kunbi	37791	1.55	17.	Kunbi	37810	1.47
	Minority							18.	Raigar	33293	1.37	18.	Nai	34417	1.34
18.	Sheikhs	14427	11.35					19.	Nai	32651	1.34	19.	Raigar	33527	1.31
19.	Pathan	4113	3.25					20.	Sargara	30592	1.25	20.	Sargar	31382	1.22
20.	Bhamhi	2589	2.05					21.	Sheikh (m)	30104	1.23	21.	Bauri	27669	1.08
21.	Bhangi	2502	1.95					22.	Bauri	27569	1.13	22.	Sad	26342	1.03
22.	Saiyad	1497	1.2					23.	Sad	25199	1.03				

Source : Census of Marwar State, 1941, Jodhpur : Govt. of Jodhpur State Press, 1942.

Castes and Type of Residence

Table 2.4 shows residence of castes. It was found that out of 37 castes (above 1% population). 16 castes (43.25%) were rural residents. 12 castes (32.45%) were urban residents and 9 castes (24.30%) were rural urban residents. Among rural castes only one caste Suthar (artisan opened their school in Jodhpur city which was later on closed for management problems. However, rural castes like: Purohits, Jats, Patels, Kumhars built hostels for their rural children for their education in Jodhpur city. Out of 12 urban resident castes, only one caste Kayastha opened their school. There were 9 (nine) castes, which resided in rural and urban localities both. Out of these nine castes Brahman, Rajput, Oswal, Maheshwari, Agarwal, Rawna Rajput (Daroga), Kumhar opened their schools in Jodhpur city. Rural castes built hostels for their children in Jodhpur, e.g., Rajput, Jat, Sanik, Kshatriya, Maheswari, Charan, Kumhar and Musalman. On the basis of above analysis it is drawn that a few castes took these activities by way of opening educational institutions and built hostels.

Table 2.4 Castes by Type of Residence in Marwar State (above 1 per cent population)

S.No	*Castes*	*Type of Residence*		
		Rural	*Urban*	*Rural & Urban*
1	2	3	4	5
1.	Balai	+	-	-
2.	Bauri	+	-	-
3.	Bhil	+	-	-
4.	Bishnoi	+	-	-
5.	Brahman	-	-	+
6.	Darzi	-	+	-
7.	Dholi	-	+	-
8.	Ghanchi	-	+	-
9.	Jat	+	-	-
10.	Gogi	-	+	-
11.	Kayastha	-	+	-
12.	Khati (Suthar)	+	-	-
13.	Khatri	-	+	-
14.	Kumhar	-	-	+
15.	Kunbi	+	-	-

Cont. Table 2.4

1	2	3	4	5
16.	Mahajan	-	-	+
17.	Mirasi	-	+	-
18.	Mochi	-	+	-
19.	Nai	-	-	+
20.	Patel	+	-	-
21.	Purohit	+	-	-
22.	Raigar	+	-	-
23.	Rajput	-	-	+
24.	Rawna	-	-	+
25.	Rebair	+	-	-
26.	Sad	+	-	-
27.	Sanik Kshatriya	-	-	+
28.	Sargara	+	-	-
29.	Sindhi	+	-	-
30.	Sirwi	+	-	-
31.	Sundar	-	+	-
32.	Bhangi	-	+	-
33.	Bhambhi	-	-	+
34.	Bhil	+	-	-
35.	Pathan	-	+	-
36.	Saiyed	-	+	-
37.	Sheik	-	-	+
	Total	16	12	9

Source : Census of Marwar State, 1941. Jodhpur: Government of Jodhpur Press, 1942.

Table 2.5 shows that there were 14 castes opened schools and built hostels in Jodhpur city. Out of these 14 castes, 6 castes opened only schools in Jodhpur city. Kayastha was urban caste so it did not require to build hostel. Brahmans, and Rawana Rajputs were rural urban residents but they did not build hostel. However, they received contribution in cash from their rural population to start their schools. Suthar (khati) was a rural based caste. However, they opened a school for education of their own children in Jodhpur city. Three castes viz. Purohit, Jat, and Patel were rural based castes, which preferred to build their hostel for education of their children. In other words they did not refer to invest money in education field. Rajputs, Sanik, Kshatriyas and Maheswaris opened schools and built hostels also. These rural-urban residing castes took care of their children's need; education and residence problem. In 1937 Muslims opened their school, which was managed by Marwar Muslim Education Society. Kayamkhanis, a group of Muslims in Jodhpur also built a hostel in 1940.

Table 2.5 Castes Opened Schools and Built Hostels in Jodhpur City

S.No	*Castes*	*Only Educational Institutions opened*	*Only hostels built*	*Educational Institutions opened and hostels built*
1.	Brahman	+	-	-
2.	Purohit (Rajpurohit)	-	+	-
3.	Rajput	-	-	+
4.	Jat	-	+	-
5.	Sanik Kshatriya	-	-	+
6.	Oswal	+	-	-
7.	Maheswari	-	-	+
8.	Agarwal	+	-	-
9.	Kayastha	+	-	-
10.	Patel	-	+	-
11.	Rawna Rajput	+	-	-
12.	Kumhar	-	-	-
13.	Suthar	+	-	-
14.	Musalman	-	-	+
	Total	**6**	**3**	**5**

Castes and Political Hold

Do these castes enjoy political hold in the society? Data were analyzed from 1952 to 1985 for M.L.A.'s and M.P's, and 1948 to 1974 for Municipal elections. Table 2.6 shows that there were nine castes, which hold political, influence in the society. These castes are: Brahman, Rajput, Sanik Kshatriya, Oswal, Maheswari, Agarwal, Suthar (khati), Sindhi and Scheduled Castes. The table confirms that only few castes hold political influence based on its numerical strength in election constituency. However, Sanik Kshatriyas and Oswals are distributed in rural and urban areas both, these castes have elected their representatives at each level. Before Independence, Brahmans, Kayasthas, and Oswals held posts of Secretary, Political Secretary, Assistant Secretary, Finance Secretary, etc. in the State Council in erstwhile princely State (Report on the Administration of Marwar State, 1941:11).

Table 2.6 Peoples Representative Castes Elected to Municipal Council, State Assembly and Lok Sabha

S.No.	*Castes*	*Number of Elected Persons*			
		Municipal	*MLA*	*MP*	*All level*
1.	Brahman	7	2	-	-
2.	Rajput	-	-	2	-
3.	Sanik Kshatriya	7	7	2	-
4.	Oswal	4	4	5	+
5.	Muslim	1	4	-	-
6.	Agarwal	2	-	-	-
7.	Suthar	1	-	-	-
8.	Sindhi	2	-	-	-
9.	Scheduled Castes	-	3	-	-
	Total	24	20	9	+

Source : 1. Collected list of members elected. However, caste-wise president-elect were shown.
2. Based on Election results published 1952 to 1985, P.78 & 102-103.

This observation further confirm that castes connected with administrative positions, political, etc. took benefit of rising opportunities available to them. B.R. Chauhan (1967)[56] has mentioned that such types of castes were quick to respond to such incentives.

Castes and Occupation

Hutton (1951)[57] has prepared a glossary of castes and described their occupation, origins, etc. The 1891 Census of Marwar[58] State has classified six-types of occupations in which populations were mainly engaged:-

- Land Lord and Agriculture (Chief Military and Class).
- Professionals (Hindu, Muslims, Jain, Priests and Jatis).
- Commercial (Traders, Peddlers and Carriers).
- Artisans and village menials (Leather, Shepherds, Wool weaving, Goldsmith, Barber and Blacksmith).
- Vagrant, Minor artisans and Performers (Earth Works, Knife grinders, Basket makers, Hunters, Fowlers, Acrobats and Jugglers).
- Races and Nationalities (Sheikhs, Pathans, Mughals, Mukranis, Wilaitis).

Rural castes (e.g., Rajput, Mahajan, Jat, Charan, etc.) were engaged in occupational groups A and C, while urban-based castes were engaged in B category occupation. The lower castes were engaged in occupational category of D and E group. In 1951, population of Jodhpur city was engaged in more or less same occupation. Table 2.7 shows that 98.5% of persons were engaged in non-agricultural work.

Table 2.7. Main Occupations of Population of Jodhpur City in 1951

S.No	*Occupations*	*No. of Persons*	*%age*
	I. Agricultural Class		
1.	Cultivators of land wholly or mainly owned and their dependents	983	0.60
2.	Unowned	511	0.30
3.	Labourers and their dependents	31	0.05
4.	Non-cultivator owner of land, Agriculture rent received and their dependents	960	0.55
	II. Non-Agricultural class		
5.	Production other than cultivation	19803	11.60
6.	Commerce	35592	20.85
7.	Transport	17013	9.95
8.	Other Services and Miscellaneous group	95724	56.10
	Total	**170617**	**100.00**

Source : Census 1951 Rajasthan and Ajmer district Census handbook. Jodhpur Pt. II Primary Census Abstract or directory. Jodhpur printed at the Government Press 1956, pp. 2-3.

Conclusions and Analysis

There were 122 castes in Jodhpur city in 1941 (Census of Marwar State, 1941)[59]. Many castes came forward in the field of education, politics, occupations, etc. with growth and development of modern education. Due to rising employment opportunities, education became a passport for entry into government service. The question is why did few castes take benefit of opportunities available in the society? Caste hierarchy and social-status were important determinants, which enjoined upon them to have access to all opportunities available in the society. For instance, castes connected with administration and occupations in princely State took benefit of all opportunities and were quick to respond to modern education. Literacy was another factor, which added to their position. In 1911, a few persons of six castes were literate in English language and other languages. It was observed that urban castes were quick in responding to rising opportunities than rural castes, or castes which resided in rural and urban areas both, responded to rising opportunities. In Jodhpur city castes above 2.00% population opened their schools and colleges and built hostels for their rural children. However, Purohits (Rajpurohit), Patels, Jats, Charans also built their hostels in Jodhpur city. They did not invest money in establishing schools. These castes were rurally predominant in numerical sense. There were other castes above 2 per cent of total population in the erstwhile Marwar State, but they did not come forward because they were in low social status and low-rank in social hierarchy. It is also evidenced that only a few castes like Brahman, Rajput, Sanik Kshatriya, Oswal, Agarwal, Maheswari, Suthar (Khati), Musalman, Sindhi and Scheduled Castes (in reserved constituency) could build their political base in Jodhpur city and Jodhpur district. Rawna Rajput and Kumahar are low in social hierarchy and low-rank could establish their schools in Jodhpur city. On the basis of above analysis, it can be said that numerical preponderance, social status, etc. determine caste's preponderance. It is a unique observation that eight castes have come forward and opened their schools and other castes built hostels. In other parts of the country, only one or two castes have opened their schools.

References

1. Misra, A.N. 1973, *Grant-in-Aid of education in India Delhi.* The Macmillan Company of India.
2. Misra, A.N. 1973, *Grant-in-Aid of education in India Delhi.* The Macmillan Company of India.
3. Kothari, D.S. (1966), *The education commission,* (1961-62). New Delhi : Government of India, Ministry of Education.
4. Sirsikar,V.M., 1965. "Use in Politics" in Seminar 70.
5. Rao, M.S.A. 1967, Education, social stratification and mobility (Chapter) in the paper's in sociology of Education in India (ed) by M.S. Gore, et. Al., New Delhi: National Council of Education, Research and Training.
6. Kapadia, K.M. 1959, "Progress of Education in Navasri Taluka" in *Sociological Bulletin,* Vol. VII, No.1.
7. Azmi, Niaz Ahmed, 1974, "Shibli Institutions: A study of the development of Education in east U.P., with special reference to Muslims". Abstracted in *Indian Dissertation.* Oct.-Dec., 1974. New Delhi :ICSSR & AIU.

8. Madan, T.N. and B.G. Haldar 1972, Caste and community in the private and public education of Mysore State (Chapter) in *Education and Politics in India: Studies in organization, society and policy* (ed.) by Susana Hoeber Rudolph and Loyd I.Rudolph, Delhi : Oxford University Press.
9. *People of India, 1998, National Series* (Delhi : Oxford University Press)
10. Hutton, J.H., 1951, *Caste in India: Its nature, function and origins.* London : Oxford University Press.
11. *People of India, 1998, National Series* (Delhi : Oxford University Press).
12. Shering, M.A. 1881, T*he Tribes and Castes of Rajasthan,* Reprint 1975. New Delhi: Cosmos Publication.
13. Ibetson, D.1916, *Punjab Castes: Races, castes and Tribes of the People of Punjab* (Lahore: Govt. Press, 1916. Reprint,1981. New Delhi: Cosmos Publication.
14. *Census of Marwar State, 1941:* Government of Marwar Press, Jodhpur.
15. Kalla, Bansi Dhar Sharma, 1916, Report of working of Sumer Pushtikar School, Jodhpur, Marwar from 8th Feb.1912 to 30 June, 1915 (Published).
16. *Marwar Mardumsumari,* 1891. Jodhpur Government of Marwar Press.
17. *Census of Marwar 1911 :* Government of Marwar Press, Jodhpur.
18. *Census of India, 1911*.Vol. I Pt.I.Calcutta: Superintendent, Government Printing Press, India, 1913.
19. Tod, Col. James 1919, *Annals and Antiques of Rajasthan* Vol. I & II (1829-32). London: Routledge and Kegan Paul.
20. *Marwar Mardumsumar, 1891*, Jodhpur: Government of Jodhpur Press.
21. *Census of Marwar, 1941*, Government of Marwar Press, Jodhpur.
22. *Marwar Mardumsumar, 1891,* Jodhpur: Government of Jodhpur Press.
23. Rose, H.A. 1919, *Glossary of the Tribes and Castes of the Punjab and N.W.F. Province.* Lahore: Civil and Militancy Gazettee Press, 1919; Reprint 1980. Delhi: Amar Prakashan.
24. Ibetson, D.1916, *Punjab Castes: Races, Castes and Tribes of the People of Punjab* (Lahore: Govt. Press, 1916. Reprint,1981. New Delhi: Cosmo Publication.
25. Crooke,W 1896, *The Tribes and Castes of NorthWestern India.* Calcutta Govt. Printing Press: Reprint 1974. Delhi: Cosmos Publications.

26. Gandhi, 1984. Gandhi, L.P., 1984, "Patterns of Genetic Variation Among the Jains," Ph. D. Thesis (Pune : Pune University) (Unpublished quoted in P.O.I. All India Series, p.2688.
27. *Marwar Mardumsumar, 1891,* Jodhpur: Government of Jodhpur Press.
28. Chakraborty, Kakali, 1980, *"Maheswari" in People of India* (Rajasthan) Bombay : Popular Prakashan.
29. *Marwar Mardumsumar,1891,* Jodhpur: Government of Jodhpur Press.
30. *Census of Marwar, 1941,* Government of Marwar Press, Jodhpur.
31. Crooke,W. 1896, *The Tribes and Castes of North-Western India.* Calcutta Govt. Printing Press: Reprint 1974. Delhi: Cosmos Publications.
32. *Marwar Mardumsumar, 1891,* Jodhpur: Government of Jodhpur Press, p.133.
33. Hutton, J.H. 1951. *Caste in India: Its nature, function and origins.* London: Oxford University Press.
34. *Marwar Mardumsumari, 1891,* Jodhpur: Government of Jodhpur Press, p.109.
35. Roychoudhary, B. 1968, *Quoted in People of India All India Series,* p.1625 1998 National Series (Delhi : Oxford University Press).
36. Singh, Munshi Hardayal, *Castes of Marward–Being.* (based on Census Report, 1891). Jodhpur: Books Treasurer (First edition). 1894.
37. *Census of Marwar, 1941,* Government of Marwar Press, Jodhpur.
38. Indira Sawhney, etc., etc. vs Union of India and others, others. Judgement delivered by Supreme Court of India, on 16.11.1992.
39. *People of India, 1998, National Series* (Delhi : Oxford University Press).
40. Hutton, J.H. 1951, *Caste in India: Its nature, function and origins.* London: Oxford University Press.
41. *Census of Marwar, 1941,* Government of Marwar Press, Jodhpur.
42. *Census of Marwar State, 1891,* Jodhpur, Government Press.
43. Jayaram. N. 1990, "Ethnicity and education": A Socio-historical perspective on educational backwardness of Indian Muslims: Sociological Bulletin Vol. 39, No. 1 & 2.
44. Hashmi, Masood, 1989, *Muslim response to western education.* New Delhi (India) : Commonwealth Publishers.
45. Azmi, Niaz Ahmed, 1974. "Shibli Institutions : A study of the development of Education in east U.P., with special reference to Muslims". Abstracted in *Indian Dissertation.* Oct.-Dec., 1974. New Delhi : ICSSR & AIU.

46. *Census of India, 1981,* Series – 18 Rajasthan. District Census hand book, Jodhpur. Rajasthan: Jaipur.
47. *People of India, 1998, National Series* (Delhi : Oxford University Press).
48. Report of Minorities, Vol.I. 1983. High Power Panel on Minorities, Scheduled Castes, Scheduled Tribes and Other Weaker Sections. Ministry of Home Affairs, Govt. of India, New Delhi.
49. *People of India, 1998,* National Series (Delhi : Oxford University Press).
50. Singh, Munshi Hardayal. *Castes of Marwar–Being.* (based on Census Report, 1891). Jodhpur: Books Treasurer (First edition). 1894.
51. Petrov Vitor, 1985, *India Spot light on population : A demographic outline,* Moscow : Progress Publishers.
52. *Census of India, 1911,* Vol. I Pt. I Calcutta: Superintendent, Government Printing Press, India, 1913.
53. *Census of Marwar State, 1911,* Government of Marwar Press, Jodhpur.
54. *Census of India, 1931,* Calcutta: Government of India Press, 1932.
55. Census of Marwar State, 1941, Government of Marwar Press, Jodhpur
56. Chauhan, Brij Raj, 1967, *Op. Cit.*
57. Hutton, J.H. 1951, *Caste in India: Its nature, function and origins.* London: Oxford University Press.
58. *Census of Marwar State, 1891,* Jodhpur Government Press, Jodhpur.
59. *Census of Marwar State, 1941,* Government of Mawar Press, Jodhpur.

3

Educational Development : Historical Perspective

Ten castes and three communities opened 25 educational institutions, e.g., boys and girls schools from the year 1887 to 1954 (See Table 2.1). Again, there were eight castes and three communities, which could upgrade their schools from lower primary or primary stage to senior higher secondary level. These eight castes were in order of their establishment: Kayastha (1887), Oswal (1896), Sanik Kshatriya (1896), Pushkarna Brahaman (1912), Rawna Rajput (1912), Maheswari (1918), Agarwal (1931) and Rajput (1875/1949).Three communities were : Christian (1937), Sindhi (1947) and Muslim (1952). These castes and communities are managing their schools from its establishment for more than four decades to a century old.

This chapter is aimed to describe growth and development of sixteen caste-managed secondary schools, which are being run, by castes and communities. Growth and development of these sixteen schools are analysed from the day these agencies were called by the State to establish their schools. Grant-in-Aid Rule,1902 (1904) further attracted private bodies to open their schools as well extended financial support to existing private-aided schools. Reorganization of education in Marwar State as per recommendations of H.T. Knowlton's report (1914) and scheme of expansion of primary education prepared by Rao Sahib K.M. Bhattji (1922) further attracted private bodies to open their schools since liberal approach and liberal grant-in-aid policy was a sequel to them.

State's Call to Prominent Castes: An Opportunity to Private Bodies to Enter in Education Sector (1887 to 1898)

Lt. Gen. Sir Pratap Singh was Regent of Marwar State. He called a meeting of members of prominent castes in 1886 and explained them need of modern education.[12] Three middle castes viz. Kayastha, Oswal and Sanik Kshatriya took an opportunity and entered in the field of education.

These castes were keen to arrange education for their children so that they could be placed on jobs.

Grant-in Aid Rule, 1902 (1904) Policy : An Encouragement to Private Bodies

State's call to private agencies had attracted only three middle castes viz. Kayastha in (1887), Oswal in (1896) and Sanik Kshatriya in (1898).These three castes are middle castes. They opened boys' schools only while they did not think of girls' education during those days. There was sociological reason for rise of such social phenomenon. Traditional system of education had always encouraged boys' education while female education was not considered at all since they were required to prepare them as good and successful mother and woman after their marriage, though State opened a girl's school known as Hewson girls School, Jodhpur, much before private agencies came forward.

The erstwhile Marwar State had always adopted and implemented education policy in different periods, which was announced by British rulers. British rulers introduced Grant-in-Aid Rule, 1902 to attract more private agencies to shoulder their responsibility to provide education to masses. After two years this State also implemented Grant-in-Aid Rule, 1902 which is known as Grant-in-Aid Rule, 1902 (1904) in Marwar State.

The aim of Grant-in-Aid Rule, 1902 (1904) was to attract more number of private agencies in the field of education. However, it was observed that private bodies did not respond to attractive policy for eight years. It was in 1912, Pushkarna Brahman caste responded to Grant-in-Aid policy and opened their boy's school first and then in 1919 a girls' school was also opened by them.

Then, Rawna Rajput caste (Daroga) came forward in the same year. No other castes responded to this policy. Maheswaris caste opened boys' school in 1918 and girls' school in 1920.Thus Pushkarna Brahmans top in caste hierarchy and Maheswari caste; middle castes were first two castes, which opened girl's schools in Jodhpur city.

Education Expansion

Grant-in-Aid Rule, 1902 (1904) attracted only three castes, viz. Pushkarna Brahman, Rawna Rajput and Maheswari castes. All of these castes have opened boys and girls school (Rawna Rajput caste opened girls school which is a middle school even now, i.e., why it has not been covered under study).

During 1912-20, only five schools have been opened. It can be understood Grant-in-Aid policy did not attract more number of private-agencies to come in the field of education. H.T. Knowlton was educational advisor in erstwhile Marwar State in 1914. On the basis of his recommendations, the erstwhile Marwar State appointed Rao Sahib K.M. Bhattji to prepare a "Scheme of Expansion of Primary Education in Marwar State" which he submitted in 1922. This scheme gave further encouragement to private agencies to open their schools throughout the State.

After implementation of the scheme of expansion of primary education in erstwhile Marwar State and liberalized grant-in-aid policy, three girls schools and two boys schools have been opened by three castes, viz. Sanik Kshatriya, Pushkarna Brahman and Agarwal and one minority community Christian (It is mentioned here that first State's girls school was named after Hewson). It is a sociologically important observation that Christians also came forward to open girl's school in this period. These schools were opened during 1925-1943. We describe and analyse growth and development of each school by managing caste in context of historical development.

A. Forward Castes

(i) The Brahmans: From Religious Education to Modern education

1. ***Sumer Pustikar Senior Higher Secondary School, Jodhpur***

Sumer Pushtikar Senior Higher Secondary School, Jodhpur is fourth private aided school which was established in 1912 by Pushkarna Brahmans caste. (Pushkarna Brahmans is one branch of Brahman caste. Pushkarnas are said to have originated and migrated from Pushkar, a religious place near Ajmer in Rajasthan State).

It is evident that three middle castes, viz. Kayastha, Oswal and Sanik Kshatriya had responded first to modern education before the end of 19th Century. While Pushkarna Brahman caste responded latter, i.e., after introduction of Grant-in-Aid Rule, 1902 (1904) and after fourteen to twenty three years of establishment of three schools by these three middle castes. Through Brahmans were literate and enjoyed occupational positions and top in caste hierarchy yet they did respond so late raised few pertinent questions. These pertinent questions are: (i) Why did not Brahmans respond to States' call to expand education? (ii) Why did not Brahman caste follow suits of other middle castes? And (iii) Why did Brahmans respond after eight years of Grant-in-Aid Rule, 1902 (1904)? Answer to these three questions brings out caste's psycho-dynamics. First, there was another school in the city which was run by Srimali Brahmans (Srimali brahmans are said to be another branch of Brahmans. They are said to have originated from Srimal, a village in Rajasthan). Since there was already one traditional boy's school which was later on merged into this school did not necessitate another school. Second, Brahmans had strong belief in oriental learning (i.e., Sanskrit) and traditional system of education, so they were not quick to respond to modern education. It was found that this school introduced 'Sandhya' (a ritual practice observed to please God those who perform worship), traditional occupation of Brahmans was priest and cook. These two occupation did not require any formal education. B.D. Kalla's (1916:93) observation partially fits into the last explanation[3]. The other historical source of records further explore out social fact to understand caste's psycho-dynamics. The school's annual magazine (Kalla, M.R. 1947)[4] carries quotable social event, which reveal social image of Brahman caste in the mind of Rajputs who were ex-rulers. In the princely State, marriage of daughter of His Highness was fixed. As usua! work was distributed among all castes on this occasion. It could not be decided who should be entrusted with the responsibility of cooking food and dinner, lunch arrangement. Someone among prominent persons pointed out towards this caste since it was known by its occupation of cook (Rasoia).Shri Harnath Talooji was Brahman. He was present in that meeting. He felt it very bad that traditional occupation is a social stigma attached to their caste. This was because there were not many literates. He called a meeting of his caste persons and decided to open a school for education of their boys. This occasion has forced them to open their school in1912.

"Pushkarna Hitachi Brahman Sabha" a caste association, called a meeting which was attended by S/Shri (i) Amba Das Kalla, (ii) Achal Das Kalla, (iii) Mag Dutta Kawalia, (iv) Gul Raj Joshi, (v) Radha Kishan Joshi, (vi) Jeth Mal Joshi, (vii) Fateh Raj Joshi (Golwala), (viii) Chatur Bhuj Purohit, (ix) Bachoo Lal Vyas, (x) Shive Lal Purohit, (xi) Shive Narain Kalla and others. These persons immediately collected Rs.18,330.The others who were present in the meeting promised to raise fund for schools' establishment and development. It was not available in historical records if fund-raising was a pre-requisite condition for this caste also like Oswal and Sanik Kshatriya castes were required to raise funds establish their schools. Also Grant-in-Aid Rules, 1902 (1904) did not contain any such conditions.

Anyhow, "Pushkarna Hiteshi Brahaman Sabha", submitted their request to His Highness Regent Sir Pratap Singh:- (i) to accord permission to open a school for education of Pushkarna Brahman boys, (ii) to allow them to name their school after Maharaj Kumar Sumer Singh, (iii) to inaugurate the opening ceremony of the school on 8.2.1912. Regent Sir Pratap Singh inaugurated the school. In his inaugural address, he commended role of this caste in the following words:

"You have made all efforts to open a caste school. I am glad to see this. Therefore, I have all sympathies with you in this work. Your forerunners have always served the Raj and Durbar with full vigor, abilities and intelligence. Your caste has always been patriotic and dutiful. For this reason this caste still enjoys confidence of the Durbar. I am sure this caste will continue to maintain their status in future. Durbar will give aid to this school like other aided schools."[5] *(translated from Marwari)*

Establishment and Upgradation

On 8.2.1912, Brahman caste opened their school in a small accommodation called "Nohra" which was given temporarily by Shri Harnath Talloji. Like two private-aided schools run by Oswal caste and Sanik Kshatriya caste, Pushkarna Brahmans had raised funds to start the school. But they did not get financial assistance from erstwhile State like earlier schools. They submitted their representation to the Finance Member to sanction grant to this school on the lines of other aided schools [6, 7]. The erstwhile Marwar State sanctioned a sum of Rs.100 P.M. recurring grant to them subject to two conditions :- (i) Satisfactory inspection report by the Education Department, and (ii) caste raised sufficient fund. Both of these conditions were fulfilled by the Pushkarna Brahman caste and they got grant from State for their school.

This was first private-aided school, which was established as a middle school in 1912. It started two sections, one English and other Hindi section. In English section this school started classes from II to VII and provided free education to all children. English, Sanskrit, Hindi, Persian, Urdu and Drawing subjects were taught in English section. While in Hindi sections subjects like Hindi, Maths and Arithmetic were mainly taught. In addition to these subjects, the school introduced 'Sandhyas' a sort of religious education to their students. It is drawn from this curriculum policy to an extent, was primarily aimed to meet needs of their traditional occupation if any in absolute terms. However, they were in line with stork's education policy.

This school was elevated to high school in 1925, i.e. after thirteen years of its establishment as a middle school. Among private-aided boys higher secondary schools, this school was third in order of upgradation to high school in the shortest period (The other two schools were: Mahesh Sr. Hr. Sec. School was upgraded to high school in eleven years and Hanuwant Sr. Hr. Sec. School was upgraded to high school in six year's period). The scheme of expansion of primary education was adopted in 1922. Thus State's education priority was horizontal expansion than to vertical expansion. This might be one of reasons for late upgradation of schools to high school stage. In 1962, the school was upgraded to the higher secondary stage and then to 10+2 stage.

2. Sarvajanik Secondary School, Jodhpur

Sarvajanik Secondary School, Jodhpur was established in 1943 as a lower primary school by a Pushkarna Brahman social worker Shri Bansi Dhar Purohit. He named it first "Sarvajanik Hindu Pathsala", i.e., it was opened for boys of all castes, creed and class, which also included untouchables. The erstwhile State recognized this school.

It was found that eleven schools were opened by different castes with a specific aim to provide education to their own boys only. A Christian community opened last school for girls' education. In this context this was the first private-aided school for children of all class of Jodhpur city. There was a shift from caste based policy to secular policy in mind of private educational entrepreneurs. This was a period of nationalistic movement when castes feelings have been drowned.

Shri Bansi Dhar Purohit, an active social worker who was involved in nationalistic movement, founded this school. During those days untouchables were deprived from education. State opened a school for education of Harijan boys in Udaimandir and Mahamandir and finally shifted to Bai-ji-ka-Talab, opposite Sir Pratap School. But the school for untouchables did not see its life and collapsed due to its own death for prevailing social prejudices in the city. [8, 9]

It is said that the managing committee of the school agreed to admit students of Harijan boys also. After the Harijans school was merged into this school it was upgraded to primary school in 1946. Again in 1950 it was further upgraded to upper primary school and finally to secondary stage of education in 1969. Among the boy's private-aided schools, it got its first upgradation in three years period while the next upgradation was after 19 years, i.e., in about two decades.

It is housed in a very inadequate accommodation.

Rajput : Ruling Caste's Realization of Need of Modern Education

The erstwhile Marwar State was ruled by Rajputs from 1459 to 1562 A.D. in the nuclear stage, then by Moghals from1562 to 1803 and again by Rajputs with Britisher's alliance from 1803 to 1949 (Kumbhat 1969). Rajputs were the ruler of the State. They had always thought of development of the State. Education was one priority in their thought. First they thought of education of Nobles and Jagirdars son who could not get admission in Mayo College, Ajmer. They opened two schools for them in 1875, which afterwards merged into one, disintegrated and lastly became one school form 1912. The erstwhile princely state financed these schools till the princely State was merged into the present Rajasthan State. After independence this school was placed under a category of private-aided school from the State. Growth and development of Chopasani School. Jodhpur which was earlier known as Rajput school is discussed here.

3. Chopasani Sr. Hr. Secondary School, Jodhpur

Chopasani Sr. Hr. Secondary School, Jodhpur is only a day-cum-boarding private-aided school. It is managed by Rajput caste. The present school is a final product of two schools, which were earlier, established in 1895 by the erstwhile Marwar State. In 1875 two small schools, the first of its kind in Rajputana known as Noble School and Thakur School were started for education of the sons of Nobles and poor Rajputs. In 1886, these schools were combined and reorganized under the name of the Powlett Nobles School so named after Col. Powlett, Resident. After ten years, the State opened another school named after Lord Elgin as Elgins school in 1896.The school expenditure of all these three schools was met by the State. This school was also merged into Powlett Nobles School in 1899,i.e., in a shortest period of three years. Merger of these schools did not last long, and fission occurred in these two schools (year not mentioned). In 1911, these two schools were again merged into the form of the present school (Annual Report on Administration of Jodhpur State, 1913-14. Jodhpur : Government of Jodhpur (pages 6-7)[10] . Figures clearly shows growth of the school from 1875 to its birth in 1912.

Chart

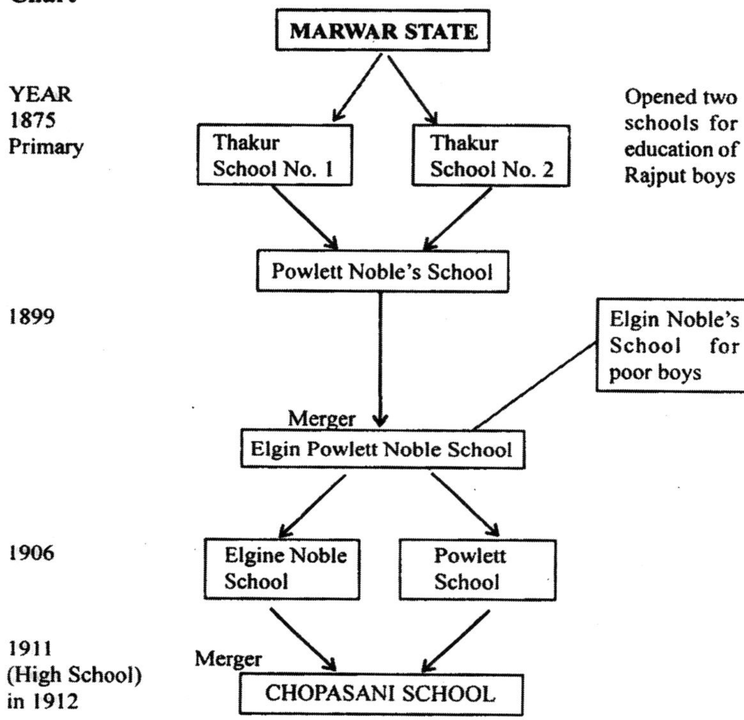

8.2 1914

Source : 1. Historical dates of Chopasani by Vikram Singh Gundoj
2. History of Chopasani in its own words by Ram Jeevan Sharma, ex-teacher, Chopasani School Diamond Jubilee Souvenir, 1976

Fig. 3.1 British of Chopasani SR. Secondary School, Jodhpur.

It is observed from this tree-chart that State took interest to open schools for education of Rajput boys. State met all expenses of the school till 1949, thus this school was not a private-aided till the erstwhile Marwar State was merged into the Rajasthan State, i.e., Rajasthan State in 1948.

Thus, it is sociologically relevant observation that Rajputs were the rulers of the Princely State, they met cent per cent school expenses, took keen interest in the school affair. This was unlike other private-aided schools, which were financed under Grant-in-Aid Rule, 1902 (1904).

However, enlightened Rajputs had conceived thought to make the school self-sufficient. It was in 1919, a committee was appointed to inquire into: (i) the finances and (ii) general working of the Rajput school. The Committee held its meeting on 30th July, 1919. The first proposal was moved by Maharaja Fateh Singh to have an endowment fund of fifteen lakh, half to be subscribed by the sardars and half by the erstwhile state. This proposal also contained one point that in case the school had to be closed the committee would be responsible to return the fund to the donors.

The second proposal was to fix maximum number of students in the school according to annual state contribution of Rs.80,000 to the school. It was also proposed to fix graduated scale of fees from students and provide free student fee-ships to a limited number of students.

Third proposal was moved by K.Chain Singhji. That a committee should first find out how much they could contribute to the endowment fund as a body and then the State should be approached to give its share of the endowment to make up the total required for the maintenance of the school.

The fourth proposal was also moved by Maharaj Fateh Singh to create a Pie-fund. All Rajputs who were in civil service had to contribute one pie-to this fund like military employees. (Note No.555 dated 23.8.1919 regarding proceedings of a meeting of a committee held on 30.7.1919 in file No.2/5/dt. I, 1903, pp. 83-84).[11]

The President of the Committee Col. R.E.A. Hamilton, C.I.E. gave a note of dissent to the first proposal, i.e., creation of endowment fund. He was only one member who submitted a note of dissent. His note of dissent carried one important observation that this school was run for nobility of Marwar and it should not be reduced parallel to other charity schools in the State. Instead he suggested levying fees from students who were from well-to-do families. (Minute of Dissent by Finance member Col. R.E.A. Hamilton (File No.2/5 Pt.I, 1903, Pt.73).[12]

However, all members of the Committee had agreed to creation of pie-fund while it was decided to appoint a Committee to decide the jubilee of endowment fund, etc. The committee submitted its report to consider measures for the improvement of the Chopasani school on 6th May, 1920. The Report was examined by the Finance Member. Finance member disagreed to place the management of the Rajput school under control of a body like other communal schools for the reasons that caste bodies had given contribution for school management since its foundation. While this school was being financed by the erstwhile Princely State. Moreover, Rajput school provided free-education, free board and lodging facilities to all Rajput boys. He agreed to creation of endowment fund for which responsibility should be entrusted to the committee of sardars.[13]

Historical development of the school shows that State first took interest to expand education among Rajput boys. State wanted to place Rajput boys on jobs in various departments after completion of school education. In this regard State sent a letter to the Principal of the school to prepare boys accordingly. It was further emphasized that Rajput school should be feeder to Mayo College, Ajmer.[14]

With the growth and development of the school, the school progressed vertically on academic horizon. The two schools were a middle school in 1886 and high school in 1912 after merger into one. This was the first school which was upgraded to middle school after 11 years of its establishment. This indicated that Rajputs did not show much interest or responded for their education in early period of its inception though it was being managed by the ex-rulers. However, State upgraded this school to high school after a period of 26 years. It was first upgraded to high school among all other private-aided schools and comparatively in less period of upgradation. This was because education was expanded from 1912 onwards after Grant-in-Aid Rule 1902 (1904) was introduced. The school was lastly upgraded to higher secondary stage in 1956 and again it was first among all private-aided schools in Jodhpur city. At present it is running classes upto 10+2 stage.

The Mahajans : Modern education a boon to trading castes in business.

We present here historical development of three schools managed by Oswal, Maheswari and Agarwal castes.

Oswal

4. Sardar Senior Higher Secondary School, Jodhpur

Sardar Senior Higher Secondary School, Jodhpur is second private-aided school in Jodhpur city. This was founded by Oswal caste in the year 1896. Oswal caste responded to a call for educational development given by the State after ten years. This was because Oswal caste is primarily a business caste and they belong to Mahajan community.

It was realized by Oswals that there were only 25 Oswal children who were studying in Durbar school (now known as New Govt. Sr. Hr.Sec.School) which was very small in number as compared to their school going population. This fact is self evident to say that Oswals were educationally backward. However, Census of Marwar State, 1941 has reported literacy figure of Mahajan community (42,027) which is above 10% of total population. Education backwardness was only motivating factor which prompted Oswals to approach the Princely State for seeking permission to start school for their own children.

Fund raising a Pre-requisite Condition for Opening a School

Mehta Bakhtawar Malji was the first prominent caste-man who submitted a few suggestions to His Highness Regent Sir Pratap Singhji for his consideration to bring change in social life of their community. On his suggestion, Regent Lt. Gen. Sir Pratap Singh sent a word to this caste to open a school for education of their children. This caste was granted permission to open a school subject to the condition that they raised fund of Rs. 40,000 to start a school.[15] In a short time the managing committee succeeded in raising fund of no less than Rs. 60,000 from the members of this community. Rs. 34,229.70 was collected on the spot. They also received Rs. 400 from Kayasthas, non-caste contributions which signifies inter-caste solidarity.Rs. 34.95 were realized by conversion of kaldar into Bijai Shahi rupee amounted to not less than Rs. 43,664.65. Late Seth Rani Raj ji who was a member of managing committee without caring for his own interest constituted to the redemption of his usu-fractuary mortgage of Nathura village and thus provided a ready opening for the investment of Rs. 21,001. Similarly Manchandji Bhandari mortgaged kurkasani of which Rs. 5,301 were invested in school.[16]

The other prominent caste persons who had contributed in cash and kind deserve to be mehtioned here: S/Shri Dewan Vijay Singhi Mehta,Dewan Sardar Singhji Mehta, Hanuwant Singhi Mehta, Hanwant Chandji Lodhi, Hanwant Chand Bhandari, Fauj Malji Mehta, Ranji Malji Mehta, Inder Nath Modi, Ganesh Chandji Lodha, Sampat Malji Bhandari, Nauratan Malji Bhandawat, Ridh Mal Singhavi, Sumer Chandji Mehta, Sumer Chandji Bhandari, Umrao Chandji Bhandari, Krishna Malji Lodha, Rikhab Rajji Karnawat, Dr. Shiv Nath Chand ji, Manohar Malji Dhadda,Ganesh Malji Saraf, Jaswant Rajji Mehta, Bhopal Chandji Lodhi, Kewal Rajji Singhavi, Moti Lal ji Mertia, Laxmi Chandji Kanoogo and Misri Malji Bafna.All of these persons had contributed their services in establishment and growth of their school. It is a notable aspect that erstwhile state asked Oswals to first raise fund and then open a school. This was a prerequisite condition for this caste while the Marwar State did not ask Kayasthas to raise fund before they were granted permission to open their school. It can be said that Oswal caste is a business caste by traditional occupation and is economically preponderant while Kayastha is a writer-caste and not economically well, through this fact cannot be substantiated with any documentary evidence.

Establishment and Upgradation

On 18th July, 1896, this school was inaugurated. In the inaugural address His Highness Regent Sir Pratap Singh emphasized that education was the need of the hour. He had always held good opinion for the caste. To quote,

" ... *Members of this community has given to Marwar State most of its pradhans, ministers, bakshi and other high officials who have not hesitated to lay down their lives in times of danger and difficulty. The successive chiefs of Marwar have recognized the meritorious services of the members of the community by grant of Jagirs and autograph letters. Even in the Council established in the reign of Maharaja Jaswant Singhji Sahib Bahadur nearly half the number of members were selected from this community." (translated from Marwari).*

(Welcome address delivered by the Oswal caste in honour of His Highness Regent Sir Pratap Singhji (undated) in File No.9/1/Pt.I, 1911, p. 50). He donated Rs.2000 to this school from his purse and announced State's donation of Rs.7000 to this school.[17] This shows that State was also generous to this caste though they were asked to raise fund before the school was opened.

Oswal caste opened their school as an Anglo-vernacular primary school in 'Niyati-ka-Nohra' near Silwato-ka-bas inside Sojati Gate. With an increase in number of students in the school, they faced difficulty to accommodate all students due to limited space. They requested His Highness Regent Sir Pratap Singhji to consider their request. State allotted them another building, known as 'Nainiji-ka-Nohra', where at present municipality office, Jodhpur is housed. The school was then shifted to the Municipality building. After the school was shifted to the present building, the school was upgraded to middle school in 1899, i.e., after three years of its establishment. The school was further elevated to high school in 1930 in the present building.[18]

Vertical growth of the school further required spacious building to run their school. Oswal caste was not keen to invest any money in government building. So they submitted a request to the State to waive off this condition. State agreed to their proposal and allotted present land for construction of the school. State also sanctioned Rs. 25,000 to this school in lieu of 'Nainiji-ka-Nohra' which is State's property.[19, 20, 21] It is an interesting observation that State paid this amount when Oswal caste vacated State building. The school was upgraded to higher secondary stage in 1958 and to 10+2 standard. This shows the school has always kept pace with educational development and educational innovation. In recent years this caste has also opened Commerce College, considering growing demands of employment in banking, public and private sectors, etc.

Maheswari

5. Mahesh Multipurpose Senior Higher Secondary School, Jodhpur

Mahesh Multipurpose Senior Higher Secondary School, Jodhpur is sixth private-aided boys school which was established by Maheswari caste in the year 1918. Till 1918, State had its own one boys school and five private-aided schools in Jodhpur city. Thus there could not be any of reasons except ideological imitations of this caste to open their own school. Because Grant-in-Aid Rule, 1902 (1904) laid down condition for private-aided schools to admit 50% students from non-managing caste. So their simple aim was to open a school of their own where Maheswaris' boys could get admission to maximum number.

This school was started as a primary school in their own building with 50 students. The school added class (VI) in 1920, i.e., after two years which was recognized by the State in 1921. In this short period strength of the school rose to 125, i.e., six times. After sixteen years, class VII was added to this school.[22, 23]

Managing committee of the school applied for recognition of the school upto middle level to the State. State granted recognition to the school upto class VIII subject to the condition that a qualified headmaster having passed matriculate should be appointed. It was found in historical records that the school appointed a headmaster having matriculate certificate in 1937[24, 25]. Thus the State recognized and upgraded this school to middle level in 1937. During that period the school was renamed to "Maheswari Anglo Vernacular Commerce Middle School, Jodhpur." By this time, the strength of the school had also increased to 150.

The school faced shortage of space due to an increase in number of students after its upgradation as a middle school. (There was another reason that Maheswari caste had opened girls school in 1920 in the same building which has caused shortage of space). It would be appropriate to clearly mention here that the managing committee for boys and girls schools are altogether separate. There may be some internal conflict among two bodies which required shift of boys school to another building besides its vertical expansion. However no historical evidence was available to substantiate the fact. Maheswari caste raised fund of approximately Rs.49,000 and purchased land near Siwanchi G ate in 1942. Construction of school building was completed in 1948. The school was shifted to the present building in that year also and got it upgraded to a high school.

In 1950, Rajasthan University inspected the school and granted recognition to this school as high school. During this year the school detached its primary section and opened a school named Mahesh School, Jodhpur. The Central Government team visited this school in 1956-57. This inspection team had recommended upgradation of the school to higher secondary stage in 1956. This was first private-aided school upgraded to higher secondary stage. As per NPE (1986), the school got its status as 10+2 school.

College Education

Maheswari caste and its founding members took keen interest in growth and development of the school. When they realized need of professional courses (e.g., B.Ed/S.T.C.), they opened a B.Ed college in 1962 and named it Mahesh Teachers Training College, Jodhpur. One year after 1963, Junior Teachers Training Courses were also started and lastly commerce college, named Somani College.

Boarding House

Maheswari caste is a Mahajan caste which reside in rural areas also. They realized that rural students should also get benefit of school and college education. In 1958, they constructed a hostel building on Chopasani road, at a cost of Rs. 3,21,000. Shri Mugni Ram Bangar donated Rs. 21,560 for purchase of land which measure to 15,000 square yards. State government also sanctioned Rs. 62,500 for construction of hostel building. In this way Maheswari caste served its population by education and residential facilities.

Agarwal

6. Hanuwant Senior Higher Secondary School, Jodhpur

Hanumant Senior Higher Secondary School, Jodhpur is the seventh private-aided boys school which was established by Agarwal caste in 1931. This school was named after His Highness Maharaja Shri Hanumant Singh ji, who was the last ruler of the princely State.

Agarwal caste opened their school when erstwhile State implemented policy of expansion of primary education throughout the State. So this caste took benefit of liberal education policy. Grant-in-Aid Rule, 1902 (1904) also encouraged private agencies to open their school. But when there were already one State run school and six private-aided schools, why did this caste open their school? Grant-in-Aid policy have also prescribed condition to admit 50% of non-managing castes students in any private-aided schools. Though historical records of the school do not indicate clearly aim of Agarwal caste to open their school yet it can be drawn that literacy percentage among Agarwals was very low in 1911 and 1941 as per Census of Marwar State reports. Secondly, Oswal and Maheswari caste cared for education of their boys only and did not give admission to sufficient number of Agarwal boys. These two factors appear to have motivated Agarwal caste to open school for education of their own boys.

Establishment and Upgradation

This school was started as primary school in Agarwal-ka-Nyat-Ka-Nohra which is situated inside Jalori Gate. There were only 21 students at the beginning. In 1944, the school was elevated to middle school and high school in 1949. This school was opened in a period of expansion of primary education, thus sooner the upgradation, better was in those days. The school was upgraded to higher secondary stage in 1966. The school faced shortage of space in the old building. Agarwal caste purchased land and constructed new building where the school is located at present.

The Writer Caste: First to Respond to State's Call Toward Modern Education

7. Sir Pratap Senior Higher Secondary School, Jodhpur

Sir Pratap Senior Higher Secondary School, Jodhpur is the first private-aided boys school which was established by Kayastha caste in the year 1887. This school has celebrated its centenary in 1987.

The history of the school has revealed that its managing caste Kayastha formed its association a year back of its establishment of caste association which is known as Kayastha General Sabha (K.G.S.). KGS's founder president was Munshi Subh Lalji Nepalia who was Superintendent Engineer in the princely State. It was an incidence that Kayasths formed its organized body as a caste-association. Coupled with this social fact, social position in occupational hierarchy of the founder president helped caste body to establish school for education of their boys in State donated building. In return to State and honour to Regent Lt. Gen. Sir Pratap Singh, this caste named their school after him. It was the occasion when Sir Pratap Singh returned from England after attending golden jubilee celebration of Queen Victoria. The school was opened on 29.8.1887.[27]

Establishment, Upgradation, Down Gradation and Restoration

This school was established as an Anglo vernacular primary school in a small accommodation (Exact location and place not mentioned in historical records). This indicates that the school was shifted to the present building from elsewhere. With financial assistance from the State, the school was elevated to middle school in 1890, i.e., in a three year's period which showed positive response of Kayasths towards modern education. A few educated Kayasthas of Jodhpur city, managed the school very well with proficiency and efficiency. Their proper management of the school brought them a boon and a reward from the State by way of sanction of two more Hindi pathsalas in 1896. The erstwhile Marwar State was also under pressure from Jodhpur-Bikaner Railway employees to grant them permission to open a school for education of their boys. The erstwhile state arranged education facilities for children of J.B. Railway employees in this school. This school was sanctioned additional grant of Rs. 40 per month to meet additional expenses.[28, 29] Upgradation of school to middle level and an increase in number of students had created necessity for more space to accommodate all children. On one school function, Kayastha caste took an opportunity and submitted their difficulty of inadequate school accommodation to Sir Pratap Singhji. He immediately accepted their request and sanctioned grant for additional construction in 1897.

Financial Crisis led to Downgradation

For first ten years the school served the society very well in sound financial position. Then it began to decline for want of financial support. As a result two Hindi pathsalas added to it in 1896, were closed in 1899, i.e., in a three year's period. It became even difficult to maintain English school properly. It was, however, kept going by its founder president late Shri Subh Lalji, until his death in 1914. The school was in extremis. State exercised its power and control and withdrew additional grant of Rs.40 p.m. sanctioned for education of Jodhpur-Bikaner Railway employees children (which was later transferred to Sardar Sr. Hr. Sec. School) and suspended payment of Rs.25 per month grant in 1915. They took this decision in view of non-payment of salary to teachers and complaint of mismanagement in the school by students. Kayastha caste could not raise fund and maintain school properly.

Sound Financial Position Led to Restoration and Upgradation of the School

In May, 1915, the Kayastha caste resolved to make one more attempt to put the school on proper footing. These measures were related to: (i) restoring its financial position by way of creation of a reserve fund, collection of donations, etc. (ii) Upgradation of the school.

Caste Sabha to Non-caste Body: Temporary Transfer of Management

It is a sociologically significant observation that State appointed a managing committee which was headed by a non-caste member and consisted of non-caste members in the management body. Sociological interpretation can be given in two ways. First, State put this school under control of non-caste members, because caste members were unable to run the school properly. This is a negative side of social fact. While, the positive approach of State was in the sense that State was keen to set the school on right form, instead to take a decision to close it down. The school management was headed by Rao Sahib K.M. Bhattji. It was in 1916. This was a first reform measure to put school in sound condition. Next reform was initiated in 1920. A ten member managing committee was formed. This committee raised funds from: (a) Individual caste-men: Among individual caste-men donation, Rs.500/- and Rs.200/- respectively were donated in sweet memory of two Kayasthas Ladies Janakibai and Tejkaurbai. Caste-men also donated money for construction of class-rooms on the occasion of birth, marriage and death of their kins. (b) Non-community members: Thanvi Sanghi Das, a non-community member, donated Rs. 9000 to this school. This shows inter-caste social solidarity in Jodhpur city. (c) State: This caste received aid for construction of gymnasium hall from State besides recurring grant. Gymnasium hall was an essential requirement considering physical well-being of students and also laid down conditions for physical well-being of students and also laid down conditions for physical growth of students in Grant-in-Aid Rule, 1902 (1904). State's regular financial support to school for its proper growth and development marked castes' loyalty towards ex-ruler. In Sir Pratap Singh's words of appreciation quotation is reproduced here in translated version:

"Kayasthas had served the Durbar on responsible jobs. This Raj had always trusted upon them. I hope Shri Durbar Sahib will also take their services. Their persons are always ready to shoulder any responsibility and prove them loyal to the Durbar. I am confident that these persons would rise further and maintain name and fame of their forerunners. I donate Rs.5000 to this school, since it has been named after me. I think Major Petterson Sahib will also try to get financial help from the State".

(Translation from Marwari quotation published in Marwar Gazettee, 1916:236)[30]

Temporary transfer of management to non-caste members put the school on sound footing which was evidenced from addition of class V again in 1916.[31] This school was further elevated to middle school in 1917 and High School in 1920. It was first private-aided school in erstwhile Marwar State which was recognized by the Allahabad University. In 1957, this school was raised to status of higher secondary stage. At present, this school provides education upto 10+2 standard in arts, science and commerce subjects. In this way school grew vertically in terms of physical, financial and educationally after a long travel on difficult roads.

College Education

Kayasthas, of course, made contribution for vertical growth of school from primary stage to 10+2 stage. However, prominent political leader of the State Late Shri Mathura Das Mathur, ex-minister of Rajasthan State opened a science college in memory of his brother popularly known as Lachoo. He established a college considering growing demands of employment in science field. This was also indirectly Kayastha caste's contribution, though individual effort at the level of college education.

Backward Castes

We discuss and analyse historical development of boys schools managed by two backward castes in Jodhpur city viz. Sanik Kshatriya (Mali) and Rawna Rajput (Daroga).

Sanik Kshatriya (Mali): Arya Samaj Preaching to reform social customs through education.

8. Sumer Senior Higher Secondary School, Jodhpur

Sumer Senior Higher Secondary School, Jodhpur is third private-aided school which was established by Sanik Kshatriya (Mali, agriculture) caste in 1898. Though literacy percentage of this caste was negligible during those days, yet this caste responded to modern education, of course, after twelve years of State's call to private agencies. Arya Samaj beliefs and Swami Dayanand Saraswati's preaching motivated Sanik Kshatriyas for education. They were influenced by preaching and ideals of Arya Samaj and Swami Dayanand Saraswati. It was realized by this caste that time had changed. Education is a prerequisite for social upliftment and progress of their caste. Education in the State was being expanded. Other castes had started taking interest in education of their own children. Kayastha and Oswal castes had already opened their schools for education of their own children. There was only one State run school in the city. These three schools are located at a far distance of 4.5 km from the area where Sanik Kshatriyas are clusterized. This caste is also a rurally predominated. There was no school on Mandore Road and non-residential school except Rajput school where only Rajput boys could study.

Fund Raising a Pre-requisite Condition to Open their School

Kshatriya Mali-Mitra Sabha (KMMS), a parent body and caste association of Sanik Kshatriya caste submitted their request to State for permission to open their own school on Mandore road. Like Oswal caste, this was required to raise fund first and then start a school. The caste association held its meeting (date not mentioned in historical records) at "Rawna-ka-chabutra" near Maghraj ji ka tank. Following prominent persons were present in the meeting: S/Shri Mistri Shiv Ramji Gehlot (Mahamandir), Purkha Ramji Sankhla, (Daroga Farash Khanna,Raj Marwar), Thekedar Pokharji, Bauji Kachawaha. Each of them donated Rs.1,000 for construction of school building where school is presently located. People from three localities and seven khedas raised the fund for construction of school building and a well. In first instance they collected Rs.7,000. The estimated total expenditure for construction of building and a well was calculated Rs.55,000. State donated land for construction of building and Rs.1,500 in cash on behalf of Maharaj Kumar Sri Sumer Singhji in whose name this school was opened.

Establishment and Upgradation

Sanik Kshatriya caste started their school as a primary school. After fifteen years, this school was elevated to the status of middle school. It is a significant observation that Kayastha and Oswal castes were granted upgradation of their schools to middle school in three years period. While this caste could not do so. Why was this so? One simple fact was that this caste did not receive any encouraging response from their own caste. This was confirmed by headmaster of the school Shri O.P. Kachawaha. Discouraging response from their own caste forced them to dilute caste-based student admission policy to general admission policy. There were other factors responsible for this state of affairs. Brahman and Rawna Rajput castes had opened their schools in 1912. The erstwhile rulers had already opened schools for education of Rajput boys in 1875 which got its recognition and upgradation to high school in 1912. Thus there were four private-aided and 2 State run schools in Jodhpur city. State was keen to expand primary education after 1922 based on recommendations of the report of scheme of expansion of primary education in Marwar State (1922) by K.M. Bhattji. For these reasons this school was given recognition and upgradation in 1945 by the State, and upgradation to higher secondary stage in 1963. Recently, this school has implemented 10+2 stage as Senior Higher Secondary School according to National Policy on Education (1986).

Boarding House

This caste is a rurally predominated students from rural areas took admission in this school. In 1945, this school opened a boarding house for rural boys. This shows that the caste had also thought of education of rural boys after forty-eight years of its establishment when the caste received donation from rural people also. The reasons maybe (i) Parents from rural areas were not ready and keen to send their boys for education to a distance school (ii) Sanik Kshatriyas might have thought of keeping construction of a hostel, a secondary priority, possibly financial factor.

Rawna Rajput (Daroga): Education a means of Social Reform
9. Umed Multipurpose Senior Higher Secondary School, Jodhpur

Umed Multipurpose Senior Higher Secondary School, Jodhpur is the fifth private-aided school which was established by Rawna Rajput caste in 1912. Rawna Rajput caste claims itself as off-spring of Rajputs. This caste entered in the field of education and opened one boys (and one girls school separately) school. Being socially, economically, educationally backward caste (SEB). Why did this caste moved into modern education? Were they keen to sanskritize them by way of modern education? Was it caste's modernization or modernization of caste? Were students of this caste deprived of admission in other private-aided schools, i.e., educational/ social inequality was there in other schools? Was there any other factor responsible for their initiatives?

Origin of caste as reported in Census of Marwar State, 1891 forced them to uplift their social status through education.

It was in the year 1906 this caste was shocked to know statement about their origin which was published in Census of Marwar State, 1891. This census report mentioned that Rawna Rajput caste is "illegitimate offspring" of Rajputs, they are slaves and servants of Rajputs (Census of Marwar State, 1891). This statement had drawn attention of Rawna Rajputs. It leads to frustration, agony and a matter of shame for all of them.

Shri Bishal Singh Sankhla was the first person of this caste who took a lead and organized a meeting on 10.6.1907. This meeting was called to take measures to bring social reform in their caste-practices. They drafted seventeen points of social reform in a letter, popularly known as 'Jai-Patra' (letter of Victory).[32] This letter was circulated among their caste members. The response to this circular was lukewarm because older people resisted to this type of social reform movement. It is evident from the fact that they could not decide anything for three years. On 26.1.1910, a meeting was organized by Rawna Rajput Sabha to frame rules and regulations for reform. Finally they could take-off as per their plan.

Establishment and Upgradation

Rishaldar Pannalal ji Chauhan was said to be connected with the princely state. He gave his house to start the school. This school was started as lower primary school in 2.4.1912 with a fund of Rs.20.50.[33] It was a monthly contribution donated by S/Shri: Moolji (Rs. 2/-), Sultan Singhji (Rs. 4/-), Arad Singhji (Rs. 1/-), Bagh Singhji (Rs. 2/-), Master Kalyan Singhji (Rs.1/-),Chauhan Panna Lalji (Rs. 3/-), Jai Singji Verma (Rs. 2/-), Rishal Singhji (Rs. 0.50.)[34], Bhairji (Rs.1/-), Aidanji (Rs. 2/-), Choga Lalji (Rs. 2/-). Rishaldar Pannalal Chauhan took his personal interest and supervised functioning of the school. Caste received encouraging response which was evidenced from an increase in number of students. An increase in number of students further required: (a) spacious building and (b) financial support. Earlier, His Highness regent Sir Pratap Singh enquired from Rishaldar Pannalal Chauhan about schools' functioning. He submitted his two difficulties to him. His Highness was kind considerate and got this school sanctioned recurring grant of Rs.40 per month and allotted Nathiji-ka-temple where they run the school there in 1913.[35, 36] After a year, the school was upgraded to middle school while the school records showed that this school became middle school in1915. It was found from historical records that State Education Department did not recognize this school upto middle level for three reasons:- (i) Not well-equipped,(ii) No play ground available (iii) No fund available.[37-40] Regent Sir Pratap Singh intervened in the matter and asked his Finance Member to find out ways to recognize this school at middle level. State supported this school by way of increasing monthly grant of Rs.25 to clear two objections made by the Inspector of Schools, Ajmer-Merwars in 1915.[41] However, one point of inadequate space remained for action for the time being. Thus the grant of Rs.65/- p.m. was more than Mali school but less than other private-aided schools. They again requested the State and were sanctioned Rs.175 pm by the State subject to the condition they raised their funds.[42-47]

Pie Fund:

It was not caste's connections with Rajputs being the ruler always eased their way as a means to an end but erstwhile Marwar State also took a serious note of financial conditions of the school. Managing caste was asked to collect one pie from all members who were well-to-do, had female relations with the State. They were asked to submit a list of defaulters and they were liable for dismissal from State's service.[48] It was a unique case which did not occur in any of private-aided schools.

Growth and development of the school showed that it has journeyed through difficult roads. In 1919, this school got its affiliation to Rajputana Middle Board (Thus the record shows school's upgradation to middle level in 1915 but recognition after four years). This school was elevated to high school level in 1945, which was very late for:- (i) Rawna Rajputs were keen to had education upto middle, (ii) other three private-aided schools had become high schools, (iii) they had to raise fund of Rs.25,000 which was a condition for upgradation of school to high school. Shri Bux Singhji Kamdar of Diggi and Shri Anand Singh ji Mehecha were among other caste philanthropists who raised funds for this school. This school was first of Jodhpur city, which got recognition as multi-purpose higher secondary school in 1959. Recently it was upgraded to 10+2 standard as Senior Higher Secondary School.

Girl's Education

Not only forward castes and backward castes show concern for boy's education, but also they were concerned for girl's education. Here we discuss and analyse the role played by two forward castes, viz., Brahman and Maheswari and one backward caste Sanik Kshatriya (Mali) and Christian, a minority community which opened schools for education of girls in Jodhpur city. (Rawna Rajput (Daroga) caste also opened a girl's school which is still at middle stage and therefore we did not cover in the study).

The Brahmans

10. Jai Narayan Vyas Kanya Secondary School, Jodhpur

Jai Narayan Vayas Kanya Secondary School, Jodhpur was the first private-aided girl's school in Jodhpur which was opened by Pushkarna Brahman caste in 1919 (It is mentioned here that Pushkarna Brahman caste had already opened their private-aided boys school in 1912.

Prior to this girl's school, there was only one State run girls school known as Hewson girl's school. Karuna Chanana Ahmed (1986:3) has rightly stated that people thought of girls education during 1921-45 when women's education had come to be accepted at least in cities and towns and among the upper and middle strata of Indian society. She discussed that: (i) Christians missionaries were motivated to introduce education with the aim of proselytization, (ii) the Hindu leaders on the other hand, hoped to reform society by ameliorating the position of women (the Idea of enlightened motherhood seemed critical). In this context, Pushkarna

Brahman caste was the uppermost in social order of the caste-hierarchy and it took up task of social reform. Late Shri Jai Narayan Vyas was political leader during those days and later he become Chief Minister of the State. This school was named after him, suggest that his support to cause of girls education was there.

Pushkarna Brahman caste submitted their request to the erstwhile Marwar State to open a girls' school. State approved their request and sanctioned them an additional amount of Rs. 2,467 and allotted a Dadiji Shri Deorajji Nohra to start their school. It was on 4th Dec., 1919. It appears that Pushkarna Brahamans started their school after 5th Dec., (exact date of its establishment not available in record).[50, 51]

Unlike other private-aided boys school, this school was upgraded to middle school in 1957 after 39 years of its establishment and to secondary school in 1967. It is drawn from this observation that upgradation of school in four decades maybe due to limited role of family to prepare and train girls for mother and wife. That is why primary education was sufficient for this task. Many scholars have found this observation all over the country.

The Mahajans : Concern for Girl's Education
Maheswari
11. Mahalaxmi Kanya Senior Higher Secondary School, Jodhpur

Mahalaxmi Kayna Senior Higher Secondary School, Jodhpur is second private-aided girls school which was established by Maheswari caste in 1920. (It is mentioned here that a separate body of Maheswaris caste had already opened their private-aided boys school in 1918.

This school was started in "Maheswari-ka-Nyati-ka-Nohra". It was named after their caste. It was established as a primary school. It got its first upgradation to middle level in 1959, i.e., after 39 years like first private-aided girls school. This school was upgraded to high school in 1971 and higher secondary in 1982. During 1986-87, this school enrolled 893 girls in Arts and Commerce subjects.

A brief history of the school only showed that there was only one State run and one private-aided girls school. They started their school to provide education to their own girls. This school has got separate managing committee than Mahesh School (boys).

Sanik Kshatriyas (Malis): Need of Girl's Education

Sanik Kshatriyas (Malis) opened two girls schools in Jodhpur city in 1925 and 1935 at two different placed by two different bodies of the managing committees other than a managing body which run boys school. They realized needs of girls education to bring in reform of early age marriage of their daughters of the adolescent age – We present here about two schools separately.

12. Umed Kanya Secondary School, Jodhpur

Umed Kanya Secondary School, Jodhpur is third private-aided girls school which was established by Sanik Kshatriya caste in 1925. This school was named after His Highness Shri Umaid Singh ji. Arya Samaj ideology and Swami Dayanand Saraswati's preaching influenced this caste to open their school. As it was stated earlier that Sanik Kshatriya caste were deeply influenced by Arya Samaj ideology and Swami Dayanand Saraswati's preaching they have already opened one boys school in 1898. Another group of this caste formed their separate caste association and decided to do something for girls education. It was late Shri Har Lal ji Sankhla who realized need of upliftment of status of women in society. In 1924 he received land from state in donation near Berion-ka-Mohalla. He collected donations in cash and kind. Late Shri Nathooji Tak donated main iron gate of the school. They constructed school building and a few shops as a source of regular income.[52]

Sanik Kshatriya caste started this school with 10 girls only, and one teacher. In one year, number of girls had increased to 31, i.e., in 1926. It was observed from the records available that Sanik Kshatriya caste first started girls school and then applied for grant-in-aid to the State.[53] It was also observed that State allotted them the land for school building and they had constructed a few shops in the building as a source of monthly income in form of rent through these shops.[54] For this reason this school was sanctioned grant of Rs. 25 pm. from 17.4.1927.[55]

Management Crisis

This school was managed well by founder president Shri Har Lal ji Sankhla for first four years then by Shri Anant Ram ji as Manager for sixteen years. After migration of Shri Anant Ram ji to Jaipur differences and infighting among members of managing committee grew. This situation forced the State to appoint an independent committee to held election of the managing committee. The committee completed its jobs in 1955 and handed over management of the school to newly elected body on 22.3.1955.

Financial Debt Held Up Schools' Growth

It was observed from the school record that the school was under financial crisis.There was excess of expenditure over income. Balance of payment position was very poor. In income side, Managing committee could raise Rs. 364 per annum and State's aid was Rs. 5583 while annual expenditure was Rs. 8254.25. Shri Tulsi Ramji Tak managed the school on loan but it was consequently resulted into half in growth and development of the school.[56]

Establishment and Upgradation

This school was upgraded to primary school in 1963, i.e. in a period of 38 years from lower primary school. After restoration and improvement of its financial position, the school was further upgraded to middle school in1964; in one years' period and lastly to secondary school in1969 after they created reserve fund of Rs. 51,000.[57]

13. Vedic Kanya Secondary Pathasala, Jodhpur

Vedic Kanya Secondary Pathsala, Jodhpur is located in Bagar Mohalla. It was established in the year 1935 by Sanik Kshatriya caste. (It is mentioned that Sanik Kshatriya caste had already opened one boys school in 1898 and one girls school in 1925, but all these three schools are managed by three different managing committees). Sanik Kshatriya caste, as it was stated earlier in the chapter had deep influence of Arya Samaj ideology and Vedic religion. This school was prefixed with name of "Vedic".

Two caste philanthropist S/Shri Ram Lal Deora and Laloo Ram Tak opened this school for upliftment of females through education. This school was opened to provide Vedic teachings to Sanik Kshatriyas women and girls.

Establishment and Upgradation

This school was established as lower primary school in 1935 by Sanik Kshatriya caste. It was upgraded in seven years period. It is observed that two Sanik Kshatriya Managing committees opened two girls schools as lower primary schools while Pushkarna Brahman caste and Maheswari caste opened their girls school as primary schools. Why was this so? It is said that Sanik Kshatriya caste believed in providing education from early stage of education because their girls were and are married at an early age, i.e.. before 12 years of age. This caste got their school further upgraded to middle school in 1949 and secondary stage in 1968.

Women's and Students Donation to the School: A Unique Observation

This school received contributions, donations in the form of cash and kind for construction of classrooms, etc. It was also observed that

Sanik Kshatriyas women also gave donation annually at Rs. one per month to this school which was a unique among private aided school.

Bad Financial Position Led the School to Downgradation

The school faced financial problems. It was under debt of Rs. 26,000. As a result of it number of students had increased in the school. Three posts of teachers were reduced. The school faced shortage of accommodation after its upgradation. The school was downgraded to Middle School in 1974.[58]

Sound Financial Position Helped the School in Restoration and Upgradation

After resignation of Shri Roop Lalji Kachawaha, the new managing committee raised funds from its caste members. Sound financial position helped the school. State Government again upgraded the school to secondary stage in 1986, i.e., after twelve years. This shows that managing committee took twelve years to restore its financial position.

Christian: Girl's Education Online of English Education
14. St. Patricks Vidya Bhavan Girls Sr. Hr. Secondary School, Jodhpur

St. Patricks Vidya Bhavan Girls Sr. Hr. Secondary School, Jodhpur is located opposite Railway Stadium behind Christian church. It was founded in 1937 by Mission sister of Ajmer, Mrs. Sterling, an Irish Catholic lady, residing in Jodhpur suggested to the Maharajadhiraj Sir Umaid Singh that unless the women of Jodhpur were educated on lines of English education his kingdom would not progress. In golden jubilee report of the school, it was mentioned that British resident Mr. Young and his wife felt the need of education of women and they impressed upon His Highness Maharajadhiraj Shri Umed Singh for the same. They submitted that an English medium school could meet the need of education of women. Rev. Mother Mary Matilda, Mother General of the Mission Sisters of Ajmer was approached for the purpose. Mission sister Ajmer accepted this responsibility and fulfilled its task. (A d.o. letter from R.T. Rev. Leo D' Mell (Retd.) Bishop of Ajmer-Jaipur to Sr. Mercia, Principal of St. Patricks Vidya Bhawan Girls Higher Secondary School, Jodhpur on the occasion of golden jubilee of the school. Souvenir : Golden Jubilee, St. Patrikcs Vadiya Bhawan, Jodhpur, 1937-87)[59].

His Highness Maharaja Shri Umaid Singh donated the land for construction of the school building. Late Seth Bijay Lal, Champa Lal of Kheechan village and Seth Jay Chand Lal of Ladnu village donated amount for construction of the school building. His Highness Sir Umaid Singh, Sir Donald field, the Chief Minister, Mr. Bilạm Chand Bhandari, the then Finance Secretary and Mr. Sterling, a great social worker associated with the Education Department took keen interest in establishment of the school. State gave recurring grant to the school under Grant-in-Aid Rule, 1902 (1904) (school's progress report by sister Mercia Principal of the school of souvenir: Golden Jubilee 1937-1987. St. Patricks Vidhya Bhawan Girls Higher Secondary School, Jodhpur)[60, 61]. This shows that it was not a missionary movement in Jodhpur city like in other parts of the country, it was an individual initiative with support from local people.

The school was started with limited classes running from First Primer to Fifth Class as a middle school with small number of 25 girls only. This school was upgraded to high school stage in a short period of eight years of its establishment in a period of expansion of primary education in the year 1945. Two boys higher secondary schools were also upgraded in the same year. In all four schools were upgraded to high school from 1922 to 1945. The school was then upgraded to higher secondary stage in the year 1960. This school was first private aided girls school which was upgraded to higher secondary stage. At present this school is running 10+2 stage classes. This school is managed and financed by Mission Sister of Ajmer.

Minority Communities

History of educational development in Jodhpur city reveal that the State not only encouraged castes but also to minority community to spread modern education among masses. Christians were the first to respond for girl's education in 1937 (that has been discussed under girl's education). Muslims also took an opportunity and responded to modern education while continuing with Madarsa education. Another numerically minority community, Sindhi, migrated from Pakistan also opened two schools in Jodhpur city; one for boys and another for girl's education in 1947. One boy's school has been closed in 1974. We discuss and analysis historical development of two schools which are run by Muslims and Sindhis.

Muslims : Theory of Compensation Benefited a Minority Community of Jodhpur City : A Case of Local Muslim Community.

Till 1931, all private-aided schools were opened by Hindu castes. There was no separate school for education of Muslim boys. His Highness Late Shri Umaid Singh made an announcement on the occasion of the foundation stone laying ceremony of Umaid Bhawan (Chittar Palace) on 21.11.1929 for opening a school for education of Muslim community as a boon in recognition of their sacrifices and services to the erstwhile State. (This announcement was published in the issue of Jodhpur State Gazette dated 24.11.1929). State opened the school on 1.12.1930 in a rented building at States' expenses. It was a unique case. Then Marwar Muslim Education Society was formed to look after the school. Muslims wanted to run this school in their own and they raised fund of Rs. 1,00,000 as per requirement of Rajputana Board of Secondary Education, Allahabad. By the time they could raise the fund our country became independent. The popular government named this school in memory of the Father of Nation Mahatma Gandhi as Mahatma Gandhi School, Jodhpur and took over its control. Muslims were sad to hear this decision since no other private-aided school was asked to change their name of secular ideology nor any of the school was taken over the State Government.

Though they continued their battle for a school in lieu of it, yet they were given permission by the erstwhile State to run Madarsa school on line of modern education pattern like other schools. Isaquia Secondary School, Jodhpur is a product of this phenomenal development which is described here. It is also mentioned that Govternment of Rajasthan has recently sanctioned them another school in lieu of this old battle which they won after 33 years.

15. Isaquia Secondary School, Jodhpur

Isaquia Secondary School, Jodhpur was established as a primary school in the year 1954 by Muslim community. This school is situated inside the city wall where Muslims are residing in large numbers.

Muslims had deep belief in traditional system of learning of Madarsa. For this reason they responded to modern education very late. Few enlightened men of Muslim community and Marwar Education Society, Jodhpur submitted a request to start their own school, Government of Rajasthan granted them permission. Thus it was after five years of takeover of Durbar Muslim School under State controlled, Mahatma Gandhi School, Jodhpur. This community had a little hope. Mohd. Hussain Sahib, Mumtaz Sahib, Mohd. Isaq Sahib and Mohd. Haji Sahib were leading philanthropist of this community who took a lead and opened the school. This school was named after Shah Mohd. Isaq Sahib.

This school was upgraded to middle school in the year 1965 and to secondary stage in 1968. It was observed that the school got its first upgradation after eleven years. This reveal that the community did not get encouragement for there were many developed and well grown schools in Jodhpur city, where Muslim boys were studying.

Sindhi: Rehabilitation through Education: A Case of Migrated Sindhi Community

India became independent on 15th August, 1947. During Independence phase, Hindustan was partitioned into India and Pakistan. Sindhi community which was residing in Sindh (Pakistan), immigrontes to Jodhpur, Rajasthan State which is across the border to save their life. Government of India and Government of Rajasthan opened a separate Department of Rehabilitation and Resettlement of refugees and settled them in different cities. (Though Sindhis were mostly residing in rural areas).

After resettlement and rehabilitation immigrant communit faced one great difficulty of language communication. Their mother tongue is Sindhi. They could speak and understand Sindhi language only. Few educated Sindhis knew English language only.

Educated Sindhis realized that they should arrange education for Sindhi boys and girls in schools in Jodhpur city. Again they were depressed to learn that medium of instruction in Jodhpur based schools was Hindi only. Sindhis could not read, write and speak Hindi language in 1947. Thus, Sindhi community decided to open two schools one for boys and one for girls for education of their children. Two separate schools for boys and girls were opened by them in 1947. One boys school was named Nehru Higher Secondary School and another school for girls was named Modern Higher Secondary School, Jodhpur.

The first school was closed in 1974, i.e., after 27 years of its functioning due to misappropriation of funds. The second school Modern Senior Higher Secondary School, Jodhpur which was earlier exclusively for girls, later it has been made co-educational school. Growth and development of this second school is discussed here.

16. Modern Senior Higher Secondary School, Jodhpur

Modern Senior Higher Secondary School, Jodhpur was established in 1947 by Sindhi community. Realizing need of education of Sindhis, Late Mr. K.K. Abhichandani, Founder Principal of the school was an educated Sindhi. He took an initiative and raised funds from its community members. He was given permission by Govternment of Rajasthan: (i) to open a school for girls education, and (ii) to teach girls through Sindhi as a medium of instruction at school level. State Government sanctioned grant to the tune of 50% of schools' annual expenditure. The Govternment also allowed the managing committee to appoint all teachers from Sindhi community as a special case so that they could teach Sindhi girls.

Prominent persons who joined in this rehabilitation programme were Dr. Pawan Das, Mr. Gandhi (Sindhi), Mr. Sant Das, Mr. K.S. Ballani, Peru Mal. These persons formed a modern education society. These persons purchased a plot for a school building, collected funds for school from community only who were residing in Jodhpur and Bombay. Seth Peru Mal, a rich business man of Jodhpur donated Rs 25,000 to this school. He was President of the modern education society.

Masked Managing Committee to a Real Managing Committee: Toward Truth

It was stated by the secretary of the committee, Advocate Shri Rewa Chand that the school was managed by one-man founder Principal Shri K.K. Abhichandani. There was a managing committee, as it was constituted as per requirement of Societies Act, 1860. All the members in the Committee were non-functional. They were masked by the founder Principal Mr. Abhichandani. After emergency was lifted in 1977, the then secretary Mr. Rewa Chand became an active member. It is not understood then (i) whether Grant-in-Aid Rule, 1963 was an effective instrument, (ii) Government of Rajasthan, Department of Education conducts regularly Annual Inspection (AI) and Panel Inspection (PI) in three years period, were on papers or ineffective. This is a question which require further probe to arrive at the truth.

The school was upgraded to higher secondary stage in 1964 and recently to 10+2 stage.

References Related to Primary Source of Data Collection

General

1. P.R. Shah (1976) : Sir P and Education, an article in Souvenir: A Diamond Jubilee of Chopasani School. Jodhpur.
2. Raghunath Singh Khichi (1976): Sir Pratap's contribution in National development (in Hindi).An article in souvenir : A Diamond Jubilee of Chopasani School. Jodhpur.

Sumer Pushtikar Senior Hr. Secondary School, Jodhpur

3. Report of working of Sumer Pushtikar School. Jodhpur, Marwar from 8th Feb., 1912 to 30th June,1915 by Kalla, B.D. Sharma, Hon. Secretary of the School, 1916.
4. Joint letter dated 8.1.1919 Pushkarna Brahman community and Sri Mali Brahman to His Highness Maharajadhiraj Regent, Sir Pratap Singh in File No.9/2, Pt.I/1912).
5. Madhulika, Annual Magazine of Sumer Pushtikar Higher

Secondary School, Jodhpur. Education by M.R. Kalla, 15.8.1947.

6. Letter from the Secretary, Sumer Pushtikar School, Jodhpur (undated) to Shri G.R. Goyder, Esquire, Finance Member, Regency Council, Marwar state, Jodhpur (received on 1.9.1912) in File No.9/2 Pt. I, 1912.
7. Extract from the proceedings of the Council of Regency Marwar State, Resolution No.5. dated 29.1.1913 in File No. 9/2, Pt., 1912.

Sarvajanik Secondary School, Jodhpur

8. Copy of letter dated July 14, 1946 from the Secretary, Marwar Harijan Sewak Sangh, Jodhpur to the Deputy Chief Minister (Subject: certain necessary wants of Harijan Sweepers of Jodhpur). In File No. C-9/9 Pt. I.
9. Letter No.13 dated 26.7.1946 from the Secretary, Marwar Harijan Sewak Sangh, Jodhpur to the Secretary, Shri Bada Maharaj Kumar Sahib (opening of Harijan School).

Chopasani Senior Hr. Secondary School, Jodhpur

10. Annual Report on Administration of Jodhpur State, 1913-14. Jodhpur: Govt. of Jodhpur Press.
11. No. 555 dated 23.8.1919 regarding proceedings of a meeting of the community held on 30.7.1919 in File No. 2/5.dt.I, 83-84.
12. Minute of Dissent by Finance Member Col. R.E.A. Hamilton in file of 2.5 Pt. File No.2.5 Pt. Minute Dissent by Finance Member 2/5 Pt. I, 1903.
13. Office Note No.1514/Education 13 dated 3.8.1920 in File No. 215 Pt.I. 1903.
14. Letter No.1238 dated 1.2.1913 from the office of the Mehkama Khas Marwar State, Jodhpur to the principal, Rajput School, Jodhpur in File No. 215 Pt. I, 1903.

Sardar Hr. Secondary School, Jodhpur

15. Diamond Jubilee, December, 1972 souvenir of Sardar Higher Secondary School, Jodhpur.
16. Report of Sardar School, 1896-1907 in File No. 9/1 Pt. I/1911 pp.14-15.
17. Report of Sardar School from 1896-1907 prepared by Managing Committee in File No. 9/1/Pt.I/1911, pp.15-17.
18. Letter dated – 19/1911 from the members of managing committee, Sardar School. His Highness Maj.Gen. Maharaja Dhiraj Sir Pratap Singh in File No. 9/11/Pt.I/1911 pp. 55, 57-58.
19. Letter No. 493 dated 10.2.1931 from the Secretary State Council, Jodhpur to the Member in waiting, State Council, Jodhpur in File No. C-9/3,Vol. I, 1930-37,p.7.

20. Letter No. 3529 dated 28.2.1931 from the Judicial Member, State Council to Jodhpur to the Director of Education, Jodhpur in File No. C-9/3, Vol. I, 1930-37, p.7.
21. Welcome address delivered by the Oswal community in honour of His Highness Regent Sir Pratap Singhji (Undated) in File No. 9/1/Pt. I, 1911, p.58.

Mahesh Senior Hr. Secondary School, Jodhpur

22. Letter No.1206 dt.30.11.1920 from the Manager, Maheswari Anglo vernacular and Commerce School, Jodhpur to the Supdt. Education Department, Jodhpur in File No. 9/10, Pt.I,1923, p.6.
23. Sanctioned vide F.M. letter No.1999, dt.22.6.1921 to Supdt., Education Deptt., Jodhpur.
24. Letter dated 8.9.1920 from Supdt. Maheswari Anglo Vernacular commerce school, Jodhpur to Supdt. Education Deptt., Jodhpur in File No. 9/10, Pt.1923, p.14.
25. Letter No.3805 of 1919-1920 dt. 22.9.1920 from Supdt. Education Deptt., Jodhpur to the Finance Member, Council of Regancy Raj., Marwar, Jodhpur in File No. 9/10 Pt. I, 1923, p.12.

Hanuwant Senior Hr. Secondary School, Jodhpur

26. Hanuwant Sr. Hr. Secondary School, Jodhpur. Annual Report 1972-73, Hanuwant Sr. Hr. Secondary School, Jodhpur.

Sir Pratap Sr. Hr. Secondary School, Jodhpur

27. A note on the Sir Pratap School, 1887-1919 dated 23-9-1919 in File No. 9/9,Pt. I, 1890, pp. 277-283.
28. Grant-in-Aid to Sir Pratap High School, Jodhpur. News item published in the Marwar Gazettee weekly newspaper, Jodhpur. Monday, August, 25, 1890, No.18,Vol XXIV, in File No. 9/9, Pt. I, 1890, p.277.
29. Grant-in-aid to Sir Pratap High School, Jodhpur. A Note in File No. 9/3 Pt. I, 1890, p.277.
30. Quotation in Marwari language published in Marwar Gazettee, 1916: p. 236, Jodhpur: Government of Marwar Press.
31. Letter No.705 dated 12.2.1916 from Regent Sir Pratap Singh to Maj. S.B.A. Petterson, Finance member of the council in File No. 9/9, Pt. I, 1890, pp.58-60.

Umed M.P.H. Sr. School, Jodhpur

32. Sudhar Saroj (in Hindi) by Risaldar Pannal Lal Chauhan, Jodhpur: Prabhakar Printing Press, 1927, pp. 39-57.
33. A Brief History of Umed High School, Jodhpur, Sri Jodhpur city, Rajput Sabha Educational Institution (No.2). Jodhpur: Manager Umed School, 1954:5.

34. Sudhar Saroj (in Hindi) by Risaldar Pannalalji Chauhan, Jodhpur, Prabhakar Printing Press, 1927.
35. Letter dated 6th March, 1913 from the President of Rawna community to His Highness Maharaj Regent Sahib Bahadur of council, Jodhpur in File No. 9/6, Pt. I, 913, pp. 1-3.
36. Letter dated 18.4.1913 from the Secretary, Raona School to Marwar State, Jodhpur Regancy Council, Marwar State, Jodhpur in File No. 9/6 Pt. I, 1913, pp.8-10.
37. Letter No.711, dated 29th August, 1913 from the Principal, Rajput School to the Finance Member, Council of Regancy, Marwar State, dated 10th Sept. 1913 in File No. 9/6, Pt. I,1913, p.17.
38. Extract from the Proceedings of the Council of Regency, Marwar State dated 10th September, 1913 in File No. 916, Pt. I, 1913, p.17.
39. Letter dated 21.7.1914 from the member of Raona community to His Highness Maharaja Regent Sahib Bahadur, Jodhpur in File No. 9/6, Pt. I., 1913, pp. 8-9.
40. Letter No. 119 dt. 27.11.1914 from the Principal,Rajput School, Jodhpur to Finance Member, Regency Council, Jodhpur in File No. 9/6, Pt. I, 1913, pp. 28-29.
41. Letter No.2743 dated 29.9.1915 from the finance member of council, Marwar State to the Secretary, Raona School, Jodhpur in File No. 9/6. Pt. I, 1913, p.45.
42. D.O. letter dated 19.12.1915 of H.H. of Maharajadhiraj Sahib Shri Pratap Singh to Maj. S.B. Petterson, finance member, Regency Council in File No. 9/6/ Pt. I, 1913, p. 46.
43. Letter No. 1231-I of 1915 dated 30.10.1915 from the Inspector of schools, Ajmer Merwara, Ajmer to Supdt. Education Deptt. Marwar State in File No. 9/6, Pt. I, 1913, pp. 51.
44. Letter dated 10.1.1916 from the Resaldar Shri Panna Lal Chauhan to His Highness Maharaja Regent Sahib Bahadur of Jodhpur in File No. 9/6, Pt. I, 1913, p. 95.
45. Letter No.1925 dated 25.9.1916 from the Finance Member of the Council, Raj Marwar, Jodhpur to the President of the Managing Committee,Raona Rajput School, Jodhpur in File No. 916, Pt. I, 1913, P.
46. Application dated 15.12.1918 from the manager, Raona Rajput School, Jodhpur to His Highness Maharaja Regent Sabib Bahadur, Marwar State, Jodhpur in File No. 9/6, Pt. I, 1913, p. 135-136.
47. Extract from the proceedings of the council of Regency Rajasthan Marwar dated 7th Feb. 1919 in File No. 9/6, Pt. I 1913, p. 141.

48. Office Note dated 2.3.1919 of vice President council in file No. 9/6, Pt. I 1913.
49. Nirman,Annual Magazine of 1957-58, Umed M.P. H.S. School, Jodhpur.

Jai Narayan Vyas Kanya Secondary School, Jodhpur

50. Office Note, dated 4.12.1919 from the Revenue Member of Council, Raj. Marwar, Jodhpur in File No. 9/3, Part. I, 1919, p. 10.
51. Extract from the proceedings of the Council of Regency Raj. Marwar dated 5th Dec. 1919 in File No. 9/3 Part. I, 1919, P.I.

Umed Kanya Secondary School, Jodhpur

52. Devi Singh Parihar, manager. A brief history of Shri Umed Kanya Pathsala. Diamond Jubilee, 1975-76.Surbhi,Umed Kanya Secondary School, Jodhpur.
53. Letter dated 2.8.1926 from the Manager, Umaid Girls School, Jodhpur to the Supdt., Education Department,Raj.Marwar, Jodhpur in File No.9.8, Part I, 1926 p.13.
54. Letter No.G-35-b/4961 dated 15.9.1926 from the Supdt.Education Department, Raj. Marwar, Jodhpur to the revenue member, state council Raj., Marwar, Jodhpur in File No. 9/8, Pt. I, 1926, P. I.
55. Letter No.G-28A/3501, dated 2.4.1927 from the Director, Education Department, Jodhpur State to the revenue member, State Council Raj. Marwar Jodhpur in File No.9/8, Pt. I, 1926, pp. 6-7.
56. Unpublished School register of Umaid Kanya Secondary School, Jodhpur.
57. Devi Singh Parihar, Manager. A brief History of Shri Umed Kanya Pathsala Diamond Jubilee, 1975-76. Surbhi, Umed Kanya Secondary School, Jodhpur.

Vedic Kanya Secondary School, Jodhpur

58. Progress Report from 1971 to 1979. Shri Vedic Kanya Upper Primary School, Jodhpur.

St. Patrick Vidya Bhavan Secondary School, Jodhpur

59. D.O. letter from Bishop Ignatius Menaces Bishop of Ajmer Jaipur to Sr. Marcia Principal of St. Patrick's Vidya Bhawan Girls Higher Secondary School, Jodhpur on the occasion of golden jubilee of St. Patrick's Vidya Bhawan, Jodhpur, 1937-87.

60. A D.O. letter from R.T. Rev. Leo D'Mello (Retd.) Bishop of Ajmer Jampur to Sr. Mercia, Principal, St. Patrick's Vidya Bhawan Girls Higher Secondary School, Jodhpur on the occasion of golden jubilee of the school. Souvenir: Golden Jubilee St. Patrick's Vidya Bhawan, Jodhpur: 1937-87.
61. School's Progress report by Sister Marcia Principal of the school in Souvenir: Golden Jubilee. Girls Higher Secondary School, Jodhpur.

4

Education Policy and its Implementation : An Analysis

Private-aided Secondary and Senior Higher Secondary Schools were established by preponderant castes of Jodhpur city. These castes established three schools at the end of nineteenth century, and thirteen schools after Grant-in-Aid Rule, 1902 (1904), i.e., during 20th Century Grant-in-Aid Rule, 1902 (1904), State's reorganization of education in erstwhile Marwar State (1914), Scheme of Expansion of Primary Education in erstwhile Marwar State (1922). The State have prescribed curriculum and courses to be followed by State and State-aided schools before independence. After Independence Secondary Education Commission (1952), Education Commission (1961-1962) have prescribed minimum number of students per class, types of courses to be followed, teachers qualifications, school environment, etc. Since these schools are sixteen in number, educational standard is bound to occur at educational differentiation among these schools. This is one of the criterion according to which private aided schools are given grant by the State under existing Rule (9) of Grant-in-Aid Rule, 1963 (Rajasthan).

This Chapter is aimed to discuss and analyse implementation of educational policies and programmes in sixteen private-aided secondary and higher secondary schools of Jodhpur city in educational perspective. It is intended to analyse and interpret data from establishment of schools, upgradation, number of students in the schools, and average number of students per class, physical and extra curricular activities, school library facilities, results at public examination, grant, fee as a source of income. The purpose of analysis of data on these variables is to measure educational prestige of these schools in the society. Statistical analysis gives an empirical base to interpret data and draw out schools which have so far created a definite educational prestige and image in the society. Educational prestige and image is a direct measure to arrive at conclusion that society has accepted their services whether educational equality or educational inequalities exists? Have these schools implemented recommendations of educational policies from beginning to NPE (1986)? Each variable is discussed in the following Sections:

1. Establishment

After state's call in 1886 to open schools in Jodhpur city, Kayastha was the first caste which opened their boy's school in 1887 in Jodhpur city. Oswal and Sanik kshatriya castes were second and third in order of establishment of their boy's schools in 1896 and 1898 respectively. It is a significant observation that no other caste responded to modern education after 1898. Grant-in-Aid Rule, 1902 was implemented in 1904 and even then private bodies did not respond to policy meant for them for first eight years. One of the sociological reasons was that there were only few persons from six castes in 1911 who knew language in English and other than English language. That is a very few persons of few castes were literate. Obviously illiterate castes did not immediately respond to education. It was wonder to observe that Brahman caste is first in rank in caste hierarchy and was first in rank in terms of literacy in Jodhpur city in 1911, but they did not respond to modern education quickly (Census of Marwar State, 1911). The reasons for delayed response to modern education by Brahman caste was discussed in the last chapter (Chapter 3 see for details Sumer Pushtikar Senior Higher Secondary School, Jodhpur). Whatever may be the reasons of delayed response of private bodies to modern education Grant-in-Aid policy did attract only three castes viz. Brahman, Rawna Rajput and Maheswari, Brahman caste opened one boys school in1912 and one girls school in 1919. Rawna Rajput caste opened one boy's school in 1912 (other girls school till now middle, hence that was not covered). Maheswari caste opened one boy's school in 1918 and one girl's school in 1920. In a period of 1912-1920 i.e., eight years period three castes had opened five schools as compared to the first period of 1887-1898, only three castes had responded. But there was an important development in Jodhpur city. These private agencies opened girl's schools too in the later period. Table 4.1 shows that private agencies did not come forward to open their schools during 1921-24. It is also mentioned that when Grant-in-Aid policy did not attract large number of private agencies, State obtained advice of its educational advisor who gave its recommendations in 1914. On advice of H.T. Knowlton and his recommendations of reorganization of education in Marwar State report (1914), State appointed a one-man Committee to frame a Scheme for Expansion of Education in Marwar State. Rao Sahib K.M. Bhattji submitted a "Scheme of Expansion of Primary Education" in Marwar State in 1922 (Directorate of Education was set up in 1920). After this report, State adopted an open door policy and encouraged private agencies to open their schools. In a period of 1925-1943, Sanik Kshatriya, Agarwal, Brahman castes and Christians opened five schools. Sanik Kshatriyas opened two girls' schools, Agarwal and Brahman castes opened one boys school each while Christians opened a girls school only. After independence Sindhis and Muslims opened boys schools in 1947 and 1954 respectively. In a period of sixty-seven years, castes and communities of Jodhpur city opened 11 boys and 5 girls schools (Ratio boys: girls school – 2.2:1), which are now senior secondary and secondary schools. Out of sixteen schools, three schools (18.75%) were established as lower primary schools (boys 1, girls 2), ten schools (62.50%) were established as primary schools (boys 8, girls 2), two schools were established as middle school (boys 1, girls 1). One boys school was established as secondary school in 1947.

Table 4.1. Caste-managed Secondary Schools (Covered) Established in Jodhpur City from 1887 to 1954

S. No.	*Period of Establishment*	*Managing Castes/ Communities*	*No. of Schools/Type of Schools*		
			Boys	*Girls*	*Total*
1.	1875	Rajput•	1 (2)*	-	1
2.	1887-98	Kayastha•	1	-	1
		Oswal•	1	-	1
		Sanik Kshatriya+	1	-	1
3.	1899-1901	-	-	-	-
4.	1902-1911	-	-	-	-
5.	1912-1920	Brahman•	1	1	2
		Rawna Rajput+	1	-	1
		Maheswari•	1	1	2
6.	1921-1924	-	-	-	-
7.	1925-1943	Sanik Kshatriya+	-	2	2
		Agarwal (1)•	1	-	1
		Christian (1) #	-	1	1
		Brahman (1)•	1	-	1
8.	1944-1946	-	-	-	-
9.	1947	Sindhi #	1(2)**	-	1
10.	1954	Muslim #	1	-	1
	Total		**11**	**5**	**16**

• Forward Caste, + Backward Castes, # Minority Communities.

* The erstwhile Marwar State opened two Thakur schools for education of Rajputs boys which became one from 1912. Later on this school got a status of private-aided in 1949 as a result of abolition of erstwhile princely state.

** Sindhis opened two schools separately one for boys (which was closed in 1974-75) and other for girls (now co-educational from 1974-75 and covered for study).

2. Upgradation

Upgradation of schools is one of the variables of vertical growth of schools. It was found that there was a variation in range of years of upgradation from 3 to 48 years at different stages of upgradation of these schools. This wide range of data required further computation at each stage of upgradation in relation to boys and girls school and also by stage of education 10+2 and 10th stage. It is because number of girls school are in ratio of 1:2.2 and student ratio 1:4.40. In other way, literacy among girls in Jodhpur city was one-fourth of boys of Jodhpur city. This is assumed as one of the reason of wide variations in between these schools at different stages of education. Secondly, was caste-factor associated with upgradation of schools?

Boys School

Table 4.2 shows that out of nine boys 10+2 schools, one school was established as middle school and another as secondary. Remaining seven schools were upgraded from primary schools to upper primary schools in 3-19 years. Mean score of year of upgradation was 9.57 years. It can be said that Kayastha, Oswal and Rawna Rajput castes got their schools upgraded in three years period while Rajput, Agarwal, Sanik Kashatriya and Maheswari castes got their schools upgraded in 11,13,15 and 19 years respectively. These schools were upgraded during 1890 to 1944. It was observed that 8 boys senior higher secondary schools were upgraded from upper primary to secondary stage (or High School) in a period of 6-32 years on an average score of 22.37 years. Agarwal, Maheswari and Pushkarna Brahman castes got their schools upgraded to high school in 6,11 and 13 years in the year 1950, 1948 and 1925 respectively. These were periods of educational expansion. The other private-aided boys schools were upgraded to high schools in 26-32 years. The first private-aided boys school was upgraded in 20 years from middle school to high school. As regard secondary to higher secondary stage, State implemented recommendations of Secondary Education Commission (1952) and National Policy on Education (1986).

Similarly, in case of two private-aided secondary boys school, one school was established as lower primary school in 1943 which was upgraded to primary school in 1946, i.e., in a three years period. (This school was opened by Pushkarna Brahman social worker Shri Bansi Dhar Purohit) while the other school is managed by Muslim community. These two schools were further upgraded to upper primary schools in a range of 11-14 years, mean 12.5 years. This is a similar observation as in case of private-aided boys schools and so their last upgradation was to Secondary Stage.

Table 4.2. Mean Score, Range of Year of Upgradation of Caste Managed Secondary Schools in Jodhpur City

S. No.	*Type of Schools*		*Lower Primary to Primary*			*Primary to Upper Primary*			*Upper Primary to Secondary*			*Secondary to Higher Secondary*		
		N	*N*	*X*	*Range*	*N*	*X*	*Range*	*N*	*X*	*Range*	*N*	*X*	*Range*
1	*2*	*3*	*4*	*5*	*6*	*7*	*8*	*9*	*10*	*11*	*12*	*13*	*14*	*15*
	Boys													
1.	Sr. Hr. Secondary	9	-	-	-	7	9.57	3-19	8	22.37	6-32	9	6	8-44
2.	Secondary	2	1	3	0-3	2	12.5	11-14	2	11	3-19	-	-	-
	Girl													
3.	Sr. Hr. Secondary	2	-	-	-	1	39	0-39	2	10	8-12	2	11	11
4.	Secondary	3	3	22.5	7-38	3	15.3	1-38	3	17.33	5-37	-	-	-

Girls School

There was, of course, marked difference in upgradation phenomenon of girls schools as compared to boys schools and as well as within and between senior secondary girls schools and secondary schools. The table indicates that Maheswari caste opened their girls school as primary school in 1929 - which was upgraded to upper primary school in 1959, i.e., after thirty-nine years. Sociological reason for this observation is that girls were married at the age of adolescent in Jodhpur city and in erstwhile Marwar State and that is why there was no educational demand for girls at middle level. Christians opened a girls school on line of English education. Both of these schools were upgraded to secondary schools in eleven and eight years respectively. These schools were upgraded in 1971 and 1945 respectively.

These two schools were then upgraded to higher secondary stage and recently to10+2 stage. A close look at the table indicate that three girls secondary schools, after a considerable period, were upgraded as compared to two girls senior secondary schools. Sanik kshatriya caste opened two girls schools in 1925 and 1935 as lower primary schools which were upgraded in a period of 7 to 38 years (Mean 22.5 year). Umed Kanya Secondary School, Jodhpur was in financial crisis as well as management problem so that it was upgraded after it was put in order by State govternment Brahman caste opened first girls school in 1919. This school was upgraded to middle school in 1957, i.e., after 38 years, like Maheswari Kanya Senior Secondary School, Jodhpur. Before independence there was no girls school which was upgraded to middle school. These three schools were lastly upgraded in 5-37 years. Mean score was calculated 17.3 years.

On the basis of above analysis it can be said that private-aided boys schools were upgraded in a shorter period than girls schools. The erstwhile State had always encouraged private agencies to grow vertically as well as horizontally (i.e., girls school by same caste). State's policy of upgradation was based on educational demand and caste factor had not played any role to influence their decision.

3. Students

Secondary Education Commission (1952:190) has recommended that each class in a school should not have more than 30-40 students in a section. Data were collected to find out whether private-aided schools are over-crowded since these are generally blamed for over crowding and profit-making institutions. Though Grant-in-Aid Rule, 1902 (1904) and 1963 did not/do not permit any school to admit extra number of students in any section of any class.

It was found that private aided schools admitted total number of 13,279 students in sixteen senior higher secondary and secondary schools of Jodhpur city in 1986-87. Out of these number of students there were 10,824 boys (81.50 per cent) and 2,433 girls (18.50 per cent), thus they were in the ratio of 4.40:1. These students were from class I to X standard (2 boys and 3 girls school) and I to XI standard (one girls senior secondary school which is managed by Maheswari caste), VI to X standard (one boys school which is managed by Brahman caste) and VI to XI standard (senior higher secondary schools). It was also found that number of student's strength varied from 202 to 1995 in 1986-87. Average number of students per school was calculated 829.93. Secondary Education Commission (1952) prescribed minimum number of students 500 in a school. There was also variation among boys schools and girls school too. Out of 10,824 boys in senior higher secondary and secondary schools, there were 9254 (85.50 per cent) in senior secondary schools in a range of 202 to 1995 students in nine schools. Average number of students per senior higher secondary school was 1028.22. There were total number of 1570 (14.60 per cent) students in boys secondary schools which varied from 436-1134 students. Average number of student per secondary school was 785. There were only 2455 girls studying in one senior secondary school and three secondary schools. In case of senior secondary schools, number of girls students varied from 257 to 842, on an average girl students per school was 520.66.

Data analysis clearly indicate wide variation in number of students in boys and girls schools. It can be correlated that physical facilities, i.e., number of class rooms was a dependent variable on number of students in the school. That is, more number of students is directly related to more number of classrooms. Hence, average number of students per class per section gives clear picture of over-crowding in the school, as it was assumed to find out. Table 4.3 shows that out of sixteen schools, 8 schools (50 per cent) admitted students in each class normal strength. These schools were 5 girls and 3 boys schools. It was found that there was only one : boys senior secondary school which admitted students as per the prescribed norm. This school is Sir Partap Senior Higher Secondary School, Jodhpur which is managed by Kayastha caste. It was also found that two boys senior higher secondary schools were below its normal strength. These schools are : Sumer Pushtikar Senior Higher Secondary School which is managed by Pushkarna Brahman caste, and Umed Multipurpose Senior Higher Secondary School which is managed by Rawna Rajput caste. Majority of boys senior secondary schools, i.e., 6 out of 9 schools were found overcrowded. These schools are : (i) Sardar Senior Higher Secondary School (Oswal caste), (ii) Sumer Senior Higher Secondary School (Sanik Kshatriya), (iii) Chopasni Senior Higher Secondary School (Rajputs), (iv) Mahesh Multipurpose Senior Higher Secondary School (Maheswari), (v) Hanuwant Senior Higher Secondary School (Agarwal) and (vi) Modern Senior Higher Secondary School (Sindhi).

Table 4.3. Student's Strength in Caste Managed Secondary Schools in Jodhpur City

S. No.	*Students Strength per class per Section*	*Higher Secondary Boys*		*Higher Secondary Girls*		*No. of School Secondary Boys*		*No. of School Secondary Girls*		*Total*	
		(N=9)	*%*	*(N=2)*	*%*	*(N=9)*	*%*	*(N=2)*	*%*	*(N=16)*	*%*
1.	Below Strength (< 30-40)	2	22.20							2	12.50
2.	Normal (30-40)	1	11.15	2	100.00	2	100.00	3	100.00	8	50.00
3.	Over Strength (> 40)	6	66.65							6	37.50
	Total	**9**	**100.00**	**2**	**100.00**	**2**	**100.00**	**3**	**100.00**	**16**	**100.00**

* Based on Secondary Education Commission Report (1952) 30-40 students per class per section.

Students strength as shown in the table indicate that 6 private-aided boys senior higher secondary schools are over-crowded while girls schools are not over-crowded. Thus there is a direct association between number of students and schools prestige. An attempt is made to compute further with all variables.

4. Physical and Extra-curricular Activities

Grant-in-Aid Rule, 1902 (1904) had emphasized need of physical exercise and games as an integral development of healthy mind and physical body of students in their growing age. Secondary Education Commission Report (1952) recommended need of health education to be introduced in all schools which is prior requisite to physical education. Health education should include properly organized school medical service, and through medical examinations of all pupils. This is done periodically in these schools. Physical education programme is organized in these schools in the form of games, both indoor and outdoor games. It was also observed that only one girls senior higher secondary and secondary girls schools organized indoor games only. This reveal that girls are not encouraged in outdoor games normally except Handball, Hockey, Kabbadi, Kho-Kho and Volleyball. Among boys schools, all schools do not organize games. These schools organized indoor games like : Badminton, Carrom, Chess, Chinese Checker, Deck-Tennis, Swimming and Table Tennis and outdoor games like : Basketball, Cricket, Football, Handball, Hockey, Kabbadi, Kho-Kho and Volleyball. These schools number 1 to 5 boys senior higher secondary schools and 1 to 2 boys secondary schools. It was further explored why do majority of schools not organize games? Because schools do not have their own playground. On the basis of this analysis it can be said that majority of private-aided schools do not give required importance on physical education aspect. Schools organize extra-curricular activities like: Scouts, N.C.C., debates, and inter-school competition. These activities help build up national character in students.

5. School Library

Library is known as brain house for every reader. Its main function is to supplement knowledge from reference-material, journals, periodicals, magazines, etc. Secondary Education Commission (1952) has also recommended need of a good library in secondary schools. It was found that all sixteen schools have got library in their schools. These libraries procured books, magazines and newspapers. It was observed that 13 schools (81.25%) had books from 1750 to 9032 in their libraries. Sardar Senior Higher Secondary School has got a big library having 24,285 books there, which was tremendously highest among all the schools. Second was Chopasni Senior Higher Secondary School which had 13,351 books and the last school is Modern Senior Higher Secondary School which had 10,095 books in their library. These three private-aided boys senior higher secondary school had more than 10,000 books in their library. Conversely, it was also observed that one girls senior secondary school (Maheswari caste) and three girls secondary schools had less number of books in their schools. Analysis of data also reveal that senior higher secondary boys schools had on an average number of books 10,015.22 (range 4387-13351) which is just double of average number of books in senior higher secondary girls schools which was 5564.5 (range 2742-8387). While there was no wide gap observed in boys and girls secondary schools.

The school libraries have also procured different types of magazines. These magazines are: Academic, comics, current events, literacy, science and health, sports, religion, women and others. These magazines carry different kinds of information which are built up for students knowledge. Total number of 270 magazines was procured by these schools in 1986-87.

The school gives due importance to Newspapers in the school library. Newspapers keep teachers and students upto date about happenings around the world. All schools display important news daily on a board. After prayer is over, a teacher of the school reads out important news under title "Today news". These news keep students knowledge upto date. These schools procure local, State and national newspapers. Out of 50 newspapers procured by these schools, only eight schools procured English newspapers. Each school procured one English newspaper only.

6. Results (Public Examinations only)

School's courses are prescribed by State Department of Education. All schools viz. government and private-aided are under obligation to abide by State education policy. This is because State have established an independent examination body known as Board of Secondary Education, Rajasthan, Ajmer. This body conducts examination at 10th and 11th standard (now 10+2 stage) to maintain uniform pattern throughout the State. Earlier to this body was Rajputana Middle and Intermediate Examination, Allahabad. In this way, private-aided schools had never been given autonomy to conduct examinations at secondary and higher secondary level independently and evaluated its students. Thus, results at these two examinations levels were right mirror image of schools whatever good/average/poor. Of course teacher's earnest hard working teaching is seen in results of students.

Table 4.4 shows results of caste-managed secondary schools in

Jodhpur city in 1986-87. It is seen from this table that one boys senior higher secondary school Shri Sumer Pushtikar Senior Secondary School, Jodhpur showed its poor result. Similarly two boys secondary schools showed its average performance. The other schools showed its good results above average results of last three years public examinations are taken into consideration while computing grant-in-aid to private-aided schools by State govt.

Table 4.4. Results of Secondary and Higher Secondary Examinations of caste managed Secondary Schools of Jodhpur City in 1986-87

S. No.	*Name of the School*	*Results % at Level of Examinations*	
		Hr. Secondary	*Secondary*
1	2	3	4
1.	Sir Pratap Senior Hr. Sec. School	80	70
2.	Sardar Senior Hr. Sec. School	78	82
3.	Sumer Senior Hr. Sec. School	75	70
4.	Sumer Pushtikar Senior Hr. Sec. School	14	29.3
5.	Umaid Multipurpose Senior Hr. Sec. School	80.11	85.61
6.	Mahesh Multipurpose Senior Hr. Sec. School	90	85
7.	Jai Narayan Vyas Kanya Secondary School	-	50
8.	Mahalaxmi Kanya Senior Hr. Sec. School	60	55
9.	Umed Kanya Secondary School	-	92
10.	Hanuwant Senior Hr. Secondary School	98.6	84.7
11.	Vedic Kanya Secondary Pathsala	-	50
12.	St. Patrick Vidya Bhawan Sr. Hr. Sec. School	99	99
13.	Sarwanjanik Secondary School	-	56.2
14.	Modern Senior Hr. Sec. School	78	75
15.	Chopasani Senior Hr. Sec. School	80	70
16.	Isaquia Secondary School	-	43

7. Grant-in-Aid

Private-aided schools are dependent largely on govternment's grant to meet their schools annual expenditure. These schools were given grants by princely state under Grant-in-Aid Rule, 1902 (1904) and now according to existing Grant-in-Aid Rule, 1963. According to Grant-in-Aid Rule, 1963, schools get different rates of grants as per their educational standards, physical and library facilities and results of examinations, etc.

Table 4.5 shows States grant to private-aide schools in 1986-87. Out of sixteen schools, 4 schools were given 90% grant according to their standards and rated special grade schools. There were three boys senior higher secondary schools namely: (i) Sardar Senior Higher Secondary School, Jodhpur, (ii) Mahesh M.P. Senior Higher Secondary School, (iii) Chopasani Senior Higher Secondary Girls School, St. Patrick's Vidya Bhavan girls school which was rated special grade school and they were given 90% grant by State government Six boys senior higher secondary schools and one girls secondary school were rated 'A' grade. These schools were given 80% grant of total annual expenditure. In case of secondary schools, 1 boys and 2 girls schools were rated 'C' grade and 1 boys school Isaquia Secondary School was given 70% grant and rate 'B' grade. There was one girls secondary school Vedic Kanya Secondary School which was rated 'A' grade and it was given 80% grant. It was also found that one girls senior secondary school, Mahalaxmi Kanya Secondary School was rated 'C' grade and given 60% grant.

Table 4.5. Percentage of Grant-in-Aid given by State to Caste-managed Secondary School of Jodhpur city during 1986-87

S.No.	*Grade*	*Percentage of*	*Number of Schools*				
			Senior	*Secondary*		*Secondary*	
			Boys	*Girls*	*Boys*	*Girls*	*Total*
1.	C	60	-	1	1	2	4
2.	B	70	-	-	1	-	1
3.	A	80	6	-	-	1	7
4.	Special	90	3	1	-	-	4
	Total		**9**	**2**	**2**	**3**	**16**

It was drawn from the above analysis that managing castes are required to raise fund to the tune of 10-40% of their annual budget expenditure. Fee is one source of income while rest is borne by castes. Castes and communities rent out schools on social functions like marriages, etc. and they raised funds in form of rents of shops built in front of school complex.

8. Fee

Fee is part of direct source of income of all private-aided schools. According to Grant-in-Aid Rule,1963, private-aided schools have been prescribed fee to charge from students, but that is not less than government school. Secondly these schools have been given partial autonomy to charge fee in name of development fund and pupils fund. It was found that schools collected 6.27 to 77.75 per cent of total school budget through fee only. Average fee per student per year varies from Rs.16.20 to 406.10. School budget also varies considerably. Table 4.6 shows percentage of fee collected to the total budget of the school. It was found that total amount of fee collected varied from Rs.52,147 to 5,13,350 in private aided boys senior higher secondary and secondary schools. Similarly in case of two boys secondary schools it varied from Rs.38,196 to 1,29,680. There was not much variation in fee collection in girls secondary schools. Amount of fee collected per year certainly depended on number of students in the school in a particular year and number of classes and sections. For this reason percentage of fee collected to total school budget was calculated as a source of income.

Table 4.6. Fee percentage of total Budget Collected in Caste Managed Secondary Schools in Jodhpur city

S.No.	*Number of Schools* / *Percentage of fee*	*Senior Secondary*		*Secondary*		
		Boys	*Girls*	*Boys*	*Girls*	*Total*
1	2	3	4	5	6	7
1.	0-10	-	-	-	3	3
2.	11-20	3	1	1	-	5
3.	21-30	2	-	-	-	2
4.	31-40	-	-	-	-	-
5.	41-50	2	-	-	-	2
6.	51-60	2	-	-	-	2
7.	61-70	-	-	-	-	-
8.	71-80	-	1	1	-	2
9.	81-90	-	-	-	-	-
10.	91-100	-	-	-	-	-
	Total	**9**	**2**	**2**	**3**	**16**

It is seen from the table that three girls secondary schools were earning around 6.45% of their total budget because girls are provided free education upto primary level. Five schools were earning in range of 11-20% fee as a source of income. Out of these five schools, there were three boys and one girls senior higher secondary school and one boys secondary school. Except two schools, one girls senior secondary school and one boys secondary school, majority of schools are earning below 60 per cent of total annual budget of the school through fee. Part of amount earned is allowed to spend on science, development activities etc. as per rule (9) of Grant-in-Aid Rule, 1963.

Analysis

In the preceding paragraphs these eight variables have shown wide variation in between schools and within schools and similarly close association between these variables. These are parameters to measure educational standards and educational facilities available at these schools. Education standards of schools form prestige in the society. An attempt was made to calculate prestige score of schools to arrive at above average, average and below average schools. Eight variables were taken for analysis: caste, number of students, number of teachers, library facilities, play ground and physical facilitates, average fee/students, results of public examinations, length of schools serving society. Each variable was given rank score from highest to lowest. For example, Brahman caste was given 8 scores because this caste occupies top position in caste hierarchy. Similarly for number of students, high score was given to highest number of students. While doing score analysis it was kept in view to form four set of groups: Boys senior higher secondary schools, Boys secondary schools, Girls senior higher secondary schools, Girls secondary schools. Again these groups were compared with each other also.

Table 4.7. Rank Score to Determine Educational Prestige of caste Managed Secondary Schools in Jodhpur city

S.	Variables Rank Scored								
No.	*Caste*	*No. of Student*	*No. of Teacher*	*Library facilities*	*Playground facilities*	*Average fee/student*	*Result*	*Length of school*	*Total*
1	2	3	4	5	6	7	8	9	10
1.	1	5	6	4	1	6	6.5	15.0	44.5
2.	2	7	9	9	1	8	6.5	14.0	56.5
3.	6	6	5	2	1	3	5.0	13.0	41.0
4.	8	1	3	1	1	5	2.0	12.5	33.5
5.	5	2	4	6	1	2	3.0	12.5	35.5
6.	7	4	7	8	1	4	7.5	16.0	54.5
7.	3	8	8	5	1	7	9.0	9.0	50.5
8.	4	3	4	3	1	9	7.5	5.0	36.5
9.	3	9	7	7	1	1	4.0	3.0	35.0
10.	8	1	1	1	0	2	2.0	4.0	19.0
11.	2	2	2	2	0	1	1.0	3.0	13.0
12.	3	4	4	2	1	4	4.0	8.0	30.0
13.	1	5	5	5	1	5	5.0	6.0	33.0
14.	8	1	1	4	0	3	1.0	12.5	30.5
15.	6	2	2	1	1	2	3.0	7.0	24.0
16.	6	3	3	3	1	1	0.0	6.0	23.0
T	**73**	**63**	**71**	**63**	**13**	**63**	**67.0**	**146.5**	**559.5**
X	**4.56**	**3.93**	**4.43**	**3.93**	**0.81**	**3.93**	**4.18**	**9.15**	**34.96**

Table 4.7 shows rank score table to determine educational prestige of caste managed secondary schools in Jodhpur city. Total score of eight variables was computed 559.5 of all sixteen schools, and mean score was 34.96. On the basis of mean score schools which fall above these score are only eight. These eight schools are all boys senior secondary schools (Except one Sumer Pushtikar Senior Higher Secondary School which is managed by Brahman caste). Two girls senior higher secondary schools and one girls secondary school scored 30.0, 33.0 and 30.5 respectively, which were close to average score of total schools. When score-analysis is looked on individual variable, then it is found something different on caste variable, mean score was found 4.56 which ticked eight schools above average (schools no. 3, 4, 5, 6, 10, 14, 15, 16). Similarly mean score 3.93 was found on number of students variable according to this score, schools which scored above mean score are No. 1, 2, 3, 6, 7, 9, 12, 13. Third variable is number of teachers in the school on this variable. Mean score was calculated 4.4. The schools which scored above their mean score are seven in number (school nos. 1, 2, 3, 6, 7, 9, 13). Fourth variable was library facilities in the schools. Mean score on this variable was found 3.93 which listed nine schools above average score. Fifth variable was playground and physical facilities. Mean score was calculated 0.84, there were thirteen schools above mean score on this variable. It is seen that schools performed above scores on one variable, but did not do it on other variables. Table 4.8 shows how schools fall on various variables. This table shows school numbers which scored above mean score on individual variables. It is found that there were number of schools which have scored their place number of times. Thus it was calculated number of times each school has scored on each variable. On the basis of total mean score 34.96 divided by eight variables, mean score was found 4.37. Only six schools have scored above this mean score. In this way statistical analysis has determined and selected only six schools which have built their prestige in society on individual scores while on general, eight schools were scored out. It was found that Kayastha, Oswal, Sanik Kshatriya, Maheswari and Rajput castes have built up their prestige in the society. Out of three communities, Christian community has also made its impact in the society. A comparative analysis of schools selected on individual schools and total scores are tabulated here to select final schools which have scored on both ways. Rajput, Kayastha, Wosal and Maheswari castes have built its prestige in the society. In other words society has accepted their services and recognized them excellent schools based on number of variables.

Table 4.8. Mean Score of Individual Variables on Individual Caste Managed Secondary Schools in Jodhpur city

S. No.	*Variable*	*Mean*	*No. of schools above mean score*	*Serial No. of schools*
1.	Caste	4.56	8	3,4,5,6,10,14,15,16
2.	Number of students	3.93	8	1,2,3,6,7,9,12,13
3.	Number of teachers	4.43	7	1,2,3,6,7,9,13
4.	Library facilities	3.93	9	1,2,5,6,7,9,13,14
5.	Play Ground/Physical facilities	0.81	13	1 to 9, 12,13,15,16
6.	Average fee/student	3.93	8	1,2,4,6,7,8,12,13
7.	Results of Public examination	4.18	7	1,2,3,6,7,8,13
8.	Length of school serving society	9.15	7	1,2,3,4,5,6,15

Table 4.9. Prestige score 4.37 to Determine and Select Caste Managed Secondary Schools in Jodhpur City

S.No.	*Above*	*Number of Schools*				
		Senior Secondary		*Secondary*		*Total*
		Boys	*Girls*	*Boys*	*Girls*	
1.	6	3 (Oswals, Sanik, Kshatriyas, Maheswarils)	1 (Christians)	-	-	4
2.	7	2 (Kayasthas & Rajputs)	-	-	-	2
	Total	5	1	-	-	6

Table 4.10. Comparative Analysis of Managing Castes Scored on Individual and Total Variables to Determine Final Scores of Schools

S.No.	*Managing caste*	*Scores obtained on individual variables*	*Scores obtained on total variables*	*Scores obtained on both variables*
1.	Brahman	-	+	-
2.	Rajput	+	+	+
3.	Kayastha	+	+	+
4.	Oswal	+	+	+
5.	Sanik Kshatriya	+	+	+
6.	Maheswari (Boys)	+	+	+
7.	Agarwal	-	+	-
8.	Rawna Rajput	-	+	-
9.	Christian	+	-	-

Analysis was done in between Brahmans schools, none of schools scored above average score of 34.96%. Similarly among Sanik Kshatriyas schools 1 boys and 2 girls schools, boys school scored 41. In schools managed by Maheswaris castes, boys schools scored 50 scores. Among Mahajan communities, three castes viz, Agarwal, Maheswari and Oswal, only later two castes scored 50 and 36.5, i.e., above average. It was also found that Rajput caste, and Sanik Kshatriya, Kayastha, Oswal and Maheswari castes of Vaishya varna scored above average score. It can be said that only a few castes are managing schools well as per society's expectation. Table 4.11 clearly indicate Mean score, SD 't' values of individual schools on eight variables and individual variable on sixteen schools to determine educational prestige of schools in society. Analysis of variance (F-test) was used to determine variance between and within schools and on eight variables. F-value was estimated 1.65 at 5% d.f. 15 and 7, which was a significant one.

Table 4.11. Mean score, S.D. and 't' values of Individual schools on eight variables and Individual variable on 16 schools to determine educational prestige in society

Individual School	*Mean*	*S.D.*	*(N=8) t*	*P (5%)*	*S. No.*		*N=16*			*P (5%)*
						Variables	*Mean*	*S.D.*	*t*	
1.	5.56	6.91	2.12	<	1	Caste	4.56	5.16	3.42	>
2.	7.06	8.05	2.31	<	2	Number of student	3.93	4.64	3.27	>
3.	5.12	6.17	2.19	<	3	Number of student	4.43	5.03	3.40	>
4.	4.18	5.71	1.93	<	4	Library facilities	3.93	4.64	3.27	>
5.	4.43	5.60	2.08	<	5	Play Ground Phy. Fac.	0.81	0.90	3.18	<
6.	6.81	7.96	2.25	>	6	Average fee/student	3.93	4.64	3.27	>
7.	6.25	6.83	2.41	>	7	Results	4.18	4.92	3.28	>
8.	4.56	5.16	2.33	<	8	Length of schools serving society	9.15	10.12	3.49	>
9.	4.37	5.18	2.27	<						
10.	2.12	3.37	1.66	<						
11.	1.62	1.83	2.33	<						
12.	3.75	4.21	2.35	<						
13.	4.12	4.51	2.41	>						
14.	3.81	5.57	1.80	<						
15	3.00	3.67	2.15	<						
16	2.75	3.55	2.04	<						

5

School Management : An Analysis

This chapter is aimed to study management process in private aided secondary schools. Management body manages private aided schools. What is the structure, and composition of management body? What is social background of members of management body? What do these bodies do? In context of policies and decisions, is there any control on management functions.

Management may thus be thought of involving two major elements, planning and control. These two aspects of management apply to all areas of organized activity, such as large firms etc represent. Planning involves decisions and actions concerning future of the organization. Control involves decisions and actions related to any organization. For management of any organization, Manager is responsible to see its activities implemented as per desired set goals. Whereas in corporate bodies or groups, a group of persons are involved in policy and decision making process. In modern management, e.g., big industrial houses etc, concept of participative management has been introduced. Participative management refers involvement of personnel who are directly or indirectly associated with policy-planning, policy-promotion and policy-implementation stages. To cite an example Secondary Education Commission (1952)[1] has recommended representation of school head master as school authority and Department of Education and ex-officio member and as a government representative respectively in the management body. Their role in management body is limited to see interest of school (in first one) and provide guidance to management body as per State's education policy (the latter one). Their role has thus been recommendatory but conceived as a positive one. Education Commission (1966)[2] has also recognized role of teacher's representative, non-community members, etc. in the management body which runs private-aided school. These two documents clearly reflect introduction of concept of participative – management in the educational sector. Why are these members given representation in school's management body? School is a complex organization which is run by: Principal/Head Master as a school authority, teachers who teach students, and students who receive education. In this way representatives of school, e.g., school Headmaster as an authority, teacher as a representative and students' representative parents form a core group and participates in management process. Similarly society is a complex organization, which is represented by persons of different social groups. Non-Community members' representation in the body has been recognized necessary since school is a part of society, and it is accountable to society. Hence their representation is essential, and more than it, to present secular character of educational institutions. This chapter focuses on three aspects:

A. Personnel and Management
B. Policies and Decisions
C. Supervision and Control

A. Personnel and Management

Who are personnel involved in management of schools? What are their social backgrounds? Do they perform their functions as a responsible member of a management body? How do they get entry into these bodies? These are few questions which are examined to understand what is management?

M.S. Gore (1982)[3] has discussed relevance of social background of members who are involved in the decision process. Robert, E. Engel and Paul P.W. Achola (1983)[4] have reviewed literature of work done on academic decision-making process in higher learning institutions. They have found that : (i) Board of management have for and against opinions about decisions taken in regard to academic affair, (ii) Perception of functional groups, and (iii) What do trustees do? Unlike it, schools have been given autonomy to choose any subject books prescribed as per approved courses and curricula. Management has no role to play in this academic-decision and any other(s) related to it. Their role is very specific related to policy and decisions.

The specific role played by personnel involved in management process depends on social background of members who are placed at different levels in structure of the management body.

Management Body: Its Structure

Table 5.1 shows that management body of all schools has three categories of members according to their positions. (i) Office-bearers, (ii) Members, (iii) Ex-officio members. It was found that office bearers represented 66.65% of total members, members 19.90% and ex-officio-members 13.45%. There were 187 members (86.55%) who formed core group in policy and decision making process (See Table 5.1).

Table 5.1 Members of Management Body of Caste – Managed Secondary Schools in Jodhpur City during 1986-87

S.No.	*Hierarchy of Members*	*Number of Members*	*%age*
1.	Office bearers	144	66.65
2.	Members	43	19.90
3.	Ex-officio-members	29	13.45
	Total	**216**	**100.00**

(i) **Office-bearers**: Office bearers are represented by President or Manager as a head of the management body, who is assisted by Vice-President(s), Secretary or Organising Secretary, Assistant Secretary, Joint Secretary (ies) and Treasurer. Data analysis show that all schools management bodies are headed by President/Manager. Only nine schools (60%) have created posts of Vice-President. The post of Secretary is a key one in any management body, since it is a functional one; every school has got it except one managed by Pushkarna Brahman. Rawna Rajput, Rajput, Maheswari, Sindhi and Muslim community have created a post of organizing Secretary (31.25%). Only one school (e.g., Maheswari caste) has additional post of Assistant Secretary. Because, this caste is running a primary school, B.Ed. and commerce colleges in addition to senior higher secondary school for boys. Kayastha, Maheswari and Sanik Kshatriya castes have created posts of Joint Secretaries (18.75%). It was found that Kayastha caste had two posts of Joint Secretaries in their management body It was wonder to note that out of sixteen, only six management bodies (e.g., Kayastha, Rawna Rajput, Agarwal, Sindhi, Sanik Kshatriya (two girls schools) have created posts of a treasurer in their schools which is very essential for maintenance of accounts while majority of nine schools did not do so. In each category of posts there was a variation in number of posts, which is a policy maker group.

(ii) **Members:**

This is a second level of important group which promotes policy planning in decision process. This group is represented by following types of members:

(a) Caste/Community members, (b) Co-opted member, (c) Teacher's representative, (d) Parents representative, (e) Ex-students' representative, and (f) Non-Community members. This structure confirms that schools have implemented recommendations of Secondary Education Commission (1952)[5] and Education Policy (1966)[6] in letter and spirit.

It was found that there was variation in number of caste members in all school's management body. Number of caste members varied from 3 to 9. Maheswari (boys), Sindhi and Brahman castes (Boys secondary school) have given representation to three members of their castes while Kayastha, Oswal, Rajput have given representation to five members of their castes. Rawna Rajput and Sanik Kshatriya (girls secondary schools;2) and Christian have given representation to six members of their community. Similarly, Maheswari castes (Girls Senior Secondary School) and Muslim community have given representation to 7 members of their caste and community. There was one caste Sanik Kshatriya, (boys senior secondary school) which gave representation to 8 members of their own caste. Pushkarna Brahman caste gave maximum representation to their caste members.

Table 5.2 shows representation of caste members in the management body. It is also observed that there is direct association between number of caste members and number of schools managed by castes according to their social position.

Table 5.2. Caste's Representatives in the Management body of Caste Managed Secondary Schools in Jodhpur City in 1986-87

S. No.	*Managing Castes*	*No. of caste member*	*No. of schools*	*%*
1.	Maheswari (Boys), Sindhi, Pushkarna Brahmans (Boys sec.)	3	3	20.00
2.	Kayastha, Oswal, Rajput	5	3	20.00
3.	Rawna Rajput, Sanik Kshatriyas (2 Girls School), Christian	6	4	26.65
4.	Maheswari & Muslim	7	2	13.35
5.	Sanik Kshatriya (Boys)	8	1	6.65
6.	Pushkarna Brahmans	9	2	13.35

As regard teacher's representation in the management body, 11 management bodies (68.75 per cent) have given representation to their teachers. This observation confirms that managing castes have implemented recommendations of Education Commission (1964-66), except five managing castes, viz. Maheswari, Agarwal and Sindhi, all are running senior secondary boys schools in Jodhpur city and one group of Pushkarna Brahmans and Muslim community are running boys secondary schools. Like it, only 10 schools (62.50 per cent) gave representation to non-community members. Managing castes which did not give representation to non-community members as per recommendation of

Education Commission (1964-66) are : Kayastha, Sanik Kshatriya, Maheswari, Agarwal, Sindhi and Sanik Kshatriya (Umed Kanya Secondary School, Jodhpur).

Parent's representatives and ex-student's representatives were very minimum, i.e., only Sanik Kshatriya, Rajput, Maheswari and Christian considered it essential to maintain close linkage with parents of students while others did not give much importance.

On the basis of data analysis of members who were in the management body, it can be said that except caste members, other categories of members were given symbolic representation in the management body i.e., to give a window show of school as a secular in its character, while it does not seem to be contrary to this empirical observation. Registration of Societies Act, 1860 do not lay down any such provisions which imbibed upon any educational institutions.

Ex-officio member:

All sixteen schools gave representations to: (i) Principal(s)/Head master(s)/Head Mistress(es) and (ii) Department of Education's personnel, in their management body. This observation also confirms implementation of recommendations of Secondary Education Commission (1952) and Education Commission (1964-66).

Table 5.3. Total Number of Members of Management Body of Caste Managed Secondary Schools in Jodhpur City in 1986-87

S. No.	*Below normal/ Above 15*	*No. of members*	*No. of schools***	*%*	*Managing Castes*
1.	<15	7	1	6.65	Pushkarna Brahman (Boys secondary)
		10	1	6.65	Sindhi
		13	1	6.65	Kayastha
		14	2	13.35	Maheswari (Boys & Girls)
2.	Normal (15)	15	7	46.65	Pushkarna Brahman (Boys & Girls), Rawna Rajput, Sanik Kshatriya (2 girls school) & Muslim, Christian
3.	>15	16	2	13.35	Oswal, Sanik Kshatriya (Boys)
		17	1	6.70	Rajputs

* Secondary Education Commission (1952) has recommended not more than 15 members in the body.

** One school Hanuwant Senior Secondary School, Jodhpur was under State Govt.

Secondary Education Commission (1952)[7] has also recommended that management body should be consisted of members not more than 15 in their bodies. It was found that there was slight variation in all these bodies from 7 to 17. Table 5.3 shows that Rajput caste had maximum number of 17 members in their management body because this caste is also running a primary school, hostel etc. Followed by it are 16 in Oswals, and Sanik Kshatriyas (Boys senior secondary school), 15 in seven schools, i.e., in Puskarna Brahmans (Boys and Girls school), Rawna Rajputs, Sanik Kshatriyas (two girls secondary schools), and Christian and Muslim communities. Maheswari caste had 14 members in management bodies of boys and girls schools both. Kayastha, Sindhi and Pushkarna Brahmans had 13, 10 and 7 members respectively in their management bodies. This shows that 46.65% of school management body has followed recommendation of Secondary Education Commission (1952), while other management body(ies) did not strictly followed, if not implemented.

It was found that management body showed its structural-variation and numerical variation at different levels. This raised a question why is it so? Did they intend to complete their two-third quorum caste members as required to form and implement policy as per their desired goals? Table 5.4 shows that 13 schools (86.65%) did not give much importance to caste's representation in their management body (ies). However, caste's representation was above 50% in all schools except Rajput caste. Sindhi and Kayastha gave representation to 80% and 75% respectively in their management body. On the basis of this empirical analysis it can be said that caste members and other members have no significant and recognized role in schools management process (In next Section of this chapter this fact will further be strengthened by response analysis of management body office-bearers, school head masters, and teachers etc.).

Social Background of Members

It was assumed that members are given place in the management body due to (i) caste background, (ii) occupational background. Data analysis showed that 46 to 80% of members belonged to managing castes (**See Table 5.4**). Madan and Halbar (1972)[8] have found that 71.0 to 96.9% of members belonged to managing castes which run schools.

Table 5.4. Caste Percentage in the Management body of Caste-Managed Secondary Schools in Jodhpur City in 1986-87

S. No.	*Below Normal, Above 2/3 or 75% members*	*Total % of caste members*	*Nos. of Schools (N=15)*	*Managing Castes*
1.	Below 75%	46.65	1	Rajput
		53.35	1	Maheswari (Girls)
		56.25	1	Oswal
		60.00	1	Rawna Rajput
		64.30	1	Christian
		66.65	4	Pushkarna Brahman Sanik Kshatriya (2 girls secondary schools)
		68.75	1	Sanik Kshatriya
		71.40	2	Maheswari (Boys) & Brahman (Boys)
		73.35	1	Muslim
2.	Above 75%	76.90	1	Kayastha
		80.00	1	Sindhi

Table 5.5 shows social background of members who were in the management body of sixteen schools studied. It was found that members belonged to various professions. However, 30 members (13.90%) belonged to service categories. Among service class, castes which represented to this group were: Kayastha, Puskarna Brahman, Sanik Kshatriya, Maheswari, Sindhi and Christian. Out of these castes and communities, two castes viz. Kayastha and Brahman were engaged in service occupation. They are not expected to play any significant role in educational management of the schools. Business/agriculturist were second in rank order which constituted to10-20%. This group helped management body in fund raising and collection of donation from caste members, etc. Similar was for industrialist, who formed 8.35% of total members. Maheswari caste gave representation to 13 members out of 14 members who belonged to industrialist group. Traditional occupation of this caste was business. The other castes were: Oswal, Pushkarna Brahman, Agarwal. Among categories of businessmen and agriculture, Oswal, Sanik Kshatriya, Rajput, Sindhi and Muslim were main castes. Sanik Kashatriya and Rajput are agriculturally predominated castes while Sindhi, Muslim and Oswal are engaged primarily in business work. Politicians have also been given representation by Sanik Kshatriya, Rajput, Pushkarna Brahman and Sindhi.

Table 5.5. Social background of Members of Managing Committee of Caste Managed Secondary Schools in Jodhpur City.

S.No.	*Social Background*	*No. of members*	*Percentage*
1.	Service	30	13.90
2.	Business/Agriculture	22	10.20
3.	Industrialist	18	8.35
4.	Educationist	11	5.10
5.	Doctor	6	2.75
6.	Politician	5	2.30
7.	Audit and Accounts	3	1.40
8.	Lawyers	2	0.90
9.	Chartered Accountant	1	0.45
10.	Journalist	1	0.45
11.	Others	117	5.20
	Total	**216**	**100.00**

Data analysis of members elected for municipal, legislative assembly and members of parliament from first democratically elected government to the present shows that these members belonged to these castes only: Brahman (9), Rajput (3), Sanik Kshatriya (16), Oswal (13) Maheswari (1), Agarwal (2), Suthar (1), Sindhi (1) Scheduled Castes (3) and Muslim (3). This data analysis show that only a few castes have strong political hold in the society.

This observation confirms that castes who have returned their representatives at different political structures have got their links in educational institutions. Gould (1972)[8] has studied relationships of politics with education in his field study of Faizabad district (U.P.). He found that political parties have controlled higher secondary schools. J.P. Naik (1963)[9] went on to say that in Uttar Pradesh Congress has abolished zamindari in land and has created educational zamindars. But this is not a case in Jodhpur city. It is generally said that politicians help management body in getting government's approval for release of grants, recognition, and upgradation of the schools. The other groups viz. lawyers, doctors, chartered accountants, journalists, audit and accounts have been elected by caste-men in the management body, but not for specific purpose.

The question is whether social background of members plays any positive role in schools management? On this aspect responses were collected from President/Secretary of all the schools. It was found that office bearers are only responsible for schools' management. Other members have been accommodated to fulfill conditions laid down in Registration of Societies Act, 1860, Secondary Education Commission

Report (1952)[10], and Education Commission Report (1964-66) and also Grant-in-Aid Rule in force from time to time. Shukla (1969)[10] has termed such groups as "pressure groups" who are occasionally locally influential and politically effective in decision-making process. Nirmal Singh (1983)[11] has reported that these groups have affiliations to religious and political parties like Hindu Mahasabha (HMS) and others which influence decision process and affect teacher's and students' condition. But the findings of this study differ from these two studies. Because teacher's and student's union of private aided schools have not been normally blessed by local, state or national political parties like in college and universities. It is a fact that private groups participating in educational enterprise are more parochial, territorial, or caste based in character.

Management Body: Its Function

Management body of a school is responsible for school management. The main responsibility of a management body is to raise fund to an extent to meet its annual expenditure. Education Commission (1964-66)[15] has reported that 67% secondary schools are private-aided. This indicates that private agencies are dependent upon government grants. In other way also private aided schools are sharing government burden let it be economic or education responsibility of State. Conclusively management body has to apply for annual grant to State Government.

Grant-in-Aid Rule, 1902 (1904) encouraged private bodies to seek financial assistance from State government After independence, Grant-in-Aid Rule, 1963 continued original grant-in-aid policy which was enunciated by Indian Education Commission (1882), but with enunciated by Indian Education Commission (1882), but with certain modifications as per need of time. According to existing Grant-in-Aid Rule, 1963, these schools are receiving grant as per A,B,C and D and Special Categories standard which is fixed on educational standard of the schools and educational facilities available there. Table 5.6 shows grant-in-aid percentage given by State to sixteen castes managed secondary schools. It was found that only four schools were given 90 per cent grant by the State. These four schools (25.00 per cent) were rated in special category for high educational standard and superb educational facilities. These four schools are three boys senior secondary schools, managed by Rajput, Oswal and Maheswari castes. One girls senior secondary school is managed by Christian community which gives instructions in English medium. Majority of schools, i.e., 7 schools (43.75 per cent) were given 80 per cent grant by the State. Out of these seven schools six schools are boys senior secondary schools, which are managed by these castes viz. Kayastha, Sanik Kshatriya,

Pushkarna Brahman, Rawna Rajput, Agarwal and Sindhi. One girls secondary school also received 80 per cent grant which is managed by Sanik Kshatriya caste. State gave 70 per cent grant to one girls secondary school which is managed by Maheswari caste and another boys secondary school run by Muslim community. These two schools were rated 'B' grade and ranked third in hierarchy. There were three schools in grade 'C' which received 60 per cent grant from the State. Out of these three schools one boys secondary school and one girls secondary school were managed by two separate managing committees of Pushkarna Brahmans. Sanik Kshatriya caste is also running one girls secondary school near Sojati Gate which received 60 per cent grant from the State in 1986-87.

Table 5.6. Grant-in-aid Percentage Given by States to Caste-Managed Secondary Schools in Jodhpur City in 1986-87

S. No.	*Grade*	*Grant in-aid %*	*Number of Schools*									
			Higher Secondary				*Secondary*				*Total*	*%*
			Boys	*%*	*Girls*	*%*	*Boys*	*%*	*Girls*	*%*		
1.	Spl. Category	90	3	33.35	1	50.0	-	-	-	-	4	25.00
2.	A	80	6	66.65	-	-	-	-	1	33.35	7	43.75
3.	B	70	-	-	1	50.0	1	50.0	-	-	2	12.50
4.	C	60	-	-	-	-	1	50.0	2	66.65	3	18.75
5.	D	50	-	-	-	-	-	-	-	-	-	-
Total			**9**	**100.0**	**2**	**100.0**	**2**	**100.03**		**100.0**	**16**	**100.0**

Analysis of data revealed that management bodies of schools are dependent upon society for their contribution to meet 40-10 per cent of schools' annual expenditure. The source of earning of schools is student fee which is charged as per approved norm of the Department of Education, Government of Rajasthan. However, it was recorded that these schools have been allowed to charge fee under two heads viz. pupil fund and development fund under Grant-in-Aid Rule, 1963. (This type of fee collection should not be confused by "Capitation-Fee" as it charged by private educational institutions which run colleges for technical courses e.g., medical, engineering, etc.). Parents' body of these castes, i.e., caste sabha or caste associations also gives contribution to schools' management body annually. Caste sabhas raised funds through rents of shops, rents of school building on occasion of marriage, etc. Was this condition earlier also? Before independence, castes were required to raise fund even to start their schools, recognition and upgradation of schools. Caste bodies have collected funds/donations in cash/kind from castes, non-caste/non-community members and the State (besides States' grant). (for details see chapter-4). Misra (1962, 1967, 1973)[12] has studied pattern of educational finances in India. He (1973:141) has compared grant-in-aid status of all States and found that all States have some common features of grant-in-aid rules like in Rajasthan.

B. Policies and Decisions

Private-aided agencies take certain important decisions, e.g., fund raising for establishment, recognition and upgradation, student admission policy and recruitment of teachers as per prescribed qualifications and conditions laid down by the State government. All of these major functions were performed by collective responsibility of members who have held different positions in the body. Social background of members, of course, play very important role in policies and decision-making process because they hold different positions in the society. Their social positions in the society build their place and exert a type of influence based on its character, local, cosmopolitan and neutral by type of residence. Robert. K. Merton (1968)[13] and Paul F. Lazarsfeld (1955)[14] have discussed types of influence and methodology to measure the influence. Three type of identified relationships viz. local, cosmopolitan and neutral are discussed are as follows:

I. *Local :* Those castes which enjoyed occupational position in administrative hierarchy of erstwhile princely state, numerically preponderant, ritually and economically high. Also perform functions of 'Policy Maker' e.g., Brahmans, Oswals, Sanik Kshatriyas, Rajputs, Kayasthas, Agarwals and Maheswaris, Rawna Rajputs, Muslims.

II. *Cosmopolitan :* Those castes which are non-traditional residents but enjoy good position in social and occupational structure of Jodhpur city, e.g. Sindhis, Christians, etc.

III. *Neutral :* Those castes which are local and they play limited role or cosmopolitan in origin but play advisory role they occupy position in school or govternment department.

Table 5.7 Participative Management of Different Groups in Relation to Pattern of Influence

Group	*Types of Decision making*	*Pattern of Influence*							
		Local		*Cosmopolitan*		*Neutral*		*Total*	
		N	*%*	*N*	*%*	*N*	*%*	*N*	*%*
I	Policy maker	143	74.10	1	11.10	-	-	144	66.65
II	Policy promoter	42	21.75	1	11.10	-	-	43	19.90
III	Policy Implementer	8	4.15	7	77.80	14	100	29	13.45
	Total	**193**	**100.00**	**9**	**100.00**	**14**	**100**	**216**	**100.00**

Table 5.7 shows that out of 216 members, 144 members fall in the category of policy maker group. This group represents to 66.65%. This group takes decision about school finances (e.g., fund raising), student's admission policy, teachers' recruitment, promotion policy etc. Except one member, all members'who were official members, local by residence, and can exert their effective influence in decision process. This group is supported by another group which is termed as policy promoter (19.90%). Out of 43 members, 42 members are local resident. In this group members are : caste members, non-community members, parents' representative, teachers' and students' representatives. These members represent 21.75% of total locally resident members. The decision taken by policy maker and policy promoter is implemented by policy implementer group. This group is represented by only two category of personnel e.g., school headmaster as a head of school, and govternment representative to guide management body in implementing state's education policy and plans. Data analysis showed variation among three levels of groups according to type of residence/pattern of influence. It was observed that there is a significant association between types of groups in management body and pattern of influence they exert in policy and decision making process. Statistical value chi-square was found X = 134.07 at d.f. 4, $P < 0.05$ and 0.01. Rene Saran (1973)[15] has also found that local group influence policies and decisions in private secondary educational institution in U.K.

There is a widespread doubt about functional aspect of "decisive social groups" which persists in schools' board of management. Frank A. Pinner (1956:20, 89-104)[16] has found that school board and school superintendent evidently varied in their orientation. Some were "local" or "cosmopolitan" in orientation. He suggests that communities of different types tend to elect people of differing orientation to the high school board. This in turn creates special circumstances which affect the interaction of the school board and school superintendent. The interaction of social group suggests definite type of relationship which is exerted out of "persistence of social groups" (Simmel, George 1898)[17] , S.N. Eisenstadt (1959)[18] reported that it was no longer relevant to report presence or absence of the type of influence in a group. Rather, it is sociologically pertinent to search out the attributes of the social structures which make for varying proportions of these identifiable groups (Fanellie, Alexander , 1956)[19] .

The persistence of social groups in a board of management can be analysed parallel to power structure in administration, management, and industrial entrepreneurship has termed it. S.K. Lall (1973)[20] has termed urban castes as urban elite based on his study in Jodhpur city. In Rajasthan middle castes are assuming leadership role, especially in rural areas. Though higher castes dominate elite stratum (Narain, 1976)[21], the numerical strength may be taken to decide dominance of higher castes in elite stratum. This trend has also been identified in the states of Tamil Nadu and Maharashtra (Beteille, Andre, 1966[22] and Sirsikar, 1970)[23].

In this context Pareto's explanation of elite group is worth mentioning. Emphasizing the inequality of individual endowment in social life, Pareto defined a member of an elite group as one who secures the highest score in specific branch by specifying the degree of individual endowment, may be in higher or lower stratum. Obviously, Pareto was conscious of the economic and political power and talks of primacy of the ruling elite (Pareto, 1935)[24]. Mosca (1939)[25] explains in a similar vein and goes further by saying that organized minority rules over unorganized minority. Understanding together the views of Mosca and Pareto, Bottomore (1968)[26] suggests that minority which rules over the majority consists of those who occupy posts of political command. The ruling minority further contends is replaceable and Pareto termed as "circulation of elites". Like Pareto and Mosca, Manneheim (1936)[27] attributes actual policy making and implementing roles to the elites.

Theoretically it becomes clear that ruling minority organized and unorganized, both economic and political dominance enjoys elitist position in power structure of the social system. In Indian society, ritually higher, numerically preponderance, caste prominence can also be added as attributes of elite status in rural as well as in urban society.

Whatever, the position, these decisive social groups hold in the management body, they are involved in management process. The nature of involvement of these members may be manifest or latent one. This type of association suggests that they are responsible members of and in the body and are answerable to society. In earlier section we have stated management body performs set of functions. An attempt was made to analyse these set of functions, first on theoretical model, which is borrowed from what Pareek and Khanna (1961)[28] have used in action research in education and on cybernetics model by Rastogi (1979)[29]. Secondly an attempt was also made to empirically justify the theoretical approach.

Pareek and Khanna (1978) have extensively reviewed the use of action research in education. The traditional concept of action research (Pareek, 1978) follows Lewin's 3-stage model of social change unfreezing-moving-refreezing. The action research process consists (with some variations) of the following steps.-

- Dissatisfaction with current state of affairs.
- Identification of a problem area.
- Identification of a specific problem to be solved through action.
- Choice of a hypothesis.
- Design of action to test and implement the hypothesis.
- Evaluation of effect of action.
- Generalization.

The variables in the present study are distributed on the three dimensions grid model and then a probability model is evolved to see how action is distributed and policy is decided in educational administration.

Certain propositions were formulated to draw results of action research model.

1. Theoretically deduction of policymaking process proposes that policy regarding recruitment of teachers (RT) distributed at three different levels. When action is oriented that is positive and potential contribution (+ + +) and action promoted (+ - +) may agree but with difference and lastly action is implemented – differ but agree to implement. Similarly, further analysis on budget expenditure (FE) and Budget finance (FB), and fee-exemption to poor students (FR), results are some what thoughtful in the sense that policy maker group agree to these policy aspects but it is not necessary policy promoter group ditto these decisions and they may differ except expenditure on library, books and science development. It is also theoretically analyzed that there may be divided opinion on fee-exemption to poor boys of their own caste students or poor boys in general, or to SC/ST students.

2. The other policy items regarding student admission policy, welfare fund, government aid, there seems to be no much variations which can be imaginatively formulated substantively.

Mathematical deduction of action research 3 grid model bring out some interesting results if we assume 7-17 members are involved in policy making then probability of taking part in policy making by each member is p=1/7 to 1/17. If we further group these members first into 2/3rd and 1/3rd; it constitutes to 86.55 per cent and 13.45 per cent (see Table 5.1) and secondly policy maker (66.65 per cent). Policy promoter (19.90 per cent), and policy implementer (13.45 per cent) (see Table 5.7). This analysis suggests that every member in the management body has formed its place in the body but only a few (e.g., policy maker) takes sole decision since they belong to managing caste. This analysis is strengthened by pattern of influence these groups exert in the management body which was statistically found significant with types of groups.

Now we see that decision in the management body is a potential contribution in policy making. In case of study of educational administration, this differs a little. First, it is a necessary contribution but not essentially a potential contribution as suggested by Pareek (1978)[30]. Secondly, it is a collaborative process both positive (+) and negative (-) but in the sense a competitive in nature based on assumption that the goal is rational in nature not in terms of buyers and sellers. When management process is collaborative then decision is consensus, if positive (+) and conflict if negative collaboration process. Microlevel analysis revel that management body and three different levels of groups decide policy consensually but individually if we measure conflict-trends emerge out that is sabotaged by majority. For example, a decision is averted by a vote of 3 very locally but group is in minority non-logical decision is taken by 4 subjectively, because they are in majority. The other point of contention of this argument is policy maker group or President and other members in the management body have no background of educational administration or educational management or think on scientific management line.

Analysis of these variables is further extended to cybernetic theory (Rastogi, 1979)[31]. This theory is borrowed to understand decision process which is operated in educational management. Organizations such as industries, military, political, labour and educational fall into different classes.

From the point of view of the present study some of variables outlined by Rastogi (1979)[32] were borrowed as a set of description and analyse the problem in context of decision process:

- Establishment/Maintenance/Expansion of educational institution.
- Facilities to students and improvement of infrastructure.
- Recruitment process for teachers and especially for Principal(s)/Headmaster(s).
- Students active dissatisfaction (agitation).
- Teacher's active dissatisfaction (agitation).
- Non-teaching staff's active dissatisfaction (agitation).
- Salary and service conditions of teacher's.
- Salary and service conditions of non-teaching staff.
- Local grievances.

- Pressures on administration.
- Government assistance.
- Political factors.

The dynamics of problem solving in decision process can be explained as shown in the figure 5.2 by using loop analysis.

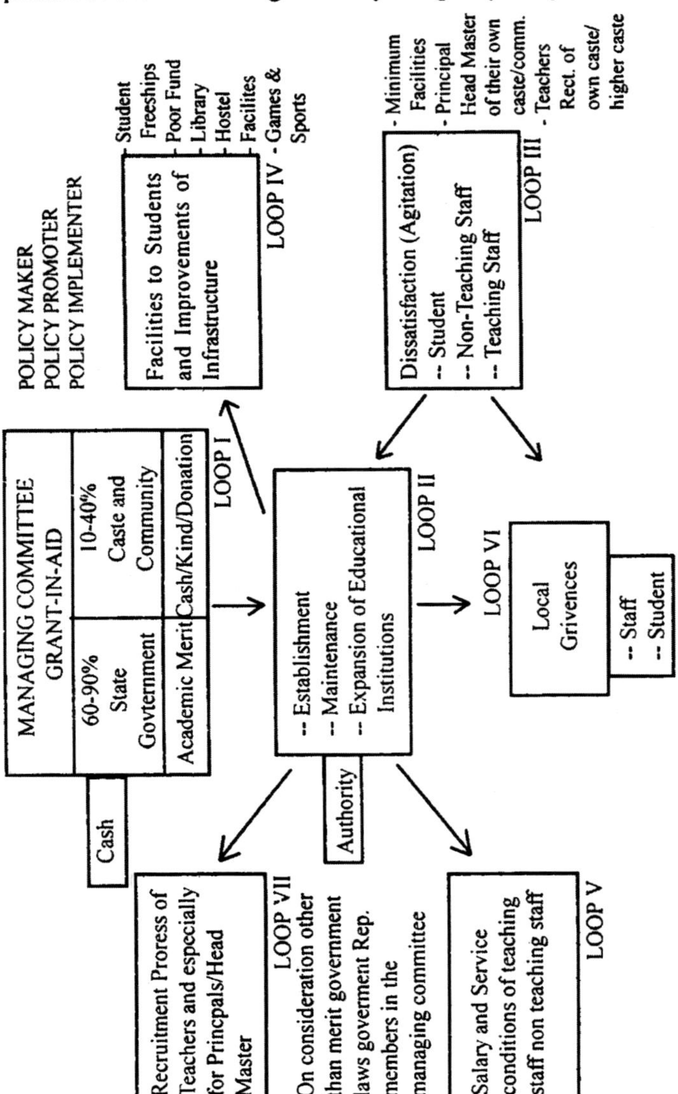

Policy Making in Private Secondary Educational Institutions : An Emperical Analysis Based on Cybernatic Theory.

Loop I explains State govternment grant to school (60-90%) on the basis of educational standards of schools and educational facilities available in the schools. Management body of schools raises 10-40% of fund which is of total annual expenditure. Loop I and VII shows intricate relationship between two which facilitate decision process. Loop II-Establishment unit of educational institutions do function for recruitment of teaching and non-teaching staff. Loop II and VII are closer in sense that recruitment is made by selection committee headed by President/Secretary of the management body and other members (e.g., Subject expert, Principal/ Head-master and government nominee as ex-officio members. Here the political factors and caste factors decide recruitment of teachers (especially of Principal/headmaster) and non-teaching staff though candidates' prescribed qualification and experience is a necessary condition of eligibility for a post. Castes' weightage is given, if he/she belongs to managing caste. This response was given by majority of respondents (i.e., secretary/manager) of management body of all schools (for empirical analysis, see for details recruitment of teachers).

On other side loop II decides salary and service conditions of teachers and non-teaching staff (loop V) and look after local grievances (loop VI). In case of present study, analysis reveal that except three schools, all schools have appointed Principals/headmasters who belonged to their own caste. This shows great and active dissatisfaction among seniormost lecturer who was eligible for the post of Principal or headmaster of the school, but could not be considered or could not get it because of caste consideration. Loop II also sees facilities to students and improvement of infrastructure of educational institutions.

Private-aided schools are managed by management body(ies) of schools so all these variables are closely interwoven in the management process that decision may be consensus in nature.

In next paragraphs an attempt is made to analyse empirical data in context of theoretical models discussed in the preceding paragraphs.

1. Grant-in-Aid and Fund raising

Grant-in-Aid to private enterprise has been the corner stone of the British policy to spread modern education in Indian society. It stimulated and encouraged the private effort and sought cooperation in difficult task of financing the education. Misra (1973)[34] has stated four principle causes of spread of education by private enterprises. These causes are:

(i) Keen desire of the people to get education in order to derive away ignorance and poverty by improving their status and earning capacity. It was often expressed by Gopal Krishna Gokhle in the legislatures and on the public platforms. R.C. Prasad (1968)[35] has found that agriculture occupation was found a failure in the Bihar state were education development was the main cause of this factor. M.S.A. Rao (1967)[36] has also stated that education was a passport to get entry into government jobs.

(ii) Rise of militant nationalism in the last quarter of the last century swept the whole continent in the first half of the twentieth century. It was very critical of government policies and intolerant of hurdles placed in the expansion of education.

(iii) Public munificence which flowed freely for the spread of education. Inspired and goaded by feelings of piety and patriotism which overtook the people as a result of several religious, social and political movements in Indian life in the last and first quarter of two centuries.

(iv) Dedication of a large number of settler's talented workers who sacrificed their careers for the cause of education.

The last point as stated by Misra was a similar observation in the present study. Besides State's aid (recurring and non-recurring) private enterprises raised funds in various forms which are discussed here.

General Fund

By 'General fund' we mean here that castes and communities raised fund for growth and development of their schools. Table 5.8 shows that Sir Pratap Senior Higher Secondary School which is managed by Kayasthas caste, raised funds in various forms. Kayasthas raised total amount of Rs. 1200 as monthly subscription, Rs. 2,100 as endowment fund, fee, interest, and non-caste's contribution. Non-caste's contribution shows inter-caste's solidarity which had existed then. This caste also collected fund on different social occasions like birth of a son, marriage, community feast and general feast besides raising fund for schools. This caste also got schools' classrooms constructed in sweet memory of their deceased, birth etc.

Table 5.8. Sources of Fund Accrued in Sir Pratap Senior Higher Secondary School, Jodhpur

S.No.	*Sources of fund*	*Amount collected*
1.	Monthly subscription	1200.00
2.	Endowment Value	2100.00
3.	Fee (from non-kayastha boys)	0.00
4.	Interest on Reserve Fund	2900.00
5.	Caste's contribution	150.00
6.	Non-caste's contribution	500.00
	Social Occasions 2	
7.	Birth of a son	1.00
8.	Marriage (a) son	3.00
	(b) daughter	2.00
9.	Niyat (community feast/sweat meat)	5.00
10.	Feet (a) Shira (Halwa)	4.00
	(b) Lapsi (sweet dish of grinded wheat)	2.00

Source : 1. Letter No. 268 of 1922-23 dated 20.1.1923 from the Secretary, Managing Committee, Sir Pratap High School, Jodhpur in File No. 9/9, pt. I. 1870.
2. Note on the Pratap Institute, Jodhpur. Undated, PPS-11 in File No. 9/9 Pt. I, 1890.

Similarly, it was found that Pushkarna Brahman caste collected Rs. 51,823.00 as caste's contribution at the time of establishment of the school. In this case also there was collection on social occasions like Gur Bhoj, Batav, marriage and yagya.

Table 5.9. Funds Raised on Different Occasions in Different Forms by Caste Contribution in Sumer Pushtikar Sr. Higher Secondary School, Jodhpur

S.No.	*Forms of Fund*	*Amount*
1.	Ek Kalin contribution	44,573 = 50
2.	Monthly contribution	206 = 00
3.	Gur Bhoj etc.	1,188 = 00
4.	From Batav	7,020 = 00
5.	Pie-Fund	865 = 80
6.	Marriage and Yagya	413 = 35
7.	Special contribution	646 = 00
	Total	**54,912 = 65**

Source : Progress report of Sumer Pushtikar School, Jodhpur, Marwar. 8.2.1912 to 30.6.1915 by Kallia, Bansi Dhar Sharma, 1916.

Table 5.9 shows different types of contributions collected by Pushkarna Brahman caste. It was found that this caste collected Rs. 44,573.00 at one time and, i.e., why it was named "Ek-Kalin Dravya Sahyata" and other funds on different social occasions. From sociological point of view it is important to analyse range of amount donated by individual members. In case of Pushkarna Brahman caste it was found that 434 members donated to Ek-kalin contributions. Amount of donation to this fund ranged from Re. 1 to Rs. 1200. It was found that 65.35 per cent of members donated less than Rs.100/- while 30.95 per cent contributed in range of Rs. 101 to 500. This means that 96.25 per cent persons (i.e., 414) donated very small amount, howsoever, they were really concerned to cause of schools' development. Only 3.70 per cent of members contributed donation above Rs.501 to Rs.1,201 Though there were only 16 persons who contributed this large amount to this fund. This shows how keen these people were to donate their saved money for good cause of the society.

It was also an interesting observation in case of Oswal caste. Two prominent persons of Oswal caste mortgaged their villages to raise fund for schools' development. They also collected Rs. 75,000 as donation immediately after the establishment of the school. The other castes, viz. Sanik Kshatriyas (Rs. 54,000), Maheswaris, Agarwals, Sindhis, Muslims raised fund at the time of establishment of the schools. (For details see chapter-3), wherein historical development of each school have been discussed individually). Oswal caste also opened another fund in 1902 in name of "Rupee fund". They resolved a system of sell of tickets to aid the institution.

Pie-Fund

There were two schools (12.50%), viz. Sumer Pushtikar Senior Higher Secondary School which is managed by Pushkarna Brahman caste and Chopasani Senior Higher Secondary School (Managed by Rajput caste), which started fund in name of Pie-Fund, i.e., one-pie contribution to the fund (see Table 5.9). In case of Chopasani School this fund was started in 1912. When the school was raised to the status of high school. It was reported that then Finance Member Lt. Col. R.E. Hamilton proposed to the judicial member to levy one pie per rupee of salary voluntarily from Rajputs serving in the State. The very purpose of this fund was to make school self-supporting as other caste and community schools in the state (Because this school was financed cent percent by the State upto 1949). In 1919 Rajput Sabha appointed a committee for school management. The committee decided to levy one pie per rupee from civil employees who belonged to Rajput caste.

High School Fund

It was realized by Rawna Rajput caste that students who passed their middle school examination had to go to other schools for study in high school classes. According to Grant-in-Aid Rule, 1902 (1904), private-aided schools were required to raise reserve fund of Rs. one lakh to start high school classes in their schools.

Shri Balkishanji Chauhan Kamdar Sahba, Digi (Jaipur) donated, Rs. 25,000 to the fund which was highest. There were 104 persons who donated amount in range of Rs. 51 to Rs. 25,000 Rawna Rajput caste and other castes generously donated this amount to this fund. Table 5.10 shows that 76 persons (73.05%) donated the amount in range of Rs.10 to Rs. 200 10 persons (9.60%) donated the amount in range of Rs. 201 to Rs. 300 to this fund. Out of total 104 persons 80 persons (85.55%) donated to this fund whiie 14.45% belonged to other castes.

Table 5.10. High School Fund Created in Umed Senior Higher Secondary School, Jodhpur

Range of donation (in Rupees)	*Managing Committe*	*Number of Donors*					
		%	*Other Castes*	*%*	*Total*	*%*
1	2	3	4	5	6	7
101-200	66	74.15	10	66.65	76	73.05
201-300	8	9.05	2	13.40	10	9.65
301-400	2	2.25	-	-	2	1.90
401-500	-	-	-	-	-	-
501-600	3	3.35	1	6.65	4	3.85
601-700	-	-	-	-	-	-
701-800	1	1.10	-	-	1	0.95
801-900	-	-	-	-	-	-
901-1000	-	-	1	6.65	1	0.95
1001-1100	6	6.75	-	-	6	5.75
1101-1200	2	2.25	1	6.65	3	2.95
5001-10000	-	-	-	-	-	-
10001-20000	-	-	-	-	-	-
20001-25000	1	1.10	-	-	1	0.95
Total	**89**	**100.00**	**15**	**100.00**	**104**	**100.00**

Source : Rajput Sabha Shikshan Sansthan (No. 2), Jodhpur. A Brief History of Umed High School, 1954. By Manager, Umed High School, Jodhpur. p. 7-10.

Endowment Fund

Management body of schools created endowment fund. For instance, Kayastha caste collected Rs. 2100 in this fund (see Table 5.8). In this fund, two endowments of value of Rs. 500 and Rs. 200 were raised in memory of two Kayasthas ladies viz. Ms. Janakibai and Ms. Tej Kaur Bai. Third endowment fund known as Petterson endowment fund of Rs. 250 was also opened in this school. These three endowments yielded interest of Rs.12-8, 26-8 and Rs.10 a year respectively and of these amount the whole of the first and a small fraction, Rs. 2-8 of the second endowment was for gifts in kind to be given to the best boy irrespective of caste, creed or sex. It was also observed that His Highness Mahrajadhiraj Regent Sir Pratap Singhji donated Rs. 5000 for construction of rooms in school building. Thakur Sanghi Das donated Rs. 9,000 to this school. He was a non-Kayastha person. There were number of well-wisher from far-off areas who sent total amount of Rs. 12,000 as donation to this school.

The other caste was Rajput. This caste is managing chopasani school. In 1919 a committee was appointed to inquire into financial condition and general condition of the school. The committee held its meeting under the chairmanship of Col. R.E.A. Hamilton, CIE, then Finance Member in the State. One member of the Committee Maharaj Fateh Singhiji put the proposal to start endowment fund of Rs. 15 lakh. Half of it to be subscribed by Sardar and half of it by the Estate. This proposal was unanimously agreed to by all members except the President who gave his note of dissent. He differed on this proposal for two reasons. First, State would get Rs. 75,000 as an interest on this amount which was less than State's grant to the school . Secondly, the school would become charitable institution by way of voluntarily contribution by members of Rajputs caste.

Lottery Method

Only Kayastha caste tried this method also to raise fund through sell of lottery tickets. This caste made two attempts to float lottery tickets. First attempt was made on 1.8.1920 for Rs. 30,000 which was unsuccessful. Second attempt was successful and they could fetch Rs. 60,000.

The historical account of growth and development of private-aided secondary schools shows that Pushkarna Brahmans, Rajputs, Rawna Rajputs, Oswals, Kayasthas, Maheswaris, Agarwals have raised funds through various methods.

2. Students' Admission Policy

In the history of modern education in India, private enterprises took the responsibility of education of their own children so that they could get occupation in government jobs where educational qualification was essentially required (Rao, 1967)[37]. This was sole aim of private educational institutions. However, it is important to note that literacy percentage was very low at the time of beginning of modern education era. In that way education was a necessity. Britishers did not object to the idea of caste-based admission policy. However, Grant-in-Aid Rule,1902 (1904) laid down one of the conditions to allow them to admit student of their own castes upto 50%. After Independence these institutions were required to show its secular character according to Constitution of India.

Madan and Halbar (1972)[38] have found that private educational institutions have succeeded in their aim of student's admission who belonged to their managing castes in three districts; Mysore, Belgaum and Dharwar district. In the present study it was found that private-aided schools which were opened before 1904 could succeed in their aim of student's admission of their own caste. This was true for boys schools only. For instance, Kayasthas opened their school in 1887. It was first private-aided school in Jodhpur city. This school admitted total number of 1009 students in different years: 1906, 1912-12, 1917-18 and 1920. Out of 1009 students, 642 (63.65%) students belonged to this managing caste.

Table 5.11 Caste-wise Enrollment of Students Caste-managed in Secondary School, Jodhpur City in Different Years

S. No.	Schools by Managing Caste	No. of Schools	Sanik Kshatriya N	Sanik Kshatriya %	Kayastha N	Kayastha %	Brahman N	Brahman %	Rajput N	Rajput %	Muslim N	Muslim %	Mahajan N	Mahajan %	Charan N	Charan %	Others N	Others %	Total N	Total %
	A. Castes																			
1.	Kayasthan	1	-	-	642	63.65	83	8.25	49	4.85	38	3.75	35	3.45	5	0.50	157	15.55	1009	100.00
2.	Oswal	1	-	-	-	-	-	-	-	-	-	-	23857	32.6	-	-	48765	67.40	72352	100.00
3.	Sanik Kshatriya (Boys School)	1	1162	39.40	-	-	-	-	-	-	-	-	-	-	-	-	1179	61.60	2941	100.00
4.	Pushkarna Brahman	1	-	-	-	-	455	100	-	-	-	-	-	-	-	-	-	-	455	100.00
	Total	**4**	**1162**	**1.5**	**642**	**0.85**	**538**	**0.7**	**49**	**0.06**	**38**	**0.04**	**23622**	**30.75**	**5**	**0.01**	**50701**	**66.09**	**76757**	**100.00**

Source :

1.(a) Letter No. 1904 of 1912-13 dated 23.8.1913, the Supt, Deptt. of Education, Rajasthan Marwar to the member of Council infile No. 1/9 Pt. I, 1890, PP 51-52

(b) Letter dated 4.9.1917 from Shri K.M. Bhattji, Manager, Sir Pratap School to Musaib Ala Rajasthan Marwar, Jodhpir infile No. A/9, Pt. I, 1890, P. 103-104

(c) A Note on the Sir Pratap High School infile No. A/9, Pt. I, 189, P. 294

(d) These figures are total of different years 1906, 1912-13, 1917-18, 1920

2. (a) Based on annual repots of administration of Marwar State, Jodhpur Govt. of Marwar Press for the period 1894-95, 96, 1901-10, 1910-14, 1918-22, 1922-26, i.e. for year

(b) Report of Sardar School, 1896-1907 in file No. (9/1 Pt. I, 1911, P. 20 indicated caste wise distribution of students in Sardar Schools as : Oswals, 565 192, 75%) Agarwals : 28 (4.60%), Maheswari (2.45%) and Sarog (0.20%), i.e. out of 607 students enrolled in a year (not mentioned)

3. (a) Annual Magzine, Sumer Higher Secondary School, Jodhpur, 1972

(b) These data are total of 1942-48

(c) Caste-wise enroliment of student for 1982-83 are : Sanik Kshatriya : 230 (25.75%), Rajput : 134(15%), Bishno and Jat : 92 (10.30%), Charan : 27(3.00), Jain Maheswari and Oswal : 112 (12.55%) Brahman : 58 (6.50%), Musliam : 23 (2.55%), SC : 68 (7.60%), ST : 6 (0.65%), Backward Castes 73 (8.15%) Total number of students enrolled were 894

4. Letter No. 742 of 1919-20 Pt. 3.1.1920 from the Supdt. Education Department, Rajasthan, Marwar to the finance member, Regency Council, Rajasthan Marwar to the finance member, Regencycouncil, Raj Marwar infile No. 9/2, Pt. I, 1912, p. 144.

This is a overall picture. Year-wise analysis further reveal that the school admitted 32 Kayasthas boys (78.05%) and 9 other boys (21.95%) in 1906 while in the year 1917-18, the figure of Kayasthas boys increased to 80%, this was situation after Grant-in-Aid Rule, 1902 (1904) was introduced. It was important to draw observation from this empirical fact that government was liberal in implementation of Grant-in-Aid policy though castes adapted to its provisions. Varma (1973)[39] has also observed similar findings. The second caste, which opened their schools in 1896, was Oswal. Oswal school admitted 565 (92.75%) students who belonged to their own caste which was high as compared to the first school. The other caste students which were given admission, they also belonged to the Mahajan community; Agarwals (4.60%) and Maheswaris (2.45%). Caste-wise enrolment of students in this school as reported in Administrative reports of Marwar State for 20 years shows that only 32.60% students belonged to Mahajan community. Among other castes include all local castes. Thus numerical analysis support theory of caste based admission policy, if analyzed individually. This caste is clusterized in rural and urban areas of Jodhpur district.

Third caste is rural based Sanik Kshatriyas. Sanik Kashatriyas opened their boys school in 1898. Data analysis for the period 1942-48 has revealed that 32.45% of students belonged to their own caste. Geographical location of the school is also a contributing factor since Sanik Kshatriyas are mostly residing in nearby areas of this school. After independence there was 25.75% students belonged to Sanik Kshatriya caste in 1982-83.

Pushkarna Brahman caste responded very late in 1912 and opened their boys school. The caste admitted all boys of their own caste. In the same year Rawna Rajput caste also opened their school but they got a luke-warm response from their own caste. It was because of low-literacy too. Rajput school was exclusively for Rajput boys till 1949, when its character was changed to private-aided. This school is a day-cum-residential school. Most of rural boys take admission in this school, they are Rajput in majority. Maheswari and Agarwal castes opened their schools in 1918 (boys), 1920 (girls), and 1931 respectively. By this time, number of schools have grown, education consciousness have also grown correspondingly. Pushkarna Brahman social worker opened another boys school for untouchables in 1943, i.e., open door policy. Sindhis and Muslims opened their schools for education of Sindhis and Muslim boys'. Government allowed the first community as a special caste to rehabilitate

Sindhi refugees after partition. The later case was upgradation from Madarsa to a formal institution.

The case of girls schools which were set up by castes Pushkarna Brahmans (1919), Maheswaris (1920, Christians (1937), Sanik Kshatriyas (1925, 1935), was found free from caste- based students' admission policy because education of girls by private bodies took late initiative.

On the basis of data analysed for boys schools, it can be said that caste and community schools achieved their aims of education of their children, adapted to grant-in-aid policy and represent its secular character. However, caste considerations exist even today. Srinivas (1966)[40] has recorded his observation that new opportunities in the field of education, economic and politics were caste-free. He further said that these opportunities were more accessible to the high castes with a tradition of learning employment in the govt. and urban residence. The present study also found that middle castes that were connected with govt. jobs were quick in responding to education. Middle castes took advantage of these opportunities and made education available for their children as compared to other castes of Jodhpur city.

3. Recruitment of Teachers

The second important aspect of policy process which influence decisions and educational character of schools is recruitment method and promotion policy of teachers. M.S.A. Rao (1967)[41] has observed that recruitment of teachers were made on (caste) consideration other than merit. It raises a few questions:

(i) Do private-aided schools recruit teachers on consideration only?

(ii) Do these schools recruit teachers without any prescribed qualification?

(iii) Do these schools recruit teachers on the basis of educational qualifications and considerations (caste)?

(iv) Do these schools observe any method of recruitment?

(v) What is the status condition of teachers in private-aided schools?

J.C. Agarwal (1988)[42] has reviewed teachers' role, status, service conditions etc. based on committees' and commissions' reports. Indian

Education Commission (1882) has prescribed educational qualification as an essential condition for permanent employment as a teacher in any secondary school, government aided. In Jodhpur city, the first private-aided school was opened in 1887 and it was upgraded to secondary school in 1920. There was no private-aided high school in Jodhpur city before 1920. However, Grant-in-Aid Rule, 1902 (1904) prescribed minimum qualification for a post of teacher so that a school could be eligible for grant-in-aid. It was strictly adhered in case of post of Headmaster of upper primary school (Middle School). Resolution of the Government of India on Education Policy, 1913 also suggested recruitment of qualified teachers in graded service (Rs. 40 per month minimum and Rs.400 per month maximum) in secondary schools. After independence, Secondary Education Commission (1952), Education Commission (1964-66), National Policy on Education (1968), National Commission on Teachers I or school teachers 1983-85, Challenges of Education Policy and Perspectives (1985), National policy on education (1986) have reported various aspects of teachers and their conditions. These documents contain observations on private-aided schools. It is because private institutions are considered as much part of national system as other institutions. Their contribution to education is as great as it has been in the past, it can be greater still in future provided they receive proper encouragement, support and recognition and give a fair deal to the teachers working with them.

In the present study it was found that private-aided secondary schools were giving certain benefits at par with govt. school teachers of Rajasthan State. Certain benefits are: age at retirement, pay scale, medical benefits, P.F. scheme in place of pension scheme, etc. As regard recruitment of teachers, Secondary Education Commission (1952) recommended constitution of a small selection committee entrusted with this responsibility. This committee may be represented by Headmaster as ex-officio member, and department of education representative as a nominee on the board. This is being followed by all private-aided schools to continue state's aid according to existing Grant-in-Aid Rule, 1963 and State education code. Before independence also, princely state took all these factors into consideration while releasing of grant to a school. Table 5.12 shows that all teachers in private-aided schools were qualified during 1919-20 except only four who were non-matric in Sardar School and Summer school which are managed by Oswal and Sanik Kshatriya caste respectively.

Table 5.12. Qualifications of Teachers in Private-aided Schools in Jodhpur City

S. No.	Name of the School	Managing Caste	Educational Qualification						Total
			Non Matric	Matric	Inter	B.A	Sanskrit	Persian & Munshi	
1	Sir Pratap School	Kayastha	-	2	2	3	-	1	8
2	Sardar School	Oswal	3	3	3	-	2	-	11
3	Pushtikar School	Pushkarna Brahman	-	9	1	1	2	1	14
4	Sumer School	Sanik Kshatriya	1	3	-	-	1	-	5
5	Umed School	Rawna	-	2	1	-	1	-	4
	Total		**4**	**19**	**7**	**4**	**6**	**2**	**42**

Source : Letter No.742 of 1919-20 dated 3.1.1920 from the superintendent, Education Department, Raj Marwar to Finance Member, Regency Council, Raj Marwar, File No. 9/2, Pt.I, 1912, p-142.

During 1986-87, there were 396 teachers in sixteen private-aided secondary schools of Jodhpur city. Out of 396 teachers, there were 103 (26.00%) teachers in the grade of lecturers, 132 (33.35%) senior teachers and 161 (40.65%) Assistant teachers. The main aim of this discussion and analysis is to find out caste wise distribution of teachers to ascertain what managing caste still holds caste-based policy on recruitment of teachers. It was found that percentage of teachers who belonged to managing caste ranged from 0 to 90.90%. Average percentage of caste teachers was calculated 38.90%. There were nine schools which showed its caste teachers' percentage below than over all average percentage. Out of these nine schools, five schools were boys schools managed by Rawna Rajput (13.65%), Maheswari (20.95%), Sanik Kshatriya (22.25%), Pushkarna Brahman (25.00%) which are running a secondary school, and Kayastha (31.60%). Among five girls schools, there was not a single Sanik Kshatriya teacher in a girls secondary school, while in another girl school managed by the same caste (but different management body) had only 11.75% of teachers from their caste. Maheswari caste recruited 25.00% teachers of their caste in girls' school. Christians too recruited 39.15% Christian teachers. This trend occurred because:

(a) Sanik Kshatriya caste is engaged in traditional occupation of agriculture. They send their girls upto school only. Also percentage of Sanik Kshatriyas working women may be very less because they are married at an adolescence age.

(b) Maheswari caste is engaged in business and trade. Literacy percentage among this caste is considerably good. However, they rarely choose this profession.

(c) Rawna Rajput caste is engaged in various types of professions, where high education is not required. So they prefer to other occupations than teaching profession.

(d) Kayastha caste is highly literate, they first go to technical and other professions. Their choice for teaching profession at school level is last one.

There were seven schools which had teachers who belonged to managing caste above 38.90% of average percentage of caste teachers. These schools are managed by Oswals (43.50%), Agarwals (52.15%), Rajputs (54.55%), Sindhis (55.00%), Muslims (63.65%), Pushkarna Brahmans (boys 76.45% and girls 90.90%). In this analysis it can be said that these castes recruited teachers more in number of their castes than other caste. Pushkarna Brahman caste topped the number in boys and superseded all in their girls school. Table 5.13 shows that except one girls secondary school which is managed by Pushkarna Brahaman caste consideration did not exist in all other four schools. Sociological fact is that women seldom go to employment due to traditional practice and prevailing local customs. Among boys' schools, caste considerations existed which varied from123.65% to 76.45%. There was also variation in caste's percentage according to its hierarchy viz. lecturers (38.85%), Senior Teachers (46.20%) and Assistant Teachers (32.90%). This analysis confirms our hypothesis that recruitment method and procedure were followed as per State government rules and procedures. However, caste considerations have played predominant role in recruitment policy of teachers and other staffs too. Madan and Halbar (1972) have found the same observation in their study of three districts of Karnataka State.

Table 5.13 Caste Percentage of Teachers in Caste-managed Secondary School, Jodhpur City in 1986-87

S. No.	*Below/Above Average caste per centage*	*Percentage of Teachers by Managing Castes*		*Secondary*	
		Higher Boys	*Secondary Girls*	*Boys*	*Girls*
1.	< 38.90 (N=9)	Rawna Rajput (13.65%) Sanik Kshatriya (22.25%) Maheswari (20.95%) Kayastha (31.60%)	Maheswari (25.00%) Christian (39.15%)	Pushkarna Brahman	Sanik Kshatriya (0.0%) Sanik Kshatriya (11.75%)
2.	>38.90 (N=7)	Oswal (43.50%) Agarwal (52.15%) Rajput (54.55%) Sindhi (55.0%) Pushkarna Brahman (76.45%)		Musalman (63.65%)	Pushkarna Brahman (90.90%)

C. Control and Supervision

State Governments have full control over private-aided schools since it gives grant to these educational institutions. In this section, what are controls and supervision exercised by State governments are discussed below?

(i) School Budget

State Government approves grant to private secondary schools at the prescribed rate of A (80%), B(70%), C (60%) and D(50%) and special category (90%) of total approved expenditure under rule of Grant-in-Aid Rule, 1963. Annual Inspection and Audit is conducted every year. Schools are supposed to utilise grant released by State as per item-wise approved expenditure. Panel inspection in every three years is also done.

(ii) Examinations and Textbooks

In all States public examinations are conducted by State Board. Board of Secondary Education, Rajasthan, Ajmer conduct examinations of Class X to XII standard. Results of these examinations for last three years are taken into consideration in deciding quantum of grant to these schools by State government.

Dy. Director, Directorate of Education Department, Jodhpur Range is responsible for supervision and control of paper setter, examination of classes below Xth standard of private-aided schools. Accordingly these schools have no autonomy on this aspect.

The second is textbooks for students at various classes. State Education Department has prescribed text books for each class. School teachers have autonomy to select books of authors which are considered suitable for learning by the students.

Summary and Conclusions

It was found that eight castes and three communities have formed a formal organized Schools management body. Each management body is composed of elected members in it. Their numbers varied from 4-17. These members were occupying their positions at three levels, viz. office bearers, members and ex-officio members. Office bearers group have been termed as policy maker group. Members have been labeled as policy promoter. Ex-officio members group was represented by school headmaster and State's education department nominee as per Secondary Education Commission (1952) recommendation. Education Commission (1964-66) have also recommended representation of parents', teachers' in schools management body which have been followed by them. Data analysis revealed that these groups occupied three identifiable position based on their pattern of influence, viz. local, cosmopolitan and neutral according to their group position also. These groups play role of decisive social groups and act as a pressure group what Suresh Shukla (1967) has termed.

Social background or members revealed a vast and wide variation which ranged from educationists, lawyers, auditors, industrialists, businessmen, politicians and largest one service class. Businessmen, agriculturist and Industrialist play effective role in fund-raising, politician help private bodies in getting their proposal cleared at state government level.

Management body play main functions of fund-raising, obtaining grant from government, decides student admission policy and recruitment of teachers as per government's policy. However, it was observed that caste considerations have played predominating role in both of these policy issues. An attempt was made to borrow theoretical model of 3 – dimensional action research model given by Kurt Lewin (1931) and discussed by Pareek and Khanna (1961), and further analysis based on cybernetics given by Rastogi (1979). These models were used and further explained by using empirical data collected in course of the present study.

This chapter suggested that schools are not independent but subjected to control and supervision of State Education Department, in respect of school budget, examinations, and textbooks, workload, school calendar, etc. It is concluded that private bodies share Government's responsibilities to run educational institutions, though they achieve their aims of caste consideration in respect of student admission and recruitment of teachers a little and latently function rather than in manifest way.

References

1. Mudaliar, A.L., *Report of the Secondary Education Commission (October 1952 to June 1953),* New Delhi. Government of India, Ministry of Education, 1954. p.188.
2. Kothari. D.S., *The Education Commission (1961-62),* New Delhi: Government of India, Ministry of Education, (1966), p.279-308.
3. Gore, M.S., *Education and Modernization in India,* Jaipur. Rawat Publication, 1982, pp.163-185.
4. Engel, Robert. E and Paul P.W. Achola, "Boards of Trustees and Academic Decision making." A review of educational research (Spring.Vol. 53, No.1), 1983, p. 55.

5. Kothari, D.S., (1966), *Ibid.*
6. Mudaliar, A.L., 1954, *Ibid.*
7. Madan,T.N. and B.G. Haldar, Caste and community in the private and public education of Mysore State (Chapter) in *Education and Politics in India: Studies in organization, society and policy* (ed) by Susana Hoeber Rudolph and Loyd I.Rudolph, Delhi: Oxford University Press, 1972, p.135.
8. Gould, Harold, Educational structure and political processes in Faizabad district, U.P. (chapter 7) in *Education and politics in India: studies in organization, society and policy* (ed.) by S.H. Rudolph and L.I. Rudolph, Delhi: Oxford University Press, p.14.
9. Naik, J.P., 1963, Selections from educational records. Vol. II, 1860-67. New Delhi: National Archives of India, 1972, p. 124-125.
10. Shukla, S., Controls and Decision-Making in the education system. (Chapter) ed. in papers in the *sociology of education in India.* M.S. Gore, I.P. Desai and Suma Chitnis, New Delhi: National Council of Education, Research and Training, 1967, p. 295.
11. Singh, Nirmal, *Education under siege: A sociological study of private colleges.* New Delhi: Concept Publication, 1983.
12. Misra, A.N., *Education Finances in India,* Bombay: Asia Publishing House, 1962. Misra. A.N, *Financing of Indian education,* Bombay: Asia Publishing House 1967. Misra, A.N., *Grant-in-aid of education in India,* Delhi. The Macmillan Company of India, 1973, p.141.
13. Merton, Robert. K., *Social Theory and Social structure,* New York. Am rind Publishing Company Pvt. Ltd., 1968, p. 44.
14. Paul, F. Lazarsfeld, pp.10-32 quoted by Robert K. Merton (1968), 1955, Ibid.
15. Saran, Rene, *Policy Making in secondary education:* A case study, Oxford: Clarendon Press 1973.
16. Pinner Frank, A, pp.20, 89-104 quoted by Robert K. Merton (1968), 1956, Ibid.
17. Simmel, George, See his essay, translated a half century ago by Albiod W. Small and published as "The persistence of social groups" in the *American Journal of Sociology 1898,* pp. 662-698, 829-836. Quoted by Robert K. Merton, 1968, Ibid. p.458.
18. Eisenstdat, S.N. "Communication on system and social structures: an exploratory comparative study". Public opinion quarterly. 1955. pp.19, 154-167. A study of a small Southern town reports that the two types of influential cannot be distinguished there;

the present suggestion holds that, with the accumulation of research, it is no longer enough to report the presence or absence of the types of influentials.Rather, it is sociologically pertinent to search out the attributes of the social structure which make for varying proportions of these identifiable types of influentials. Quoted by Robert. K. Merton, 1968, Ibid, p.459.

19. Fanellie, Alexander. A typology of community leadership based on influence and interaction within the leader sub system". Social forces. 1956, p.35, 332-338. Quoted by Robert. K. Merton. 1968, Ibid, p.459.
20. Lall, S.K. *Urban Elite.* New Delhi: Thompson Press (India) Limited, 1974.
21. Narain, Iqbal, K.C.Pande and M.L.Sharma. *The Rural elite in Indian State: A case study of Rajasthan,* New Delhi : Manohar Book House, 1976, p.26
22. Beteille, Andre. "Pattern of Status Groups" in Seminar, 70, 1965, p.66.
23. Siriskar,V.M. *The Rural Elite in a Developing Society,* Delhi: Orient Longman Ltd., 970.
24. Pareto, V. *The Mind and Society Eng.* Trans by Bongiorano and Arthur Livingstone, New York: Harcourt Brace. Co. 1935, p.1422-23.
25. Mosca,G. The Ruling Class, New York: Macgraw-Hill, 1939, p.50-53.
26. Bottomore, T.B. "The Administrative Elite". Chapter in *New Sociology: Essays in social science and social theory* (In Honour of C. Wright Mills) ed. By I.L. Horowitz, New York, a galaxy book, Oxford University Press. 1965, p.7-23.
27. Manneheim, Karl and W.A.C. Stewart. *An Introduction to the Sociology of Education,* London: Routledge and Kegan Paul. 1962
28. Pareek Udai, "The role of action research in building self-sustaining system", Indian Journal of Social Work, Vol. XXXVIII, No. 4, Jan. 1978, p.124.
29. Rastogi.
30. Pareek, Udai. "The role of action research in building self-sustaining system". *Indian Journal of Social Work,* Vol. XXXVIII, No.4 Jan. 1978, p.124.
31. Pareek, Udai. "The role of action research in building self-sustaining system". *Indian Journal of Social Work,* Vol. XXXVIII, No.4 Jan. 1978, p.124.
32. Rastogi.

33. Rastogi, p.102.
34. Misra, A.N. *Grant-in-aid of education in India,* Delhi. The Macmillan Company of India, 1973, p.118.
35. Prasad, R.C., "Educational Development in Bihar" in seminar (107), 1968, p.68.
36. Rao, M.S.A., Education, Social Stratification and mobility (Chapter) in the papers in *Sociology of Education in India* (ed) by M.S.Gore, et.al. New Delhi: National Council of Education, Research and Training. 1967, pp.134, 142.
37. Rao, M.S.A., Education, Social stratification and mobility (Chapter) in the papers in *Sociology of Education in India* (ed) by M.S. Gore, et.al. New Delhi : National Council of Education, Research and Training, 1967, pp.134, 142.
38. Madan,T.N. and B.G. Haldar. Caste and community in the private and public education of Mysore State (Chapter) in *Education and Politics in India: Studies in organization, society and policy* (ed) by Susana Hoeber Rudolph and Loyd I.Rudolph, Delhi : Oxford University Press, 1972.
39. Verma, G.C., *Modern education: Its growth and development in Rajasthan 1818 to 1983.* Jaipur: Publication scheme, 1984.
40. Srinivas, M.N. *Social change in Modern India,* New Delhi: Orient Longman, 1966, p.90.
41. Rao, M.S.A., Education, social stratification and mobility (Chapter) in the papers in *Sociology of Education in India* (ed) by M.S. Gore, et.al., New Delhi: National Council of Education, Research and Training. 1967, pp.135, 142.
42. Agarwal, J.C. *Teacher's Role, Status, Service Conditions education in India: A Reference to committees and commissions.* Delhi : Doaba House, 1988.
43. Mudaliar, A.L. Report of the Secondary Education Commission (October 1952 to June 1953), New Delhi. Government of India, Ministry of Education. Ibid, 1954.
44. Kothari, D.S. The Education Commission (1961-62). New Delhi: Government of India, Ministry of Education - Ibid. (1966).
45. National Policy on Education: New Delhi. Department of Education, Government of India, Ibid, 1968.
46. National Committee on Teachers – Schools (1983-85). New Delhi: Government of India, J.C. Agarwal, 1988 - Ibid.
47. Challenges of Education: Policy and Perspective. Government of India Report, New Delhi. Ministry of Human Resources, Department of Education, 1985.

6

Selected Case Studies

This chapter is aimed to present profile of selected caste-managed secondary and higher secondary schools of Jodhpur city. Private bodies have played their contributory role in growth and development of their schools. They opened their schools for education of their own children when education was considered a necessity and the erstwhile Marwar State was backward in educational development. Grant-in-Aid policy did not encourage private bodies immediately. However, they responded very late. In the first period, only three middle castes, viz. Kayastha (1887), Oswal (1896) and Sanik Kshatriya (1898) had responded to modern education. All these three middle castes opened only boys primary school. While in the second stage of development, Grant-in-Aid policy (i.e., Grant-in-Aid Rule, 1902 (1904) did attract only three castes after eight years of its implementation which opened three boys and two girls schools. These three castes were: Pushkarna Brahman (1912, 1919), Rawna Rajput (1912) and Maheswari (1918, 1920). It is noteworthy to observe that only two castes, viz. Pushkarna Brahman (1919) and Maheswari castes (1920) took a lead for girls education in Jodhpur city. The first caste belonged to higher social hierarchy and first in caste hierarchy; the second one is in middle in caste hierarchy.

Third period in development of modern education era in Jodhpur city began from 1925 to 1943. This period is marked by educational reorganization, introduction of a scheme of expansion of primary education (1922). In view of these developments on the line of national development, the development period was classified into educational expansion. Three girls schools were opened by Sanik Kshatriya caste (1925, 1935) and Christian's community (1937). Two boys schools were opened by Agarwal caste (1931) and Pushkarna Brahman (1943). A continuity was observed in rise of private enterprises in the field of girls' education which began from 1919 till 1937.

After independence national and social development have given rise to an opportunity to migrated community; Sindhis to rehabilitate and resettle them in Jodhpur city. Sindhis opened their two schools (1947) after partition of Hindustan (one school was later on closed in 1974). Their sole need was instruction in their own language. Government granted permission to Sindhis to open their own schools. Another community Muslim suffered a great loss in the sense that Muslim school, Jodhpur was converted into name of Mahatma Gandhi School and is run by State Government after independence. They were a little compensated in 1954; a school was upgraded from Madarsa to a centre of formal learning. Another important development after independence was change of status of Rajput school converted one school managed by Rajput caste from state-financed run school to a private-aided school.

A brief history of rise of private-aided schools has revealed historical development more or less with little variation as per period of establishments. However, these schools have related impact in the society and built its educational and social prestige. Society has accepted these private-aided schools, while social differentiations existed before and differentiation was also observed in terms of their educational standard and educational facilities. These indexes were measured and calculated on eight variables individually and total scores. These variables are: caste, number of students, number of teachers, library facilities play-ground/ physical facilities, average fee/students, results, length of schools serving society. (For details see Tables 4.7 and 4.8). On these variables average score was measured 34.56 and scores on individual items varied from 0.81 to 9.51. Overall analysis of scores obtained gave a clear indication about five castes viz. Rajput, Kayastha, Oswal, Sanik Kshatriya and Maheswari which were found the best among all sixteen schools studied. (For details see Table 4.9). The Rajput schools were opened in 1875 and cent per cent financed by State till 1947. This school is dropped out in selection of case-studies because (i) This school got status of private-aided from 1949. (ii) Caste's contribution was in form endowment fund and pie-fund which were created in 1919 on the recommendation of a committee to make the school self-sufficient. Another school is run by Maheswari caste, which was opened in 1918. It was also not included in selection of case-studies, though it scored on all variables because it was opened in the period when State encouraged private bodies to open their school by giving grant-in-aid. There was no specific sociological or educational features served in development of this school like other schools, which are discussed now. Kayastha, Oswal and Sanik Kshatriya opened their schools for education of their own children in the first leg of development of modern education in Jodhpur city from 1887 to 1989.

These castes are middle castes; first one Kayastha is urban caste while two castes Oswal and Sanik Kshatriya are urban-rural predominant and rural pre-dominated respectively. In this chapter case-studies of three caste managed secondary schools are discussed here.

I. Sir Pratap Senior Higher Secondary School, Jodhpur

Kayastha caste is known as "Writer-caste", since they mostly worked in administrative and record keeping work. In caste-hierarchy, they occupy place in middle position. Literacy percentage of this caste was highest in many parts of the country. These two factors placed them in privileged position. This is the reason Kayasthas responded to modern education quickly and first among all castes of Jodhpur city. This caste is a urban-dominated which was always conscious and aware of all round development in the city and state.

Kayasthas opened first private aided school in Jodhpur city in 1887 when State gave a call to private bodies to expand education in Jodhpur city. Incidentally, Kayasthas formed their caste association in 1886. This caste has celebrated its centenary after passing through upheavals in its growth and development.

Founder President of Kayastha General Sabha (KGS), late Shri Subh Lal ji Nepalia held the post of Superintendent Engineer, P.W.D. Department in the erstwhile Marwar state. This factor coupled with education a necessity made a way for this caste to avail first opportunity and opened their school. (There was only Durbar School, now known as New Govt. Senior Higher Secondary School, Jodhpur in Jodhpur city. This school was run by erstwhile State). Kayasthas named their school in honour of Regent Sir Pratap Singhji of erstwhile Marwar State. Sir Pratap Singhji had generously helped this school in many ways (e.g. allotment of State building to start a school, non-recurring and recurring grant, etc.). It is only caste in Jodhpur city which was not required to raise fund before the school in Jodhpur city.

Kayasthas opened their school on 29.8.1887. It was anglo-vernacular primary school. The school was started in a small accommodation (Exact location and place not mentioned in historical records). This indicates that the school had been shifted to the present building, which was donated by the State. In three years period the school was elevated to middle level which showed a positive response of the school which brought them boon and a reward from State by sanction of two more Hindi Pathsalas in 1896. State was also under pressure from employees of Jodhpur-Bikaner Railway to open a school for education of their children. This school was entrusted with additional responsibility and additional grant of Rs.40 p.m. was also sanctioned. Addition of two Hindi Pathsalas and additional class for education of children of Jodhpur-Bikaner railway employees had necessitated requirement of more space. State sanctioned grant for their purpose in the allotted building in 1897.

However, Kayastha caste could go well with additional responsibilities for first ten years. Then they faced great financial difficulties to an extent which resulted in withdrawal of additional grant sanctioned for education of Jodpur-Bikaner Railway Employees and closure of two Hindi Pathsalas. Further school's financial position worsened to an extent that a stage had come to close the present school. As fortunes were, the school survived its life when Kayasthas resolved to take appropriate measures to improve its financial position by way of reserve fund, lottery methods, endowment fund, etc. and upgraded it again to middle school. The school management was put under chairmanship of a non-caste member Rao Sahib K.M. Bhat ji in 1916. It is a sociologically significant observation that school management was transferred from caste body to non-Kayastha caste. It is, of course, a temporary phenomena and state had prerogative to exercise its power of control on private-aided schools. This was also a unique case observed in this school only. Temporary transfer of school control by body in bringing out school from financial crisis as well was to put the school on sound footing. Their contribution was well evidence of re-upgradation of the school to middle school in 1917 and high school in 1920. It was first private-aided high school in the erstwhile Marwar State which was recognized by Allahabad University. After independence and implementation of eleven year's schooling as per recommendation the school was upgraded to higher secondary school in 1957. At present the school provides educational facilities upto 10+2 stage as per recommendation of National policy on Education (1986).

Historical records of the school have revealed that Kayasthas provided educational facilities in form of night classes for poor students and boarding house facilities to those students who came from outside Jodhpur city. It was a notable contribution of this caste Lin Jodhpur city. Another contribution was fund raising fund from non-Kayasthas caste. (For details see Table 5.8). Thanvi Sanghvi Das, a prominent Pushkarana Brahman donated Rs.9,000 to this caste for school's development. There existed inter caste solidarity between two castes of Jodhpur city. Other non-kayasthas also contributed Rs.500 to Kayastha caste.

At present the State government gives 80% grant to this school and rated "A" grade under Grant-in-Aid Rule, 1963. This school falls on educational standard equal to majority of private aided schools and has completed its hundred year, it should have built its educational prestige, then why it is ranked "B" Grade? It was observed that this school has never undertaken new experimental projects in educational research. Nor did it ever implement multipurpose scheme. Also this caste enjoys middle level economic status and that is why Kayasthas could not afford to invest-money more than schools' annual expenditure.

Educational prestige of a school is generally conceived by high number of students in a school. Physical space is a determinant and dependable variable to calculate class wise strength of students in a school. Secondary Education Commission (1952) has recommended that each class should have normally 30-40 students in each section. It was found that this school was only one boys senior higher secondary school which admitted students in each class as per recommended strength (**See Table 5.3**). While in this category there were five girls school and 2 boys secondary schools. Comparing class-wise and section wise strength of students of this school with other boys senior higher secondary schools all schools had over strength in their schools.

However, strength of students from high to low of a school can not be taken as one variable to measure educational prestige on one variable but total eight variables viz. caste, no. of students, no. of teachers, library facilities, play ground/physical facilities, Average fee/student, results of a school and length of serving society were ranked in order of high to low to calculate rank score on all these variables and on individual variable (See Table 4.7). Average score on total scores was obtained 34.96 and mean scores on individual variables varied from 0.81 to 9.51. (See Table 5.7). It was found that this school scored 44.5 on total variable which was above mean score 34.96. Out of eight schools which scored above mean score this school stood fourth in rank. On individual scores this school obtained scores above average on library facilities, play ground, Average fee/ students, results, and length of school except on caste hierarchy. A combined score on total variables and individual variables ranked out this school for selection of case students based on its educational prestige (Table 4.9).

Educational prestige of a school is dependent on teachers, Principal and schools' management body. Teachers and Principal of a school are directly responsible for providing effective educational instructions. Teachers' working conditions are influenced by recruitment and promotion policy in private-aided schools. M.S.A. Rao (1967) has said that recruitment of teachers is made on consideration other than merit. It was found that Grant-in-Aid Rule, 1902 (1904) and Grant-in-Aid Rule, 1963 have prescribed educational qualification for teachers in secondary schools, so management body have never been given any leverage to select a candidate of their choice irrespective of qualifications, etc. (see Table 5.12). Secondary Education Commission (1952) and Education Commission (1964-66) have suggested for a small selection committee, having representation of Principal as ex-officio member and State's official as government nominee. Response analysis revealed that caste consideration existed and exist even today provided candidate of their caste fulfils minimum prescribed qualification. In this school it was found that there were 19 teachers during 1986-87. Out of 19 teachers, only 6 teachers (31.60%) belonged to Kayastha caste. This analysis further reveal that Kayasthas did not follow caste-based policy in recruitment of teachers. Mean score on all schools was 38.90; this school scored less than mean score on caste wise percentage of teachers among all aided schools (see Table 5.13). Among nine boys' senior higher secondary schools, it was found that only 26.30% of teachers have been working in this school for more than 15 years. This was the lowest among all, is a clear indication of teachers instability, i.e., they move from this school to other schools (govterment or private-aided). It may also be a reason management body recruit temporary staff and change teachers after a few years. If this was not the case then teacher's service conditions might not be satisfactory like in other schools.

The other important variable is student admission policy. Kayasthas opened their school for education of their children. Kayasthas admitted 63.65% students of their own caste, which is a similar observation, found in private-aided schools studied in Mysore State by Madan and Halbar (1972). Comparing with other caste schools, Pushkarna Brahmans admitted 100% boys from their own caste. (For details see Table 5.11 and Note 1(a) (b) and (c)).

It is concluded from the above caste-study analysis that the Kayasthas adapted to States policy in terms of student admission policy (e.g., from 100% to 50%), transfer of management to non-Kayasthas to survive as is seen today. This school has implemented recommendations of education policy from time to time. However, it could not undertake any innovative educational researches, etc. to come up to level of special category of schools, i.e., 90% grant.

II. Sardar Senior Higher Secondary School, Jodhpur

Sardar Senior Higher Secondary School, Jodhpur is second private-aided school in Jodhpur city. This school was founded by Oswal caste in the year 1896. Oswal caste responded to a call given by erstwhile ruler for expansion of education in 1896, i.e., after ten years, which was given by the State. It was because traditional occupation of Oswals was business and a very few of them were also connected with administrative work. In other words, there were only 42,027 literate Mahajans in Jodhpur city according to Census of Marwar State, 1941. Comparing the position in early years, it was found that Census of Marwar State, 1911 did not list Mahajan community among literate caste. This was one of reasons for delayed response to modern education.

Oswals realized that only 25 children of their castes were studying in Durbar School, Jodhpur (now known as New Govt. Senior Higher Secondary School) that was very small in number as compared to their population among other castes. Mehta Baktawar Malji was the first prominent caste-man who submitted a few suggestions to Regent Sir Pratap Singhji for his consideration to bring social change in their life. One of the suggestions was to open a school for education of their children. Regent Sir Pratap Singhji accepted his suggestions and advise them to open a school for education of their boys subject to the condition they raise Rs.40,000 to start a school. In a short time Oswal Sabha could raise fund of Rs.60,000. They also received a donation of Rs.400 from Kayasthas, another middle caste, which signifies inter-caste solidarity among them in Jodhpur city.

It was also observed that the Seth Rang Rajji (who was a member of the management body) without caring for his own interest constituted to the redemption of his Usu-fractury mortgage of Nathura village and thus provided a ready opening for the investment of Rs.21,001. Similarly Man Chandji Bhandari mortgaged Kurkasni village of which Rs.5301 were reinvested in school.

Castes contribution to growth and development of their school was a unique and notable. Oswals mortgaged their property and did a lot of sacrifice for their school. It was a unique example, which was found in the history of this school only. No other caste did any such sort of things. It is a fact Oswal were and are economically rich, being a business and industry caste. This caste was also required to raise fund to start their school unlike Kayasthas.

Oswals opened their school on 18.7.1896. This school was named after His Highness Sardar Singhji. Regent Sir Pratap Singhji donated Rs. 2,000 to this school from his own purse and announced State's donation of Rs. 7,000 to this school. This school was started as an anglo-vernacular primary school in Niyati-ka-Nohra near Silawato-ka-bas inside Sojati Gate. Oswal caste received encouraging response from their caste and community. Encouraging response of caste had resulted into increase in student's strength. This has further caused shortage of space. Oswals could get another building from the State, which was "Nainiji-ki-Nohara". The school was then shifted to this building. After upgradation of this school to middle school in 1899, it again required more space. The State agreed to construct more classrooms in the same building provided Oswals also agreed to invest fund for this purpose. Oswals were, instead, prevailed upon the State and got the land from the State owned building. It was again a unique case State agreed to their request in such a manner. The school was further upgraded to high school in 1930, which was third in order then. (The other private aided high schools were : Sir Pratap Senior Higher secondary School (1920), and Sumer Pushtikar Senior Higher Secondary School (1925). Caste members constructed large spacious building for the school among all other schools. For this reason, and its high educational standard State gives 90% grant to this school (The other two boys school are: Chopasani Senior Higher Secondary School and Mahesh Senior Higher Secondary School; and girls school St. Patrick Vidya Bhavan girls Senior Higher Secondary School). Under Grant-in-Aid Rule, 1963, this school is getting grant in special category of schools since it conducts innovative educational researches.

Spacious building and school in special categories has attracted large number of students from class VI to XI standard. This school stood third in number of students among nine boys higher secondary school. Secondary Education Commission (1952) has recommended that each class and section should have normal student strength of 30-40.Data analysis have revealed that each class and each section was overcrowded in the school like other five boys higher secondary schools which are managed by Sanik Kshatriyas, Rajputs, Maheswaris, Agarwals and Sindhis. (see Table 5.3). While there was only one boys senior secondary school managed by Kayasthas which showed normal strength. It cannot be said that the school overcrowded each class for profit making. However, it would be a correct statement that these schools have built their educational prestige in society. Society has also accepted these schools.

An attempt was made (in Chapter 4) to empirically verify education prestige of private-aided schools by rank-score analysis method like for all schools. This school was also given ranks on eight variables viz. caste, number of students, number of teachers, library facilities, play ground, Average fee/students, results of public examination, length of school serving society. Mean score of all schools was calculated 34.96 on all these eight variables. It was found that this school scored highest score 56.5 among all sixteen private aided schools. On the basis of this analysis the school was ranked first and superb in its educational standard and educational facilities. (see Table 4.7). On individual scores, this school achieved scores above mean scores on: No. of students (7), No. of teachers (9), library facilities (9), play ground (1), Average fee/student (8), results (6.5), length of school serving society (14.0). These scores show that the school achieved highest score and second in order also on some variables (Average fee/student, and length of school) on both variables i.e., individual scores and total scores (see table 4.9). Thus the school has built its prestige in the society. Private enterprises have entered in the field of education to educate their own children. Their sole aim was to provide education to their own children and recruit teachers of their own caste on consideration other than merit (Rao, 1967). It was found that Oswal caste admitted 25857 of Mahajan community students (32.60%) in twenty years period from 1894-95 to 1922-26 (for details see Table 5.11). As compared to other castes, Oswals admitted 100% of their children, Kayasthas admitted 63.65% and Sanik Kshatriyas admitted 39.40% indifferent periods. Caste percentage in student admission had existed even after Grant-in-Aid Rule 1902 (1904). Though Grant-in-Aid Rule 1902 (1904), allowed private-aided schools to admit children of their own caste upto 50% after independence, Constitution of India and Grant-in-Aid Rule, 1963 did not permit any of these bodies to continue caste based policy.

The second important aspect was recruitment of teachers on caste consideration other than merit. Historical records of the school have shown that qualified teachers were recruited in this school. During 1919-20, three teachers out of eleven teachers in the school were non-matriculate (see Table 5.12). Grant-in-Aid Rule, 1902 (1904) had laid down prescribed qualifications for each post of teacher. However, rule was flexible for primary and middle schools, and strict for high school and science teacher posts. After independence, Grant-in-Aid Rule, 1963 do not permit caste based policy in recruitment of teachers. It was found that 43.50% of teachers belonged to Oswal caste, which was above mean score of 38.90% of all schools. (see Table 5.13). There were other castes viz. Agarwals (52.15%), Rajputs (54.55%), Sindhis (55.05) and Pushkarna Brahmans (76.45%) have recruited teachers from their own caste. Comparing these figures, it can be said that caste consideration exists even today provided their caste candidate fulfill prescribed qualifications and experience etc.

It is important to analyse teachers' stability in the school, when caste consideration exist there because it affects teacher's status conditions in the school. Out of 46 teachers in the school, 24 teachers (52.15%) have rendered more than 15 years of service in the school. It was also observed that 11 teachers (91.65%) out of 15 teachers in lecturer grade have rendered more than 15 years of service. On this basis, it can be said that teacher's condition, status, and service conditions are generally satisfactory that is why teachers have stayed well. However, teachers in second and third hierarchy i.e., Senior teachers and Assistant teachers, the observation was quite contrary and opposite to lecturer one. It was because teachers in early age, if get service in government schools have preferred to go for better one or any other better occupation. This theory also applied to first case i.e., those teachers who have crossed their age of entry into government service stayed in this school. One unique observation that this school was first among all private-aided schools to introduce P.F. scheme for teachers. Before independence not a single private-aided school introduced this scheme.

Concluding that Oswal caste raised funds first as a prerequisite condition and opened a school for education of their own children. This school has progressed well with castes contribution. Caste-members sacrificed to an extent that they mortgaged their villages and donated money for school's growth and development. Oswals did follow caste-based policy on preferential terms in student admission policy and recruitment of teachers. But they also provided better service conditions to teachers as compared to other schools.

III. Sumer Senior Higher Secondary School, Jodhpur

Sanik Kshatriya caste was third traditional caste of Jodhpur city which responded to modern education. They were influenced by Swami Dayanand Saraswati's ideology and preaching. They also believe in Arya Samaj philosophy. These two factors led them to introduce social reform in their caste. Social reform was conceived through modern education. They also realized that two middle castes, viz. Kayastha and Oswal have already opened their schools in Jodhpur city in 1887 and 1896 respectively. There was only one State run school for general population. All these three schools are situated at a far distance from outskirts of Jodhpur city where clusters of Sanik Kshatriyas caste reside. This caste is rurally predominated also. All of these factors enlightened Sanik Kshatriyas to open their school.

Kshatriya Mali Mitra Sabha (KMMS), a parent body and caste association of Sanik Kshatriya caste submitted their request to State for permission to open their own school. Like Oswal castes, State granted them permission on the condition they raised their funds before hand. State gave them land for construction of building like to other schools. Sanik Kshatriyas raised fund of Rs. 55,000.

Sanik Kshatriyas opened their school as primary school in 1898 for education of Sanik Kshatriya boys only. It was observed that this school was second private-aided boys higher secondary school in Jodhpur city which was upgraded to middle school after fifteen years. (The first private-aided school was Mahesh Senior Higher Secondary School, Jodhpur) The other schools have been upgraded in lesser period. Similarly, this school was also elevated to high school after thirty-two years of its first upgradation. Again it was very late. On being asked this question to the present Headmaster of the school, it was told that Sanik Kshatriyas did not get encouraging response from their own caste Discouraging response from their own caste diluted their aim of caste based student admission policy.

Data analysis revealed that this school enrolled 40% of Sanik Kshatriyas students, which was more as compared to Oswal caste. Figures are total of 1942-48, when there were large number of schools which have already been opened (For details see Table 4.11). As this caste is rurally distributed also, rural children turned up after construction of boarding house in1945. This was also the reason of poor response of their caste.

After independence the school has built its prestige in the society. The school was found four in rank order among private-aided schools. Secondary Education Commission (1952) has recommended that each class and section should have normal capacity of30-40 students. Analysis revealed that this school showed over strength (see Table 5.3, chapter 5). In 1982-83 there were 25.75 per cent of Sanik Kshatriyas student in the school. This shows castes based admission policy continue to exist in this school like other caste-own private-aided schools.

The second aspect is recruitment of teachers based on caste consideration. It was found that out of five teachers only one teacher was non-matriculate during 1919-20 (see Table 4.12) like in Sardar Senior Higher Secondary School, Jodhpur that is managed by Oswal caste. Caste-wise analysis of teachers reveals that there were 22.25% Sanik Kshatriya teachers in the school, which was below than the overall average of 38.90% of teachers of all private-aided schools. A very simple reason is traditional occupation of Sanik Kshatriya caste are business, agriculture, etc. Hence they did not prefer to turn toward teachers' occupation. As regard status, conditions etc. of teachers in this school comparing from schools managed by Kayasthas and Oswals, it was found that 55.55% of teachers have served this school for more than fifteen years of service, which shows teachers stability and better service conditions provided by the management in the school. Among boys higher secondary schools, this school showed its uniqueness in respect of teachers service conditions, etc.

Like for other two private-aided schools, rank score analysis on eight variables was – one for this school also. On total scores this school achieved 41.0 which was above over all average score of 34.96 (see Table 5.7). Though Chopasani Senior Higher Secondary School (managed by Rajput caste) has achieved 54.5 scores second to Oswals and Mahesh Senior Higher Secondary School (managed by Maheswari caste) has achieved 50.0 score were not included for the reason that the first school was State run till 1949 and the second was established in the period when there were number of other aided schools and State encouraged all private bodies to open their schools by giving Grant-in-Aid to them. On the basis of above analysis the case study of this school was chosen for discussion since it outnumbered other schools on other parameters.

Summary and Conclusion

Three middle castes viz. Kayastha, Oswal and Sanik Kshatriya opened their own boys schools in the period when education was a necessity. There was only one State run school for students of general population in Jodhpur city. Rajputs had their own school which was exclusively opened for Rajput boys only. These castes were quick to respond to modern education and States' call given by Regent Sir Pratap Singhji. While the upper most caste Pushkarna Brahman did respond to modern education in 1912, which was very late, of course, and even after eight years of Grant-in-Aid Rule, 1902 (1904) was made into force. The reason of its delayed response was Srimali Brahmans had their one school which was later on merged into this school. Another reason was they were engaged in their traditional occupation of priest, etc, though brahmans topped in literacy also.

It was found that Kayasthas, Oswals and Sanik Kshatriyas raised funds for schools establishment, upgradation and etc. Except Kayasthas, the latter two castes were required to raise fund first and then they were granted permission to start their schools. After Grant-in-Aid Rule, 1902 (1904), these castes adapted to student admission policy based on "Cattiest" approach, (upto 50%) though these schools were opened for education of their own children. In this regard Kayasthas topped Oswals and Sanik Kshatriyas.

As regard recruitment of teachers on caste consideration, data analysis revealed that Kayasthas recruited 31.60 per cent teachers of their own caste (Rank 2), Oswals recruited 43.50 per cent of their own caste (Rank 1) and Sanik Kshatriyas recruited 22.25 per cent teachers of their castes (Rank 3). Similarly rank score analysis gives Sanik Kshatriyas teachers 22.25 per cent. Similarly rank score analysis gives order in this fashion Oswals (56.5%), Kayasthas (44.5), and Sanik Kshatriyas (41.0). A clear picture on three aspects viz. students, teachers, and rank scores on all eight variables are shown below to select the best school which has built its prestige in the society.

From the above table it is seen that rank score varied on these three aspects. For correct assessment of one school, weighted average score method is used because, when figures on each variable of each school, is summed up then Sir Pratap School gives total 139.75 (Rank 1), Sardar School's total figure 132.6 (Rank 2) and Sumer School's total figure 102.65 (Rank 3). While weighted average score given 1.54 to first school (Rank 2) 1.49 to second school (Rank 3) and 2.61 to third school (Rank 1). Thus weighted average score has helped us to correctly state the prestige position of the school No. 3, i.e., Sumer School, which is managed by Sanik Kshatriya caste.

7

Conclusion and Analysis

In India, educational institutions are mainly managed by three types of agencies, viz. official (or government), missionaries and private bodies (Mudaliar 1952[1], Kothari 1966[2]: Table 10.1, Desai 1967[3], Damle 1967[4], Verma 1984[5]). One third of educational institutions were managed by non-governmental organizations in 1960-61 (Kothari 1966[6]). The rise of non-governmental organizations was noticed from the beginning of modern education era throughout the country when the first charter of 1854 (Wood's dispatch) and Indian Education Commission (1882)[7] recognized role and involvement of private agencies in the development of modern education of India. There was a rise in number of privately managed and publicly managed educational institutions from 1901-02 to 1955-56 which was 1.57 times (Misra 1962) because then British government and all princely states introduced grant-in-aid policy in the form of Grant in Aid Rule 1902 on the recommendations of Indian Education Commission (1882). Grant-in-Aid Rule, 1902 further attracted private bodies to start activities in the field of education. (Misra 1973)[8] has stated four factors which led private bodies to open schools, colleges and built hotels in the country: (i) keen desire of the people to spread education among masses, (ii) public donation, (iii) rise of militant nationalism, (iv) dedicated workers who sacrificed even their careers. After independence there was decline in growth in number of privately managed educational institutions because people experienced effect of Second World War and price inflation. They were not keen in spread of education rather than to think for bread and butter. In Rajasthan State, there was 3.5 per cent non-governmental organizations in 1960-61 which was second state from lowest rank among fifteen states of the country (Kothari 1966)[9]. However, there were fourteen castes, which were rural, urban, or both which came forward and established schools and hostels in Jodhpur city from the beginning of modern education period. Private efforts in the field of modern education began from 1887 in Jodhpur city.

Preponderant Castes: A Concept Formation

This research study analzed characteristics of preponderant castes based on literacy status, population, type of residence, educational institutions or hostels opened, political hold, occupational, economic status. This study found that nine castes opened schools in Jodhpur city. (Suthar/ Khati) was managing one boys secondary school which was closed later on. This analysis present discussion of eight preponderant castes. Table 7.1 shows characteristics of eight preponderant castes on six variables: literacy, population, type of residence, educational institutions, hostels established, political hold in society, occupational and economic status of the caste.

Table 7.1. Characteristics of Preponderant Castes in Jodhpur City

S. No.	*Preponderant Caste*	*Literacy (1941 Census)*	*Characteristics/Rank Score*					
			Population	*Type of residence*	*Edu/ Hostel*	*Political Hold*	*Occupation /Economic*	*Total*
1.	Brahman	3	6	3	1	1	3	17
2.	Rajput	2	5	3	2	1	3	14
3.	Oswals	4.5	5.5	3	1	1	2	17
4.	Maheswari	4.5	5.5	3	2	1	2	18
5.	Agarwal	4.5	5.5	3	1	1	2	17
6.	Kayastha	1	2	1	1	0	2	7
7.	Sanik Kshatriya	0	4	3	2	1	2	12
8.	Rawna Rajput	0	1	3	1	0	1	6

Literacy of population : Highest to Lowest
Type of residence: 1 = urban caste, 2 = Rural caste, 3 = Rural urban residence
Edu. Institution = 1, Hostels & Edu. Institutions = 2, Political hold = 0, No hold, 1 = Yes
Occupation/Economic Status = High = 3, Medium = 2, Low = 1

Rank score analysis was done from highest to lowest. It was observed that Oswal, Maheswari and Agarwal castes scored highest score in the sense that a few of their persons were educated in English language and native languages as compared to other castes which scored low, viz. Brahman, Rajput and Kayastha. While on population, Brahman scored the highest rank 6 and then were the following castes: Oswal, Maheswari, Agarwal, Sanik Kshatriya, Rajput, Kayastha and Rawna Rajput. Except one Kayastha caste which was urban based, all other seven castes were distributed in rural and urban areas both. There were only three rural castes: Rajput, Sanik Kshatriya and Maheswari which opened hostels also. It was observed that two castes, viz. Kayastha and Rawna Rajput did not have political hold at city level (However, Kayastha enjoyed their political hold at State level due to ex-minister of Rajasthan State Shri Mathura Das Mathur, and late Shri Harish Chandra Mathur, ex- M.P.). At occupational level or economic status Brahmans and Rajputs held high positions while others were in middle rank except Rawna Rajputs which have always held low occupational position.

A combined score-analysis suggest that except Rawna Rajput caste which obtained 6 scores only other seven castes obtained scores in range of 12-18, which was around average of all.

B. The rise of Castes and Communities in Spread of Modern Education from 1887 to 1954

Castes have established schools, colleges and hostels in Jodhpur city before and after independence. These castes have contributed in many ways in growth and development of their schools from lower primary and primary stage of education to college education. Rural castes preferred to build hostels instead of establishment of educational institutions because they could get education of their children in educational institutions run by State and other private bodies.

The erstwhile State had always considered and examined matter as per State's education policy, grant-in-aid rule, etc. Nine castes viz. Brahman, Rajput, Sanik Kshatriya, Oswal, Maheswari, Agarwal, Kayastha, Rawna Rajput and Suthar (Khati) opened schools for education of boys and girls in Jodhpur city. Three minority communities viz. Christian, Sindhi and Muslim also opened their schools for education of boys and girls in the city. Their activities continued upto 1954.

After independence the erstwhile Marwar State was merged into the present Rajasthan State in 1949 and the Chopasani Sr. Hr. School which is managed by Rajput caste, was sanctioned 90% grant, i.e., reduction by 10% annually as per Grant-in-Aid Rule in force that time. Two developments occurred as a result of abolition of princely State: (i) Rajput school was financed cent per cent by the erstwhile State got status of aided school in 1949. (ii) Muslim school was established by Marwar Muslim education society which was later on taken over by the popular and democratically elected government and renamed it to Mahatma Gandhi School, Jodhpur. This decision had frustrated to a great extent to local Muslims and they approached the Rajasthan government again. In1954, they were allowed to start a primary school known as Isaquia school, Jodhpur which has been covered in the study because it was a case of theory of compensation of local minority community. However, Government of Rajasthan has compensated local Muslims by land and permitted to start a senior higher secondary school. Muslims have opened their school in name of Maulana Abdul Kalam Azad Senior Higher Secondary School, Kamala Nehru Nagar, Jodhpur in 1990.

India became independent in 1947. As a result of partition, Sindhis migrated to Jodhpur city from Pakistan (Sindh) (Though Sindhis were residing in rural areas). A Department of Resettlement and Rehabilitation was set up to rehabilitate them. They were first given shelters in refugee camps. They faced great difficulty of communication because they were knowing Sindhi language. Due to this reason they could not take education benefit immediately in any school. A few educated Sindhis approached Government of Rajasthan to start their own school. Government of Rajasthan gave them permission to start one boys and one girl's school in Jodhpur city as a special case on these grounds: (i) They were allowed to admit Sindhi children only, (ii) They were allowed to use medium of instructions in Sindhi language, (iii) They recruited Sindhi teachers only. This was a case of rehabilitations of immigrant community through education.

In Jodhpur city the rise of private bodies can be conveniently grouped into three phases: (i) castes and communities came forward and opened their schools. It was a period of education as a necessity to educational expansion. (ii) local Musiim community was given permission to start a school, a theory of compensation and (iii) rehabilitation of immigrant Sindhi minority community.

The reason for emergence of castes and community in the field of modern education in Jodhpur city were: (i) realization of need of modern education, and (ii) reform through educational advancement. This phenomenon was unlike the educational movement of non-brahmans movement in the field of education in the States of Andhra Pradesh, Karnataka (Mysore), Maharashtra and Tamil Nadu (Rao,1967)[10]. While Rudolph and Rudolph (1972)[11] classified educational movement into: (i) nationalist, (ii) sectarian, (iii) caste and community. The fundamental difference lies between educational movement by certain castes in certain States and in Jodhpur city is that in the later case it was State's initiative to involve private bodies to spread modern education in 1886 (Singh, Vikram 1983)[12]. Though the erstwhile rulers were not keen on education for masses in earlier period (Erskine, K.D. A.P. III, 162), yet the development of modern education began when Sir Pratap Singh was the Regent in the erstwhile State. Sir Pratap Singh had always thought of education and development and in particular of Rajputs to place them in high offices (Vanwart, Robert 1926)[13] . It was on his initiative a meeting of prominent persons was called. He advised them to spread education among masses. The other ruler Maharaja Umaid Singhji also took interest in development of modern education of Jodhpur city and the erstwhile Marwar State. It was observed that out of nine castes which opened schools, seven castes named their schools after erstwhile rulers viz. Maharaja Sardar Singh, Maharaja Kumar Sumer Singh, Sir Pratap Singh, Regent of the State, Maharaja Umaid Singh and Maharaja Hanuwant Singh.

Three middle castes Kayastha, Oswal and Sanik Kshatriya (Mali) were quick to respond to a call given by the State to spread modern education. Kayastha was urban caste. A few educated English knowing persons who held key posts in administration of princely state took advantage of rising opportunities opened their Anglo-vernacular boys primary school in 1887 atter the in name of Sir Pratap Singh, Regent of the erstwhile State. This caste received full support from him in particular and from State also. The second middle caste was Oswal. Oswal was rural and urban caste, economically well-being. A few educated persons of this caste realized need of modern education though their traditional occupation was business which also require formal education for better advancement. Oswals also held key portfolios in the princely State. They opened their Anglo-vernacular boys primary school in 1896. These two castes were connected with administration of princely State and took advantage of their position in the establishment of schools. This is a similar observation made by Chauhan (1967)[14] . Third middle caste was Sanik Kshatriya (Mali). This is a rural caste and its traditional occupation is gardening and flower growing and numerically dominant. They were influenced by Swami Dayanand Saraswati and Arya Samaj ideology. These were factors, which motivated a few persons to arrange education for their children so that customs of their caste e.g., early marriage can be of girl reformed. For instance, girls were married at an early age in this caste and in Rajasthan also. After the Mandal judgment in 1992, this caste was also in the Central's list of Backward Classes as Sociolly and educationally Backward caste. This caste had an advantage of numerical preponderance, wealth and political power which was similar to observations made by Desai (1969)[15] for rural castes in context of position of caste hierarchy and status.

Though education was a necessity and the erstwhile rulers took initiative first by a call given to prominent castes and second by introduction of Grant-in-Aid Rule 1902 in 1904. In other States and country as a whole there was rise in number of privately managed educational institutions but in case of Jodhpur city under erstwhile Marwar State, the situation did not improve for first eight years. Why did not private bodies come forward in Jodhpur city? It can be interpreted that grant-in-aid policy contained conditions such as adoptions of courses and curricula as per state's education code for uniform educational standard. Before Grant-in-Aid Rule, 1902 there was no such conditions.

In 1912, two castes came forward and opened their schools. Pushkarna Brahmans opened their Anglo-vernacular middle school for boys. They opened their school after twenty-five years of first middle caste Kayastha who opened their school in 1887. They reacted to the situation very lately because: (i) there was already one traditional school run by Srimali Brahmans in Jodhpur city, (ii) Brahmans realized need of modern education very late because they were engaged in traditional occupation of priests and cooks, (iii) they were insulted on one social occasion being known as cook which led this caste to open their school. The other backward caste was Rawna Rajput. They opened their school in1912 also because they were shocked to read statement about their caste origin in 1891 Census of Marwar State. They considered that education could only bring social reform in their caste customs. This caste opened a lower primary Anglo-vernacular boys school in 1912 and girls school later on. This caste named their boys school after Maharaja Umaid Singhji and girls school after Maharaja Kumar Sumer Singhji.

The erstwhile rulers thought to reorganize education in erstwhile Marwar State because education was not progressing well after Grant-in-Aid Rule, 1902 was introduced in 1904. H.T Knowlton (1914) gave his report on reorganization of education in the erstwhile Marwar state. This report suggested: (i) adoption of liberal approach in grant-in-aid policy, (ii) evolving a scheme of expansion of primary education. The princely State accepted all recommendations. Liberal grant-in-aid policy attracted two more castes, viz. Pushkarna Brahman and Maheswari. Pushkarna Brahman had already opened a boy's school in 1912 and later they opened a girl's primary school in 1919. This girls school was named after the ex-Chief Minister of Rajasthan State, Shri Jai Narain Vyas. Maheswari caste also opened Anglo-vernacular primary school for boys in 1918 and a girls school in 1920. This indicates that castes of Jodhpur city realized need of education for girls too.

On the recommendations of H.T. Knowlton (1914)[16], State prepared a scheme of expansion of primary education in erstwhile Marwar State in 1922 (Bhattji, K.M. 1922)[17]. The erstwhile State was keen on expansion of primary education than upgradation of schools. As a result of this policy of Marwar State education policy could attract castes and communities to open their schools for education of boys and girls upto 1943. (i) Sanik Kshatriyas opened two girls' schools in1925 and 1935. Both of these schools are situated at different locations and managed by two separate management bodies. One school was named after Maharaja Umaid Singhji, which is situated at Berion-Ka-Mohalla, Sojati Gate. The other school was named after their religious belief in Vedas, i.e., Vedic Kanya Pathshala, Bagar-Mohalla, Jodhpur. (ii) Agarwal caste being a trader's caste, opened their Anglo-vernacular boys school in1931. This caste took advantage of erstwhile State's liberal policy of grant-in-aid. (iii) Till now upper and middle castes thought of education of upper and middle caste children only. They did not consider education for scheduled caste boys as prevailing customs did not allow them. But a Pushkarna Brahman local worker Shri Bansi Dhar Purohit took an initiative and opened a school for children for all class irrespective of caste, creed or sex which included Scheduled Castes children. The school was named Sarvajanik school and was opened in 1943. His efforts to admit Scheduled Caste students in general school did not succeed like erstwhile government also made unsuccessful efforts. This observation was similar to Chauhan (1967:235) that caste differentiation had existed during those days.

Not only did castes played role in spread of modern education but also minority communities – Christians, Muslims and Sindhi also came forward in the field of education. Before independence, a few Christian ladies who had connections with British officials in the princely State took initiatives to start a girl's school on the line of English education. They obtained support of locally influential, and rural economically elite persons. Thus, in Jodhpur city the efforts made by Christian ladies were different from missionary movements in spreading education as in other parts of the country. It is a fact that the school is managed by Mission Sisters, Ajmer.

After independence, two minority communities Sindhi and Muslim opened their schools. Sindhi was a immigrant community which opened two schools one for boys and another for girls education 1947. The first boy's school was named after the first Prime Minister of Independent India, Pandit Jawaharlal Nehru. Nehru Higher Secondary School was closed in 1974 due to financial impropriety. Later on, second school known as Modern Senior Higher Secondary School was converted from girls school to co-educational school in 1974. This was a case of rehabilitation of migrant communities through education. Third minority community was local opened their primary school in 1954 and named it after their founder person Mohd. Isaq. Sahib.

Development of modern education in Jodhpur city and the erstwhile

Marwar State began during Maharaja Jaswant Singhji II (1873-1895). Sir Pratap Singhji, Regent of the erstwhile Marwar State and Maharaja Sri Umaid Singhji, ex-rulers took all interest in the development of modern education in the erstwhile State (Cox, A.P. 1968:166)[18]. It was stated that the erstwhile rulers were not keen on spread of education because: (i) they considered it below their dignity (Erskine, K.D.) and (ii) rulers thought educated people would seldom bow down to aristocratic rule of one man and purposefully neglected education (Agarwal, B.D. 1979)[19] But this was not true because there were few females who had received education at home in nineteenth century (Shah, P.R.)[20]. Also the erstwhile rulers opened a state school in 1867 which was earlier named Durbar School and is now known as New Govt. Senior Secondary School, Jodhpur. The ex-rulers also opened two schools in 1875 for education of Rajput boys. The erstwhile State implemented recommendations of India Education Commission (1882) in 1886 and in two years Grant-in-Aid Rules, 1902 in 1904, which was not considerably late to recognize role of private bodies in spread of modern education. Later on there was rise in number of State and State-aided schools from beginning of twentieth century to 1949.

The present work found that castes and communities started their schools and other activities in different phases: (i) education was a social necessity; it was on State's call to private bodies (1887 to 1898). (ii) Grant-in-Aid policy: An encouragement to private bodies (1902 to 1923). (iii) Education expansion (1922-1943). In the first period only Kayastha caste was not required to raise the fund when they started their school in 1887, while it was a pre-requisite condition for Oswals and Sanik Kshatriyas (Mali) to raise their fund first and then only were they allowed to open their schools in 1896 and 1989. The erstwhile state allotted building to Kayastha caste only to run their school while Oswals started their school in their own building and Sanik Kshatriyas started their school after construction of the building. The condition of fund raising then was made a rule for all private bodies that came forward in such activities. This might be the one of the reason that the Kayastha caste got the benefit of being the first caste that responded to modern education. Also Oswal and Sanik Kshatriya caste were economically well being. While upgradation of their schools, all of them were required to raise funds as per rule. The study also found that:

(i) In the first phase (1887-1989), three Anglo-vernacular boys schools were opened by Kayastha (1887), Oswal (1896) and Sanik Kshatriya (1989).

(ii) In the second phase (1902-1921), 3 boys and 2 girls schools were opened. Pushkarna Brahmans opened first Anglo-vernacular boys middle school in 1912 and then Anglo-vernacular girls primary school in1919. Rawna Rajput first opened Anglo-vernacular lower primary boys school in 1912 and then girls school later one. Maheswari caste opened first Anglo-vernacular primary school for boys in 1918 and then a girl's school in 1920. In this period private agencies initiated efforts for girls education.

(iii) In the period of educational expansion (1922-1943), 3 girls schools and 2 boys schools were opened. Sanik Kshatriya caste opened two girls' schools in 1925 and 1935. The schools are located at different places and managed by different management bodies. Agarwal caste and Pushkarna Brahman social worker opened two boys' schools in 1931 and 1943 respectively.

(iv) Christian (local ladies of Jodhpur city) opened one girl's school in 1937 online of modern education. Two minority communities Sindhis and Muslim opened their boys school in 1947 and 1954 respectively.

(v) After merger of the erstwhile Marwar State in the present Rajasthan state, Rajput school got status of private-aided schools from 1949.

After establishment of these private-aided schools, upgradation of these schools from lower primary or primary stage to higher stage varied from school to school (see Table 4.2). The variation in upgradation period was from 3 to 43 years at different stages of upgradation of schools. There was also difference in upgradation period of boys and girls schools. Out of nine boys senior higher secondary schools, two schools were established as middle school and secondary school. Seven schools were upgraded from 3-19 years. Mean score of upgradation of school was 9.57 years. It can be said that Kayastha, Oswal and Rawna Rajput got their schools upgraded in three years period while Rajput, Agarwal, Sanik Kshatriya and Maheswari got their schools upgraded in 11, 13, 15 and 19 years respectively. There was variation at each stage of upgradation. Upgradation from primary stage to secondary stage or senior secondary stage of education is one parameter to measure vertical growth of these schools. Growth of schools is judged by number of students in these schools (see Table 4.3). There were 13,279 students in sixteen schools studied. The purpose of this study was to find out if these schools overcrowded number of students in a class, as is generally said about them. There were 6 senior higher secondary boys schools where students strength was more than recommended by Secondary Education Commission (1952). On other side there were two schools which were below strength. One boys, two girls senior higher secondary schools and five secondary schools admitted students as per recommended strength. These schools are providing physical and library facilities also which varied from school to school.

Fee is considered one important source of part of income. It was observed that it also varied to a great extent in range of Rs. 52,147 to 5,13,350. Six schools raised fee more than 50% of total budget (see Table 4.6).

It was assumed that private-aided schools have been serving society for more than four decades; could they build educational prestige in the society? The study measured educational prestige of schools on eight variables viz. caste, number of students, number of teachers, library facilities, play ground/physical facilities, average fee/student, results, length of school serving society. Rank score analysis on these eight variables was done (see Table 4.7). Mean score was found 34.96 on total variables and mean scores varied from 0.81 to 9.15 on all these individual variables (Table 4.8). Statistical analysis indicated further that there was large variation among all these schools. Over all mean score was found 4.37 (see Table 4.9) which scored out six schools managed by Oswals, Sanik Kshatriyas, Maheswari, Christian (6 scored) and Kayastha and Rajput (7 scores). A comparative analysis of scores obtained by these schools on total variables and individual variables (see Table 4.10) gave a clear picture that only five schools managed by Kayastha, Oswal, Sanik Kshatriya, Rajput and Maheswari scored on both these variables. Rank-score analysis has given us a base to select schools for detailed case study. The first three schools were selected which have sociological, historical relevance in context of the present study. Chopasani school is managed by Rajput caste. This school got status of private-aided in 1949, and received princely state's cent per cent fund, so this school was dropped. Also Rajputs did not contribute to the growth of the school initially but later on endowment fund was created. Similarly Maheswari caste opened one boys and one girls school in the period of educational expansion. When there were already numbers of State and State-aided schools in Jodhpur city.

These schools are managed by management body. Management body of the schools have three types of members viz. office bearers, members (caste and non-managing caste members), and ex-officio members (school principal and government representative). The study found that all schools have implemented recommendations of Secondary Education Commission (1952) and Education Commission (1960-61) and gave representation to other category of members. Office bearers decide policies and decision issues related to educational administration and educational management. There was variation in number of members in the management body from 7 to 17. It was found that members in the management body belonged to different social backgrounds (see Table 5). Do they play any decisive role (Shukla 1967)[21] or perform manifest functions (Baranbas and Kashyap 1965)[22] ? Data were collected from key functionaries of management body, principals and teachers to analyse management process.

Majority of key functionaries or respondents stated that members in the management body are show pieces. It depends on how effective office bearers are? Who takes what decision and how do they take decisions? Was observed in this study as reported by Gore (1982)[23] . Management body performs these functions : (i) Fund raising: Before independence caste contribution, inter-caste contribution in form of cash and kind were there. After independence they raised funds through rents of shops, rents of school on occasion of marriage, etc. (ii) Student admission policy: Castes founded their schools to admit students from their own caste before Grant-in-Aid Rule, 1902, they adapted to the rule and allowed 50% students from other castes. After independence, caste base student admission policy is not allowed but it is still practiced in schools and even in higher learning institutions, i.e., why they were known as caste-colleges, caste schools, etc. (Sirsikar, 1965)[24] ; (iii) Recruitment, promotion, service benefits, etc. to teachers: It was found that there were only few educated persons among managing castes during 1911 to 1941. This was the reason that they recruited staffs from other castes and from other States. After Independence recruitment of teachers were made through selection process as per prescribed qualifications, which was initiated from Grant-in-Aid Rule, 1902. Response from teachers showed that private-aided schools follow all procedures but they recruit teachers and principals from their own caste provided they fulfill minimum qualifications.

This research study used three dimensional action-research model given by Pareek and Khanna (1978)[25] and cybernetic model by Rastogi (1979)[26] . This purpose of using these two model was to analyse policy and decision process in private-aided schools. It was found that castes played their role in all policy and decision aspects (see chapter – 5).

The purpose of using case study technique and preparing case-studies of selected schools was to understand and analyse role played by castes in development of these schools. Chapter 6 described case studies of three schools which were: (i) Sir Pratap Senior Higher Secondary School, Jodhpur. It is managed by Kayastha caste. It was established as an Anglo-vernacular primary boys school. Kayasthas was the first middle caste which responded to modern education in the State. A few educated persons of this caste held important occupational position in the princely State like Oswals. The school progress well after a difficult journey of financial crisis which led this school to downgradation etc. (ii) Sardar Senior Higher Secondary School, Jodhpur. It was established in 1896 by Oswal caste. This school was opened as Anglo-vernacular boys school. Oswals also realized need of modern education though their traditional occupation was business. They were rural-urban resident caste. A few educated persons of this caste took initiative and opened their school. They raised fund and shifted their school to the present building. (iii) Sumer Senior Higher Secondary School was established by Sanik Kshatriya caste. It is agriculturally and numerically dominant caste. They were influenced by Arya Samaj ideology and Swami Dayanand Saraswati preaching which motivated them to start a school for education of their boys. They did not get encouraging response from their caste members and hence there was delayed upgradation in the school.

This study concluded that educational measures and legislative measures are not effective instruments to weaken castes in Indian society since castes contribute to society by way of educational development, and raise funds, etc. These bodies expect, if not, economic return (these are not profit making institutions) at least social return to benefit their members. Then the question of educational inequality among upper-upper castes, upper-middle castes, middle-middle castes exist. Educational inequality widen social inequality. If the issue of caste differentiation between upper and backward caste, general and Scheduled Castes are given a serious thought then it is contemplated that society will be in danger in future. There may be number of riots and violence which occurred in last few years on Mandal Commission report implementation. The last question is: Should we discontinue practice of educational management by private bodies? This is not the solution. In India, the time has neither come to do privatization of education; it is a social development sector. In developed countries also private and public agencies are managing schools, colleges also. Educational inequalities exist there also between upper and lower economic class, Black and White, etc. Finally what should be planned to minimize caste-differentiation, and reduce gap of social inequality? Education is a State subject and State Government may consider tempering down of grants to make them self-sufficient upto 50 per cent.

Then what will be the difference between recognized-unaided schools and recognized aided schools. There are large number of recognized unaided schools in the country but these are at primary and upper primary stage and hence this idea of tempering down grant at secondary or senior higher stage may not fit well. If it is allowed to run like these institutions may take form of professional colleges like medical, engineering etc. Then supervision and control of government will end. They will have their autonomy. There will be large number of litigations in the country. Politicians may form their umbrellas on such institutions and became educational zamindars as in Faizabad (Gould,1972)[27]. Finally, this study suggests evolving checks and counter checks to make education an open market available for have's and have not.

Reference

1. Mudaliar, A.L., *Report of the Secondary Education Commission (October 1952 to June 1953).* New Dělhi: Government of India, Ministry of Education, 1954.
2. Kothari, D.S., *The Education Commission, (1961-62).* New Delhi: Government of India, Ministry of Education. (1966).
3. Desai, A.R., Social change and educational policy (chapter) in papers in the *Sociology of Education in India* (ed) by M.S. Gore, I.P. Desai and Suma Chitnis, New Delhi : National Council of Educational Research and Training, 1967.
4. Damle, Y.B., The School and college as a social system (chapter) in paper in the Sociology of Education in India (ed) by M.S. Gore, New Delhi : National Council of Educational Research and Training, 1967.
5. Verma, G.C., *Modern education: Its growth and Development in Rajasthan 1818 to 1983.* Jaipur : Publication scheme, 1984.
6. Kothari, D.S., *The Education Commission, (1961-62).* New Delhi: Government of India, Ministry of Education. (1966).
7. Indian Education Commission (1882).
8. Misra, A.N., *Grant-in-aid of education of India,* Delhi. The Macmillan Company of India, 1973.
9. Kothari, D.S., *The Education Commission,* (1961-62). New Delhi: Government of India, Ministry of Education, (1966).
10. Rao, M.S.A., Education, Social stratification and mobility (Chapter) in the papers in *Sociology of Education* in India (ed) by M.S. Gore, et. al., New Delhi: National Council of Education, Research and Training, 1967.
11. Rudolph, S.H. and L.I. Rudolph, *Education and Politics in India* (Studies in organization, society and policy) New Delhi : Oxford University Press. 1972.
12. Singh, Nirmal, *Education under siege: A sociological study of private colleges,* New Delhi : Concept Publication, 1983.

13. Vanwart, Robert, B., *The life of Lt. General His Highness Sir Pratap Singh,* London: Oxford University Press. 1926.
14. Chauhan, B.R., Special problems regarding education among the Scheduled Castes (chapter) in the papers in the *Sociology of Education in India* (ed) by M.S. Gore, etc. al New Delhi : National Council of Educational Research and Training, 1967.
15. Desai, A.R., Social change and educational policy (chapter) in papers in the *Sociology of education in India* (ed) by M.S. Gore, I.P. Desai and Suma Chitnis, New Delhi : National Council of Educational Research and Training, 1967.
16. Knowlton H.T., *Report on the conditions of education in Jodhpur State.* Jodhpur : Government of Marwar State, 1914.
17. Bhattji, K.M., *Scheme for Expansion for Primary Education in Marwar State in Administrative Report of Jodhpur State 1921-22.* Jodhpur : Government of Marwar, 1922.
18. Cox, A.P., *Forty years of reminiscences,* New Zealand: Christchurch. 1968.
19. Agarwal, B.D., Education and culture (Chapter XV) in *Rajasthan District Gazettes: Jodhpur.* Jaipur : Directorate Gazetteers, Government of Rajasthan, 1979.
20. Shah, P.R., *Raj Marwar during British Paramountancy (A study in Problems and Policies upto 1923).* Jodhpur: Sharda Publishing House, 1981.
21. Shukla, S. Controls and Decision-Making in the education system. (Chapter) ed. in papers in the *Sociology of Education in India.* M.S. Gore, I.P. Desai and Suma Chitnis, New Delhi: National Council of Education, Research and Training, 1967.
22. Barnabas, A.P. and Subhas, C. Mehta, "Caste in changing India". (Mimeograph), New Delhi : IIPA, 1965.
23. Gore, M.S., *Education and modernization in India.* Jaipur, Rawat Publications, 1982.
24. Sirskar, V.M., "Use of Politics" in *Seminar*, 70, 1965.
25. Pareek, Udai, "The role of action research in building self-sustaining system in Indian Journal of Social Work" Vol. xxxviii, No. 4, Jan. 1978, p. 124.
26. Rastogi, P.N., cybernatic studies,
27. Gould, Harold.Educational structure and political processes in Faizabad district, U.P. (chapter 7) in *Education and politics in India: studies in organization, society and policy* (ed.) by S.H. Rudolph and L.I. Rudolph, Delhi : Oxford University Press. 1972.

Appendix I

Number of Recognised Educational Institutions in India 1950-51

Primary/Junior Basic

S.No.	*State/Uts*	*Boys*	*Girls*	*Total*
1.	Andhra Pradesh	0	0	0
2.	Assam	9432	1266	10698
3.	Bihar	21574	2125	23699
4.	Bombay	26292	2215	28507
5.	Madhya Pradesh	7936	595	8531
6.	Madras	38443	0	38443
7.	Orissa	9582	219	9801
8.	Punjab	3254	1061	4315
9.	Uttar Pradesh	29459	2520	31979
10.	West Bengal	14033	750	14783
11.	Hyderabad	7749	1056	8805
12.	Madhya Bharat	3859	313	4172
13.	Mysore	9702	583	10285
14.	Pepsu	679	107	786
15.	Rajasthan	3563	372	3935
16.	Saurashtra	2186	224	2410
17.	Travancore-Cochi	3968	0	3968
18.	Ajmer	320	80	400
19.	A&N Islands	19	0	19
20.	Bhopal	238	34	272
21.	Biaspur	28	0	28
22.	Coorg	84	1	85
23.	Delhi	361	169	530
24.	Himachal Pradesh	377	22	399
25.	Kutch	223	43	266
26.	Manipur	430	25	455
27.	Tripura	397	7	404
28.	Vidhya Pradesh	1582	114	1696
29.	Jammu & Kashmir	0	0	0
30.	N.E.F.A.	0	0	0
31.	Kerala	0	0	0
32.	L.M. & A Island	0	0	0
33.	Pondicherry	0	0	0
	India	**195770**	**13901**	**209671**

Source : Growth of Schools, 1950-1992 (Statewise). Govt. of India, Ministry of Human Resources Development, Department of Education (Planning, Monitoring and Statistics Division), 1997, Table I, Table I, p.1.

Appendix II

Number of Recognised Educational in India 1992-93

Primary / Junior Basic

S.No.	State/Uts	Boys	Girls	Total
1.	Andhra Pradesh	48297	309	48606
2.	Arunachal Pradesh	1149	1	1150
3.	Assam	29080	482	29562
4.	Bihar	49136	3927	53063
5.	Goa	1033	0	1033
6.	Gujarat	13881	195	14076
7.	Haryana	4596	862	5458
8.	Himachal Pradesh	7581	27	7608
9.	Jammu & Kashmir	6613	3171	9784
10.	Karnataka	23424	398	23822
11.	Kerala	6679	40	6719
12.	Madhya Pradesh	66581	4741	71322
13.	Maharashtra	38746	1238	39984
14.	Manipur	2966	63	3029
15.	Meghalaya	3994	5	3999
16.	Mizoram	1065	1	1066
17.	Nagaland	1305	0	1305
18.	Orissa	40774	430	41204
19.	Punjab	12279	183	12462
20.	Rajasthan	30501	1953	32454
21.	Sikkim	527	0	527
22.	Tamil Nadu	30098	0	30098
23.	Tripura	2113	0	2113
24.	Uttar Pradesh	74889	4332	79221
25.	West Bengal	48248	487	48735
26.	A & N Islands	188	0	188
27.	Chandigarh	56	0	56
28.	Dadra & Nagar Haveli	126	0	126
29.	Daman & Diu	46	0	46
30.	Delhi	1093	979	2072
31.	Lakshadweep	19	0	19
32.	Pondicherry	325	16	341
	India	**547408**	**23840**	**571248**

Source : Growth of Schools, 1950-1992 (Statewise). Govt. of India, Ministry of Human Resources Deveopment, Department of Education (Planning, Monitoring and Statistics Division), New Delhi 1997, Table XLIII, p.43

Appendix III

Number of Recognised Educational Institutions in India 1950-51

Upper Primary / Middle

S.No.	State/Uts	Boys	Girls	Total
1.	Andhra Pradesh	0	0	0
2.	Assam	812	105	917
3.	Bihar	2055	117	2172
4.	Bombay	347	33	380
5.	Madhya Pradesh	759	76	835
6.	Madras	221	61	282
7.	Orissa	469	33	502
8.	Punjab	861	88	949
9.	Uttar Pradesh	2386	468	2854
10.	West Bengal	1084	177	1261
11.	Hyderabad	169	39	208
12.	Madhya Bharat	279	52	331
13.	Mysore	597	114	711
14.	Pepsu	220	25	245
15.	Rajasthan	602	91	693
16.	Saurashtra	69	8	77
17.	Travancore-Cochi	507	110	617
18.	Ajmer	28	11	39
19.	A&N Islands	0	0	0
20.	Bhopal	20	2	22
21.	Bilaspur	5	1	6
22.	Coorg	38	0	38
23.	Delhi	45	29	74
24.	Himachal Pradesh	80	8	88
25.	Kutch	12	0	12
26.	Manipur	68	3	71
27.	Tripura	34	6	40
28.	Vidhya Pradesh	155	17	172
29.	Jammu & Kashmir	0	0	0
30.	N.E.F.A.	0	0	0
31.	Kerala	0	0	0
32.	LM. & A Island	0	0	0
33.	Pondicherry	0	0	0
	India	**11922**	**1674**	**13596**

Source : Growth of Schools, 1950-1992 (Statewise). Govt. of India, Ministry of Human Resources Deveopment, Department of Education (Planning, Monitoring and Statistics Division), New Delhi 1997, Table XLIV, p.44

Appendix IV

Number of Recognised Educational Institutions in India 1992-93

Upper Primary/Middle/Sr. Basic

S.No.	State/Uts	Boys	Girls	Total
1.	Andhra Pradesh	6131	41	6172
2.	Arunachal Pradesh	274	0	274
3.	Assam	6267	462	6729
4.	Bihar	12344	1072	13416
5.	Goa	109	0	109
6.	Gujarat	16574	1577	18151
7.	Haryana	1231	170	1401
8.	Himachal Pradesh	1071	18	1089
9.	Jammu & Kashmir	1986	682	2668
10.	Karnataka	16459	698	17157
11.	Kerala	2908	20	2928
12.	Madhya Pradesh	14747	1499	16246
13.	Maharashtra	18417	898	19315
14.	Manipur	632	20	652
15.	Meghalaya	824	4	828
16.	Mizoram	553	0	553
17.	Nagaland	357	0	357
18.	Orissa	11199	161	11360
19.	Punjab	1376	53	1429
20.	Rajasthan	8779	1234	10013
21.	Sikkim	122	0	122
22.	Tamil Nadu	5608	0	5608
23.	Tripura	423	8	431
24.	Uttar Pradesh	14120	3610	17730
25.	West Bengal	2443	536	2979
26.	A & N Islands	46	0	46
27.	Chandigarh	32	0	32
28.	Dadra & Nagar Haveli	42	0	42
29.	Daman & Diu	20	0	20
30.	Delhi	447	72	519
31.	Lakshadweep	2	2	4
32.	Pondicherry	107	11	118
	India	**145650**	**12848**	**158498**

Source : Growth of Schools, 1950-1992 (Statewise). Govt. of India, Ministry of Human Resources Development, Department of Education (Planning, Monitoring and Statistics Division), New Delhi 1997, Table LXXXVI, p. 86.

Appendix V

Number of Recognised Educational Institutions in India 1950-51

High / Post Basic

S.No.	*State/UTS*	*Boys*	*Girls*	*Total*
1.	Andhra Pradesh	0	0	0
2.	Assam	234	35	269
3.	.Bihar	608	35	643
4.	Bombay	812	151	963
5.	Madhya Pradesh	211	47	258
6.	Madras	922	195	1117
7.	Orissa	165	7	172
8.	Punjab	389	40	429
9.	Uttar Pradesh	833	154	987
10.	West Bengal	957	150	1107
11.	Hyderabad	95	35	130
12.	Madhya Bharat	40	10	50
13.	Mysore	174	36	210
14.	Pepsu	84	9	93
15.	Rajasthan	148	7	155
16.	Saurashtra	43	9	52
17.	Travancore-Cochi	364	102	466
18.	Ajmer	17	3	20
19.	A&N Islands	1	0	1
20.	Bhopal	4	1	5
21.	Bilaspur	1	0	1
22.	Coorg	8	2	10
23.	Delhi	49	20	69
24.	Himachal Pradesh	20	4	24
25.	Kutch	5	1	6
26.	Manipur	10	1	11
27.	Tripura	16	8	24
28.	Vidhya Pradesh	14	2	16
29.	Jammu & Kashmir	0	0	0
30.	N.E.F.A.	0	0	0
31.	Kerala	0	0	0
32.	L.M.& A Island	0	0	0
33.	Pondicherry	0	0	0
	India	**6224**	**1064**	**7288**

Source : Growth of Schools, 1950-1992 (Statewise). Govt. of India, Ministry of Human Resources Deveopment, Department of Education (Planning, Monitoring and Statistics Division), New Delhi 1997, Table LXXXVII, p. 87

Appendix VI

Number of Recognised Educational Institutions in India 1992-93

High / Post Basic

S.No.	*State/Uts*	*Boys*	*Girls*	*Total*
1.	Andhra Pradesh	6209	538	6747
2.	Arunachal Pradesh	83	1	84
3.	Assam	2703	477	3180
4.	Bihar	3189	648	3837
5.	Goa	328	10	338
6.	Gujarat	3536	184	3720
7.	Haryana	1826	279	2105
8.	Himachal Pradesh	967	35	1002
9.	Jammu & Kashmir	836	203	1039
10.	Karnataka	4091	430	4521
11.	Kerala	2262	238	2500
12.	Madhya Pradesh	2135	208	2343
13.	Maharashtra	8313	834	9147
14.	Manipur	411	49	460
15.	Meghalaya	392	20	412
16.	Mizoram	271	2	273
17.	Nagaland	188	1	189
18.	Orissa	4199	541	4740
19.	Punjab	1837	267	2104
20.	Rajasthan	2811	448	3259
21.	Sikkim	60	3	63
22.	Tamil Nadu	2867	336	3203
23.	Tripura	314	18	332
24.	Uttar Pradesh	2308	350	2658
25.	West Bengal	3659	1032	4691
26.	A & N Islands	29	0	29
27.	Chandigarh	49	2	51
28.	Dadra & Nagar Haveli	6	0	6
29.	Daman & Diu	17	0	17
30.	Delhi	244	66	310
31.	Lakshadweep	9	0	9
32.	Pondicherry	66	15	81
	India	**56215**	**7235**	**63450**

Source : Growth of Schools, 1950-1992 (Statewise). Govt. of India, Ministry of Human Resources Development, Department of Education (Planning, Monitoring and Statistics Division), New Delhi 1997, Table LLXXIX, p. 129.

Appendix VII

Number of Recognised Educational Institutions in India 1950-51

High Sec. / Sr. Sec.

S.No.	*State/Uts*	*Boys*	*Girls*	*Total*
1.	Andhra Pradesh	0	0	0
2.	Assam	0	0	0
3.	Bihar	0	0	0
4.	Bombay	0	0	0
5.	Madhya Pradesh	0	0	0
6.	Madras	0	0	0
7.	Orissa	0	0	0
8.	Punjab	0	0	0
9.	Uttar Pradesh	0	0	0
10.	West Bengal	0	0	0
11.	Hyderabad	0	0	0
12.	Madhya Bharat	0	0	0
13.	Mysore	0	0	0
14.	Pepsu	0	0	0
15.	Rajasthan	0	0	0
16.	Saurashtra	0	0	0
17.	Travancore-Cochi	0	0	0
18.	Ajmer	0	0	0
19.	A&N Islands	0	0	0
20.	Bhopal	0	0	0
21.	Bilaspur	0	0	0
22.	Coorg	0	0	0
23.	Delhi	0	0	0
24.	Himachal Pradesh	0	0	0
25.	Kutch	0	0	0
26.	Manipur	0	0	0
27.	Tripura	0	0	0
28.	Vidhya Pradesh	0	0	0
29.	Jammu & Kashmir	0	0	0
30.	N.E.F.A.	0	0	0
31.	Kerala	0	0	0
32.	L.M. & A Island	0	0	0
33.	Pondicherry	0	0	0
	India	**0**	**0**	**0**

There were no Hr. Sec. Schools for this period, Statewise break-up of 128 intermediate Colleges are not available.

Source : Growth of Schools, 1950-1992 (Statewise). Govt. of India, Ministry of Human Resources Development, Department of Education (Planning, Monitoring and Statistics Division), New Delhi 1997, Table LLXXX, p.130.

Appendix VIII

Number of Recognised Educational Institutions in India 1992-93

Higher Sec. / Intermediatre / Sr. Secondary

S.No.	State/Uts	Boys	Girls	Total
1	Andhra Pradesh	761	107	868
2	Arunachal Pradesh	54	1	55
3	Assam	431	32	463
4	Bihar	233	26	259
5	Goa	48	1	49
6	Gujarat	1559	201	1760
7	Haryana	388	91	479
8	Himachal Pradesh	196	9	205
9	Jammu & Kashmir	194	42	236
10	Karnataka	1226	106	1332
11	Kerala	257	3	260
12	Madhya Pradesh	2177	473	2650
13	Maharashtra	1986	147	2133
14	Manipur	35	2	37
15	Meghalaya	8	0	8
16	Mizoram	6	0	6
17	Nagaland	0	0	0
18	Orissa	425	24	449
19	Punjab	559	114	673
20	Rajasthan	908	200	1108
21	Sikkim	17	2	19
22	Tamil Nadu	1810	355	2165
23	Tripura	132	16	148
24	Uttar Pradesh	2947	510	3457
25	West Bengal	1106	210	1316
26	A & N Islands	40	1	41
27	Chandigarh	17	13	30
28	Dadra & Nagar Haveli	6	0	6
29	Daman & Diu	3	0	3
30	Delhi	588	314	902
31	Lakshadweep	2	0	2
32	Pondicherry	29	10	39
	India	**18148**	**3010**	**21158**

Source : Growth of Schools, 1950-1992 (Statewise). Govt. of India, Ministry of Human Resources Development, Department of Education (Planning, Monitoring and Statistics Division), New Delhi 1997, Table LLLXXII, p.172.

Appendix IX

Table 1.02

Number of Selected Educational Institutions by Management

Type of Institutions	*Institutions managed by*				
	Government	*Local*	*University*	*Private bodies*	*Total*
Higher Secondary Schools (10+2 pattern)	7916	426	7	11698	20047
	(39.49)	(2.13)	(0.03)	(58.35)	(100.00)
High/Post Basic Schools	22625	5615		35210	63450
	(35.66)	(8.85)		(55.49)	(100.00)
Middl/Senior Basic Schools	70042	50182		38274	158498
	(44.19)	(31.66)		(24.15)	(100.00)
Primary/Junior Basic Schools	273828	256869		40551	571248
	(47.93)	(44.97)		(7.10)	(100.00)
Pre-Primary/Pre-Basic Schools	7930	3038		6182	17150
	(46.24)	(17.71)		(36.05)	(100.00)
Total	**382341**	**316130**	7	**131915**	**830393**
	(46.04)	**(38.07)**	**(0.00)**	**(15.89)**	**(100.00)**

Note : *Figures in Parenthesis indicate percentage to total number of institutions.*

Source : Education in India, 1992-93 Vol. I (S), Govt. of India, Ministry of Human Resource Development (Deptt. of Education), Planning, Monitoring and Statistics, Division, New Delhi. Table 1.02.

Appendix X

Number of Selected Educational Institutions by Management

School for General Education

(a) Higher Secondary (10 + 2)

State/Union Territory	*Govt.*	*Local Bodies*	*Univer-sities*	*Private body Aided*	*Private body Unaided*	*Total*	*% age of Instt. managed by Govt. to Total*
Andhra Pradesh	26	-	-	3	21	50	52.00
Arunachal Pradesh	51	-	-	4		55	92.73
Assam	461	-	-	-	2	463	99.57
Bihar	190	-	-	12	8	210	90.48
Goa	12	-	-	37	-	49	24.49
Gujarat	94	84	-	1562	20	1760	5.34
Haryana	350		-	58	71	479	73.07
Himachal Pradesh	177	5	-	11	12	205	86.34
Jammu & Kashmir	210		-	16	10	236	88.98
Karnataka	460	9	-	490	373	1332	34.53
Kerala	194		-	34	32	260	74.62
Madhya Pradesh	1841	40	-	345	424	2650	69.47
Maharashtra	45	140	-	1828	120	2133	2.11
Manipur	31	-	-	-	6	37	83.78
Meghalaya	8	-	-	-	-	8	100.00
Mizoram	-	-	-	-	-	-	-
Nagaland	-		-	-	-	-	-
Orissa	208	6	-	-	-	214	97.20
Punjab	479	2	7	139	46	673	71.17
Rajasthan	821	-	-	193	94	1108	74.10
Sikkim	16	-	-	3	-	19	84.21
Tamil Nadu	901	68	-	699	497	2165	41.62
Tripura	125	-	-	23	-	148	84.46
Uttar Pradesh	505	65	-	2843	44	3457	14.61
West Bengal	34	1	-	1249	32	1316	2.58
A & N Islands	40	-	-	1	-	41	97.56
Chandigarh	24	-	-	5	1	30	80.00
Dadra & Nagar Haveli	5	-	-	-	1	6	83.33
Daman & Diu	2	-	-	1	·	3	66.67
Delhi	574	6	-	146	176	902	63.64
Lakshadweep	-	-	-	-	-	-	
Pondicherry	32	-	-	2	4	38	84.21
INDIA	**7916**	**4267**	**7**	**9704**	**1994**	**20047**	**39.49**

Source : Education in India, 1992-93 Vol. I(S), Govt. of India, Ministry of Human Resource Development, (Deptt. of Education), Planning, Monitoring and Statistics Division, New Delhi. Table III, p. 21.

Appendix XI

Number of Selected Educational Institutions by Management
School for General Education
(b) High / Post Basic School

State/Union Territory	*Govt.*	*Local Bodies*	*Univer-sities*	*Private body Aided*	*Private body Unaided*	*Total*	*% age of Instt. managed by Govt. to Total*
Andhra Pradesh	810	4472	-	688	777	6747	12.01
Arunachal Pradesh	80	-	-	4		84	95.24
Assam	1828	-	-	960	392	3180	57.48
Bihar	3595	-	-	179	63	3837	93.69
Goa	61	-	-	273	4	338	18.05
Gujarat	112	260	-	3319	29	3720	3.01
Haryana	1726	-	-	174	205	2105	82.00
Himachal Pradesh	867	3	-	71	61	1002	86.53
Jammu & Kashmir	916	-	-	65	58	1039	88.16
Karnataka	1406	27	-	2119	969	4521	31.10
Kerala	969	18	-	1362	151	2500	38.76
Madhya Pradesh	1560	10	-	91	682	2343	66.58
Maharashtra	185	677	-	5368	2917	9147	2.02
Manipur	193	-	-	82	185	460	41.96
Meghalaya	22	-	-	364	26	412	5.34
Mizoram	90	-	-	99	84	273	32.97
Nagaland	72	-	-	46	71	189	38.10
Orissa	394	-	-	2799	1547	4740	8.31
Punjab	1764	4	-	237	99	2104	83.84
Rajasthan	2912	-	-	107	240	3259	89.35
Sikkim	60	-	-	2	1	63	95.24
Tamil Nadu	1894	83	-	352	874	3203	59.13
Tripura	323	-	-	7	2	332	97.29
Uttar Pradesh	462	50	-	1662	484	2658	17.38
West Bengal	3	6	-	4682	-	4691	0.06
A & N Islands	27	-	-	-	2	29	93.10
Chandigarh	36	-	-	1	14	51	70.59
Dadra & Nagar Haveli	4	-	-	1	1	6	66.67
Daman & Diu	14	-	-	3	-	17	82.35
Delhi	172	5	-	34	99	310	55.48
Lakshadweep	9	-	-	-	-	9	100.00
Pondicherry	59	-	-	15	7	81	72.84
INDIA	**22625**	**5615**	**0**	**25166**	**10044**	**63450**	**35.66**

Source : Education in India, 1992-93 Vol. 1(S), Govt. of India, Ministry of Human Resource Development, (Deptt. of Education), Planning, Monitoring and Statistics Division, New Delhi. Table 111, p. 22.

Appendix XII

Number of Selected Educational Institutions by Management
School for General Education
(c) Middle/Senior Basic School

State/Union Territory	*Govt.*	*Local Bodies*	*Univer-sities*	*Private body Aided*	*Private body Unaided*	*Total*	*% age of Instt. managed by Govt. to Total*
Andhra Pradesh	346	4708	-	401	717	6172	5.61
Arunachal Pradesh	271		-	3	-	.274	98.91
Assam	5820	146	-	648	115	6729	86.49
Bihar	12961	-	-	384	71	13416	96.61
Goa	95	-	-	13	1	109	87.16
Gujarat	68	15552	-	982	1549	18151	0.37
Haryana	1197	1	-	14	189	1401	85.44
Himachal Pradesh	1012	16	-	28	33	1089	92.93
Jammu & Kashmir	2426	-	-	29	213	2668	90.93
Karnataka	14016	6	-	1621	1514	17157	81.69
Kerala	960	28	-	1852	88	2928	32.79
Madhya Pradesh	12199	933	-	360	2754	16246	75.09
Maharashtra	264	17549	-	976	526	19315	1.37
Manipur	308	-	-	94	250	652	47.24
Meghalaya	60	-	-	733	35	828	7.25
Mizoram	239	-	-	266	48	553	43.22
Nagaland	235	-	-	91	31	357	65.83
Orissa	3650	1420	-	6010	280	11360	32.13
Punjab	1291	-	-	36	102	1429	90.34
Rajasthan	8139	-	-	221	1653	10013	81.28
Sikkim	119	-	-	3	-	122	97.54
Tamil Nadu	3290	417	-	1888	13	5608	58.67
Tripura	421	-	-	4	6	431	97.68
Uttar Pradesh	254	9397	-	1765	6314	17730	1.43
West Bengal	3	1	-	2975	-	2979	0.10
A & N Islands	45	-	-	1	-	46	97.83
Chandigarh	13	-	-	-	19	32	40.63
Dadra & Nagar Haveli	37	-	-	3	2	42	88.10
Daman & Diu	19	-	-	1		20	95.00
Delhi	199	8	-	27	285	519	38.34
Lakshadweep	4	-	-	-	-	4	100.00
Pondicherry	81	-	-	6	31	118	68.64
INDIA	**70042**	**50182**	**0**	**21435**	**16839**	**158498**	**44.19**

Source : Education in India, 1992-93 Vol. 1(S), Govt. of India, Ministry of Human Resource Development, (Deptt. of Education), Planning, Monitoring and Statistics Division, New Delhi. Table 111, p. 23.

Appendix XIII

Number of Selected Educational Institutions by Management
School for General Education
(d) Primary/Junior/Basic School

State/Union Territory	*Govt.*	*Local Bodies*	*Univer-sities*	*Private body Aided*	*Private body Unaided*	*Total*	*percent-age of Instt. managed by Govt. to Total*
Andhra Pradesh	3311	42121	-	1968	1206	48606	6.81
Arunachal Pradesh	1136	-	-	14	-	1150	98.78
Assam	26699	1849	-	669	345	29562	90.32
Bihar	52511	-	-	521	31	53063	98.96
Goa	976	-	-	3	54	1033	94.48
Gujarat	66	13264	-	198	548	14076	0.47
Haryana	5248	-	-	72	138	5458	96.15
Himachal Pradesh	7482	12	-	22	92	7608	98.34
Jammu & Kashmir	9094	-	-	171	519	9784	92.95
Karnataka	22272	12	-	489	1049	23822	93.49
Kerala	2521	68	-	3983	147	6719	37.52
Madhya Pradesh	56517	9269	-	1112	4424	71322	79.24
Maharashtra	189	36343	-	1589	1863	39984	0.47
Manipur	2109	-	-	429	491	3029	69.63
Meghalaya	6	2799	-	954	240	3999	0.15
Mizoram	914	-	-	101	51"	1066	85.74
Nagaland	1216	-	-	42	47	1305	93.18
Orissa	40607	-	-	561	36	41204	98.55
Punjab	12145	12	-	119	186	12462	97.46
Rajasthan	2838	26688	-	250	2678	32454	8.74
Sikkim	527	-	-	-	-	527	100.00
Tamil Nadu	23840	1134	-	5105	19	30098	79.21
Tripura	863	1235	-	12	3	2113	40.84
Uttar Pradesh	88	71550	-	885	6698	79221	0.11
West Bengal		48735	-	-	-	48735	0.00
A & N Islands	181	-	-	-	7	188	96.28
Chandigarh	30	-	-	-	26	56	53.57
Dadra & Nagar Haveli	115	-	-	10	1	126	91.27
Daman & Diu	43	-	-	3	-	46	93.48
Delhi	-	1778	-	56	238	2072	0.00
Lakshadweep	19	-	-	-	-	-	100.00
Pondicherry	265	-	-	7	69	341	77.71
INDIA	**273828**	**256869**	**0**	**19345**	**21206**	**571248**	**47.94**

Source : Education in India, 1992-93 Vol. 1(S), Govt. of India, Ministry of Human Resource Development, (Deptt. of Education), Planning, Monitoring and Statistics Division, New Delhi. Table 111, p.24.

Appendix XIV

Number of Selected Educational Institutions by Management

School for General Education

(e) Pre-Primary/Pre-Basic School

State/Union Territory	*Govt.*	*Local Bodies*	*Univer-sities*	*Private body Aided*	*Private body Unaided*	*Total*	*percent-age of Instt. managed by Govt. to Total*
Andhra Pradesh	5	19	-	4	1	29	17.24
Arunachal Pradesh	249	-	-	-	-	249	100.00
Assam	450	13	-	19		482	93.36
Bihar	1	-	-	-	-	1	100.00
Goa	-	-	-	-	-	-	-
Gujarat	-	596	-	1596	183	2375	0.00
Haryana	27	-	-	-	-	27	100.00
Himachal Pradesh	13	-	-	-	1	14	92.86
Jammu & Kashmir	-	-	-	-	-	-	-
Karnataka	2519	176	-	705	1820	5220	48.26
Kerala	55		-	102		157	35.03
Madhya Pradesh	309	59	-	86	641	1095	28.22
Maharashtra	208	1601	-	311	387	2507	8.30
Manipur	1	-	-	-	-	1	100.00
Meghalaya	-	-	-	-	-	-	-
Mizoram	-	-	-	-	-	-	-
Nagaland	-	-	-	-	-	-	-
Orissa	-	-	-	-	-	-	-
Punjab	2	-	-	-	-	2	100.00
Rajasthan	18	-	-	-	3	30	60.00
Sikkim	723	-	-	9	-	723	100.00
Tamil Nadu		-	-	22	-	22	0.00
Tripura	3295	-	-	111	-	3406	96.74
Uttar Pradesh	1	5	-	22	9	37	2.70
West Bengal	-	-	-	-	-	-	-
A & N Islands	4	-	-	-	19	23	17.39
Chandigarh	-	-	-	-	-	-	-
Dadra & Nagar Haveli	-	-	-	-	-	0	-
Daman & Diu	-	-	-	-	-	0	-
Delhi	-	569	-	-	-	569	0.00
Lakshadweep	9	-	-	-	-	9	100.00
Pondicherry	41	-	-	-	131	172	23.84
INDIA	7930	3038	0	2987	3195	17150	46.24

Source : Education in India, 1992-93 Vol. 1(S), Govt. of India, Ministry of Human Resource Development, (Deptt. of Education), Planning, Monitoring and Statistics Division, New Delhi. Table 111, p.25.

Selected Bibliography

Agarwal, B.D. Education and culture (Chapter XV) in Rajasthan District Gazetteers : Jodhpur, Jaipur Directorate Gazetteers, Govt. of Rajasthan, 1979.

Agarwal, J.C., Teacher's Role, Status, Service conditions education in India. A Reference to committees and Commissions. Delhi; Doaba House, 1988.

Acharya, Poromesh 1986. English and Elite Education. Paper presented at Regional Conference of Sociology of Education held from 16-17 August, 1986 in New Delhi.

Administrative reports of Jodhpur State from 1923-45, Government of Marwar Press, Jodhpur.

Ahmed, Karuna Chanana, 1986. Social Reform or social change: education of women in Pre-Independence India. A paper presented at Regional Conference of Sociology of Education held on 16-17 August, 1986.

Atal Yogesh, 1972. "Changing Pattern of caste". A working paper presented in Indian Sociological Society Eleventh All-India Sociological Conference Panel III (April 28-30), 1972).

Bacchu, M.K. 1990. A critical Review and Analysis of early developments in Education in the British West Indian colonies. Sociological Bulletin, Vol. 39, No.1 & 2.

Basu, Aparna. 1974. The Growth of education and political developments in India, 1989-1920. Delhi: Oxford University Press.

1982. Essays in the History of Indian Education. New Delhi : Concept Publishing Company.

Basi, A.N. 1947. Education in Modern India.

Bottomore, T.B. The Administrative Elite. (Chapter) in New Sociology : Essays in Social Science and Social Theory (In honour of C. Wright Mills) (ed.) by I.L. Horowitz, New York : A Galaxy book, Oxford University Press, 1968.

Bowles, Samuel 1977. Unequal education and the reproduction of the social division of labour (ch. 5) in Power and Ideology in Education by Jerome Karber and A.H. Halsay, New York : Oxford University Press.

Buch, M.B. 1987 . The Third survey of Research in Education : 1978-83, New Delhi : NCERT.

Census of India. 1891. Calcutta : Superintendent, Government Printing

Press, India, 1913.

Census of India, 1931, Calcutta : Government of India Press, 1932.

Census of India Rajasthan, 1951, New Delhi: Government of India.

Census of India,1981. Series – 18 Rajasthan. District Census hand book, Jodhpur, Rajasthan : Jaipur.

Census of India,1991 : Rajasthan District Census hand book, Jodhpur, Jaipur : Rajasthan.

Census of Marwar State, 1981. Jodhpur: Government Jodhpur Press.

Census of Marwar State, 1931, Jodhpur: Government of Jodhpur Press, 1932.

Chanana, Karuna 1990: The Dialectics of Tradition and Modernity and Women's Education in India in Sociological Bulletin, Vol. 3, No. 1 & 2.

Chauhan,Risaldar Pannalal, 1927. Sudhar Saroj, Jodhpur Prabhakar Printing Press.

Chesler, Mark. A and William. M. Cane, 1981: Community Groups and Community Schools (Chapter 4) in Sociology of Education, New York : Macmillian Publishing Co. Inc.

Chitnis, Suma, 1980. "Second Review and Trend Report on the sociology of Education in India." Prepared for the ICSSR.

Chitnis, Suma. 1982. Sociology of Education in India : Emerging Trends and Needed Research. (Chapter-8) in Sociology in India Retrospect and Prospect (ed) by P.K.B. Nayar, Delhi : B.R. Publishing Company.

Cohn, Bernard.S, 1968. Notes on the History of the study of Indian Society and culture. (Ch.(1) in structure and change in India Society (ed) by Milton Singer and Bernard S. Cohn, Chicago : Aldine Publishing Company.

Crooke, W 1896. The Tribes and Castes of North Western India. Calcutta Govt. Printing Press : Reprint 1974, Delhi : Cosmos Publications.

Desai, A.R. 1948.Social background of Indian nationalism Bombay: Oxford University Press

Desai, A.R. (ed) 1969. Rural sociology in India Bombay : Popular Prakashan

Dhangare, D.R. 1980 . "Literacy and structural change in Rural Society in colonial India." The Journal of Social Studies, Dacca, No. 7, pp. 45-64.

Dumont, Louis 1970. Homo Hierarchicus – the caste system and its Implications (eng. Ed) Delhi : Vikas Publications.

Durkheim, Emile 1909. On education and society (Chapter 2) translated version published in Power Ideology (ed) by Jerome Karbel, et. al. 1977.

New York. Oxford University Press.

Erskine, K.D. Rajputana Gazetteer,Vol. III A & B.

Faure, Edgar, Felipe Herrera, Abdul-Razzak Kaddoura, Henri Lopes, Arthur.V. Petrovsky, Majid Rehman, Fredrick Champion Ward 1973.

Learning to be : The work of education today and tomorrow. Delhi : Sterling.

Gadgil, D.R. and V.M. Dandekar, 1955. Report of two investigations : Primary education in Satara District. Poona : Gokhale Institute of Politics and Economic Change.

Gore, M.S. 1982. Education and Modernization in India. Jaipur: Rawat Publications.

Gore, M.S. and I.P. Desai 1967.The Scope of sociology of education chapter (ed) in papers in the sociology of education in India (edited) by M.S.Gore, et. al. New Delhi: National Council of Educational Research and Training.

Gore, M.S. and Suma Chitnis, 1967. Sociology and educational research (Chapter) in papers in the sociology of education of India (ed) by M.S.Gore etc, al. New Delhi : National Council of Educational Research and Training.

Gore, M.S. 1970. Field studies in sociology of education in India, New Delhi : National Council of Educational, Research and Training.

Ghurye, G.S. 1957. Caste and class in India, Bombay : Population Book Depot.

Hashmi, Masood 1989, Muslim response to western education, New Delhi (India) : Commonwealth Publishers.

Harber, Edward. B. 1968. A Comparative analysis of caste: the United States and India.Chapter (3) in structure and change in Indian Society (ed) by Milton Singer and B.S.Cohn. Chicago Aldinel Publishing Company.

Ibetosn, D. 1916. Punjab Castes : Races, castes and Tribes of the People of Punjab (Lahore : Govt. Press, 1916. Reprint, 1981, New Delhi : Cosmos Publication.

Jeojnu, Hee-Chun Kang. 1984. "Equality of educational opportunity ideas and Politics: 1900-1918. British Journal of educational studies (Vol. XXXII, No.1 997-1005).

Joshi, P.C. 1967. Literacy and Education in backward regions (mimeographed).

Joshi, P.C. and M.S.A. Rao, 1964. "Social and Economic factors in literacy and education in rural India". Economic weekly 4, January, Bombay.

Joshi, P.C. and M.S.A. Rao, 1965. "Changes in Literacy and education study of villages in U.P. and Punjab". Economic Weekly, July.

Kalla, Bansi Dhar Sharma, 1916, Report of working of Sumer Pushtikar School, Iodhpur, Marwar from 8th Feb., 1912 to 30 June, 1915 (Published)
Kalla, M.R. 1947. Madhulika: A souvenir of Sumer Pushtikar Hr.Sec. School, Jodhpur.

Kamat, A.R. 1967. "Education in Gulumbi in India Education Review No. (2).

Kamat, A.R. 1968. "Some features of the growth of education in Rural Maharashtra". Indian Education Review No.3 (2).

Kamat, A.R. 1979. " The emerging situation: A socio structural analysis." Economic and Political Weekly, annual number, Bombay (Feb.).

Kamat, A.R. 1985. Education and Social change in India, New Delhi : Somaya Publications Pvt. Ltd.

Karabel, J. and A.H. Halesy 1977. Power and Ideology (ed). New York: Oxford University Press.

Karabal, Jerome 1977. Community colleges and social stratification: Submerged class conflict in American Higher Education (Chapter 11) (ed) in Power and Ideology, by Jerome Karabel and A.H. Hasley, New York: Oxford University Press.

Kaur, Kuldip 1985. Education in India (1981-1985): Policies, Planning and Implementation, Chandigarh: Centre for Research in Rural and Industrial Development.

Kerchoff, Alan.K. 1982. "Dimensions of educational and occupational attainment in Great Britain" in American Journal of Sociological Review, Vol. 47, June, No.3.

Kerr, Norman.D. 1964. "The School Board as an agency of legitimation" in sociology of education, No.1, Vol.38.

Khare, R.S. 1970. The changing Brahmans : Associations and elites among the Kanya-Kubja of north India. Chicago: The University of Chicago.

Kob. J. 1964. Definition of Teacher's role (Chapter.34) in Education, Economy and Society (ed) by A.H. Halsey Jean Flould and Charles. C. Anderson. USA : Free Press, Glencon Inc.

Kumar, Nita 2000. Lessons from Schools The History of Education in Banaras, New Delhi : Sage Publication.

Kumbhat, P.C. 1969. Urban geography of Jodhpur. Unpublished Ph.D dissertation.

Lall, S.K. Urban Elite. New Delhi : Tompson Press (India) Limited. 1974
Siriskar, V.M. The Rural Elite in a Developing Society, Delhi : Oritent Longman Ltd., 1970.

Madan, T.N. and B.G. Halbar. Caste and community in the private and public education of Mysore State (Chapter) in Education and Politics in India : Studies in Organisation, Society and Polity (ed.) by Susana Hoedar Rudolph and Loyld. I Rudolph, Delhi : Oxford University press, 1972.

Marton, Robert. K. Social Theory and Social structure, New York. Am rind Publishing Company Pvt. Ltd. 1968.

Manneheim, Karl and W.A.C. Stewart. An introduction to the Sociology of Education, London : Routledge and Kegan Paul. 1962

Madan,T.N. 1965. Facts and the Future. Seminar (June) 70.

Marwar Gazettee, 1916. Jodhpur Government of Marwar Press.

Mathur, M.L. 1978. "Caste and educational institutions in Jodhpur city : A sociological study". The Journal of Social Sciences. Samaj Vigyan Jagat, Vol.1, No.1 & 2, June/Dec 1978.

Mathur, M.L. 1980. "Caste, Elite and education: a sociological analysis of school's board of Management" in the journal of Social Sciences: Samaj Vigyan Jagat, Vol. 3, No.1 & 2. June/Dec. pp.36-46.

Mathur, M.L., 1986, "Caste and Education: A sociological analysis." A paper presented at Regional Conference on sociology of education held at New Delhi 16-17 Aug., 1986.

Misra, A.N. Education Finances in India. Bombay : Asia Publishing House. 1962.

Misra, A.N. Grant-in-Aid of Education in India Delhi : The Macmillan Company of India, 1973.

Mills, C. Wright 1956.The Power elite, New York: Oxford University Press.

Narain, Iqbal; K.C. Pande, and M.L. Sharma. The Rural Elite in Indian State : A Case Study of Rajasthan. New Delhi : Manohar Book House, 1976.

Naik, J.P. 1965. The status of private enterprises in Indian education (in the post independence period). Mimeo, New Delhi.

Naik, J.P. 1972. The role and problem of private enterprises in education in I.S.S. Feres consultation of principles of Christians colleges, Tambram.The Christian college and National Development 1967 (comment recorded in Gould 1972).

National Committee on Teachers-schools (1983-85), New Delhi, Government of India.

National policy on education: 1968, New Delhi, Department of Education, Government of India.

National Commission on Women Development (1959), New Delhi. Department of Education, Government of India.

National Policy on Education, 1968, New Delhi. Department of Education, Government of India.

National Policy on Education, 1986: Programme of Action, New Delhi : Government of India, Ministry of Human Resource Development, Department of Education.

Nurullah, S. and J.P. Naik, 1943. A History of Modern education in India: During the British Period, Bombay: Macmillan and Co.

Oommen,T.K. 1970: " The concept of dominant caste some queries" in contributions to India sociology (New Series) No.V.

Pareto, V. The Mind and Society Eng. Trans by Bongiorano and Arthur Livingstone, New York : Harcourt Brace. Co. 1935. P. 1422-23.

Parsons, Talcott, 1959. "The school class as social system: some of its functions in American society" Reprinted from Harvard educational review, XXIX (Fall, 1959, p.297-318) in education, economy and society (ed) by A.H. Halsey, Jean Floud and Charles C. Anderson, USA: Free Press, Clencoe Inc.Ltd.

Paulston, Rolland.G., 1971.Educational stratification and cultural hegemony in Peru (chapter 24) in Power and Ideology (ed) by Jerome Karabel and A.H. Halsey, New York: Oxford University Press.

Oersell, Caroline Hodges,1977. Education and Inequality: The roots and results of stratification in America's schools, New York: The Free Press Macmillan Publishing Co.

People of India, 1998. National Series (Delhi : Oxford University Press)

People of India, 1998. Rajasthan (Bombay : Popular Prakashan)

Petrov, Victor, 1985. India-Spot light on population: A Demographic outline, Moscow: Progress Publishers.

Phadke, Sindhu, 1967. Special problems of the education of women in papers in the Sociology of education in India (ed) by M.S. Gore, etc, al. New Delhi : National Council of Education, Research and Training.

Petrov,Vitor, 1985, India Spotlight on Population: A Demographic outline, Moscow: Progress Publishers.

Raza, Moonis, 1986. Educational planning long term perspective (ed) New Delhi: NIEPA.

Reu, B.N. 1940: Marwar-ka-Itihas, (Part II) (from Maharaja Man Singh to 1938). Jodhpur Archeological Department.

Reid. F.L. 1905. Report on the State of education in the native States of Rajputana.

Richey, J.A. 1922. Selection from educational Records (Pt.II)

Rose, H.A. 1919. Glossary of the Tribes and Castes of the Punjab and N.W.F. Province.

Rossana Rossanda M. Cini and L. Berlingver 1977. Thesis on education: A Marxist views (Chapter 38) in Power and Ideology (ed) by Jerome Karabel and A.H. Halsey, New York: Oxford University Press.

Ruhela, S.P., 1981. Education and Social transformation: Religion, caste and tribe. (Chapter) in the Teacher and Education in emerging Indian society (ed) by C.L. Anand, et. al. New Delhi: National Council of Education, Research and Training.

Saran, Rene. Policy making in Secondary Education : A Case Study. London : Oxford & Claredon Press, 1973.

Saran, Rene. Policy Making in secondary education : A case study : Oxford: Clarendon Press 1973.

Saxena, R.N. 1967. Traditional systems of education in India (Chapter) Papers in the sociology of education in India by M.S. Gore et. al., New Delhi : National Council of Education, Research and Training.

Seminar, 1965. Special issue on caste ('The Problem').

Shering, M.A. 1881. The Tribes and Castes of Rajasthan, Reprint 1975, New Delhi : Cosmos Publication.

Shukla, Suresh. Controls and Decision-making in the education system (chapter) ed. in The Papers in the Sociology of Education in India (ed) by M.S. Gorc, et.al, Ibid. 1967.

Sharma, M.L.,1975. A critical study of the role and contribution of private enterprise in education in Punjab from 1854 to 1966. (Unpublished Ph.D. Dissertation) Abstracted in third study of Education Research (ed) by Buch, M (1987).

Sharp, I.H. 1920. Selections from educational records (Pt.I)

Simkus, Albert and Rudolf Andorka, 1982. "Inequalities in Educational attainments in Hungary": 1923-1973 in American Sociological Review (Vol. 47, No. 6).

Siriskar, V.M. The Rural Elite in a Developing Society, Delhi : Orient Longman Ltd., 1970.

Singh, Munshi Hardayal. Castes of Marwar-Being. (based on Census Report, 1891). Jodhpur: Books Treasurer (First edition). 1894.

Singh, Nirmal, Education under siege: A sociological study of private colleges. New Delhi: Concept Publication. 1983

Singh,Vikram, 1983. Sir Pratap and his contributions, Jodhpur: Rajasthan Shodh Sansthan, Chopasani.

Singh, Yogendra, 1973. Modernization of Indian Tradition, New Delhi : Thompson Press (India) Limited.

Srivastava, H.S. 1973, Growth of private enterprises in education in Madhya Pradesh from 1860 to 1970 (Unpublished Ph.D. Dissertation) Abstracted in Third survey of Education Research by M.B. Buch.

Srinivas, M.N. 1959. The Dominant caste in Rampura" in American Anthropologist Vol.61, No. (Fen.).

Srinivas, M.N. 1962.Caste in Modern India and other essays, Bombay : Asia Publishing House.

Srinivas, M.N. 1968. Mobility in the caste system (Chapter 8) in structure and changes in Indian society (ed) Milton Singer and Bernard S. Cohn, Chicago: Aldien Publishing Co.

Srivastava, H.A., 1973. Growth of private enterprises in education in Madhya Pradesh from1860 to 1970 (unpublished Ph.D. Dissertation).

Surve, D.S. 1974. "Social and Political Influence on India education during the later half of the nineteenth century." Indian dissertation Abstracts, Oct-Dec, 1974.

Tilak, Jandhyala, B.G. 1986. Education in an unequal work chapter (2) in education planning long term perspective, New Delhi. NIEPA.

Tod, Col. James 1919. Annals and Antiques of Rajasthan Vol. I & II (1829-32). London: Routledge and Kegan Paul.

UNESCO. 1955. Financing of Education. Geneva: UNESCO.

Velaskar, Padma, 1990. "Unequal schooling as a factor in the reproduction of social inequality in India" in Sociological Bulletin. Vol.39, No.1 & 2.

Verma, G.C. Modern Education: Its growth and development in Rajasthan 1818 to 1983. Jaipur: Publication scheme, 1984.

Walter, C.K. 1877.Gazetters of Marwar, Mallani and Jeysalmer.

Weber, Max, 1968. Educaiton system in relation to the power structure of society (ch.) Education, Economy and Society, Halsey, A.S. et.al., 1968. New York; Free Press.

Index